# Uchida Hyakken

## A Critique of Modernity and Militarism in Prewar Japan

Harvard East Asian Monographs 310

# Uchida Hyakken

## A Critique of Modernity and Militarism in Prewar Japan

Rachel DiNitto

Published by the Harvard University Asia Center
and distributed by Harvard University Press
Cambridge (Massachusetts) and London, 2008

Printed in the United States of America

The Harvard University Asia Center publishes a monograph series and, in coordination with the Fairbank Center for Chinese Studies, the Korea Institute, the Reischauer Institute of Japanese Studies, and other faculties and institutes, administers research projects designed to further scholarly understanding of China, Japan, Vietnam, Korea, and other Asian countries. The Center also sponsors projects addressing multidisciplinary and regional issues in Asia.

Library of Congress Cataloging-in-Publication Data

DiNitto, Rachel.
Uchida Hyakken : a critique of modernity and militarism in prewar Japan / Rachel DiNitto.
p. cm. -- (Harvard East Asian monographs ; 310)
Includes bibliographical references and index.
ISBN 978-0-674-03112-8 (cloth : alk. paper)
1. Uchida, Hyakken, 1889-1971--Criticism and interpretation. I. Title.
PL818.C5Z65 2008
895.6'09--dc22

2008032982

Printed on acid-free paper

Last figure below indicates year of this printing

18 17 16 15 14 13 12 11 10 09 08

# *Acknowledgments*

This project began as a dissertation and has taken many years to complete. I would like to acknowledge my gratitude to all those who offered help along the way.

I was fortunate to have conducted my graduate studies at the University of Washington, where I was welcomed into a dynamic community of faculty and graduate students. I miss the rainy Seattle afternoons spent sharing beer and good conversation. I worked under the guidance of John Whittier Treat, and I am appreciative for his frank assessment of my work, rigorous disciplinary training, savvy advice, and continued guidance and friendship. Although I had only a few seminars with Jay Rubin, I learned from him what it meant to read modern Japanese literature, and I can only hope someday to have such a sensitivity to literary language. I first read Hyakken in a seminar taught by Motoo Kobayashi. Robert Omar Khan enthusiastically encouraged and guided me through some of my early translation attempts at Hyakken's *Realm of the Dead*.

Many friends and colleagues kindly and carefully read and commented on individual chapters. Davinder Bhowmik, Bill Burton, James Dorsey, Charles Exley, and Melek Ortabasi found time in their busy schedules to respond to my last-minute requests for comments, and they continue to provide intellectual support and warm friendship. Regina Root, Silvia Tandeciarz, and Sibel Zandi-Sayek offered their support and insightful, cross-disciplinary comments in a reading group that gave me a reason to leave my office. Kuroko Kazuo procured difficult-to-find materials on Suzuki Seijun. Francie Cate-Arries offered much needed mentorship and encouragement at critical points in the writing process. Maryse Fauvel and Bruce Campbell kindly guided me through the rigors of the academic review process. Wakaba Tasaka patiently and carefully read through my translations of Hyakken's stories. Hiroshi Kitamura generously assisted in acquiring a photograph from Japan. Finally, I would like to thank my colleagues in the Department of Modern Languages and Literatures at the College of William and Mary for their support and interest in my project.

I would like to thank Uchida Hyakken's family, especially Okuno Kikumi and Uchida Mine, for their support and cooperation, for sharing their memories, and for trusting me to translate Hyakken's literature. I am terribly indebted to Professor Uchida Michio, who generously shared his insight and research on Hyakken, and to his wife, Kinuyo, who kindly read and commented on early versions of my English translations of Hyakken's stories. Professor Uchida also worked tirelessly to track down copyright holders for the images of Hyakken used in this book. Figures 1 and 2 were secured with the assistance of Fujita Mitsuo, former president of Kobikisha, and the Okayama Culture Foundation (Zaidan hōjin Okayama-ken kyōdo bunka zaidan). I would like to extend my thanks to Koishi Yasuo for allowing me to reprint the picture of Hyakken taken by his father, Koishi Kiyoshi, the well-known prewar avant-garde photographer. I would also like to thank the Yasukuni Shrine and the National Diet Library for allowing me to reprint images from their collections.

I had the opportunity to explore ideas for the book in lectures presented at Harvard University, Princeton University, and at a number of national and regional Japanese studies conferences. I was able to concentrate on this project full-time thanks to a postdoctoral fellowship from the Edwin O. Reischauer Institute of Japanese Studies at Harvard University, and two faculty summer grants from the College of William and Mary. I would especially like to thank the Reischauer Institute for supporting the project and the kind staff for accommodating me. I conducted the research for this book at the libraries of the College of William and Mary, Harvard University, Keiō University, Tsurumi University, and the University of Washington, and I am grateful to their staff members as well.

I also want to thank the staff at the Harvard University Asia Center and the anonymous readers whose comments and suggestions helped shape the book in its final stages. William M. Hammell was especially helpful in guiding me through the Byzantine process of permissions, patiently answering my endless stream of emails, and smoothing out my language.

Portions of the Introduction and Chapter 2 first appeared in "Return of the *zuihitsu*: Print Culture, Modern Life, and Heterogeneous Narrative in Prewar Japan" *Harvard Journal of Asiatic Studies* 64, no. 2 (December 2004): 251–90, reprinted here with permission of the editor and the Harvard-Yenching Institute. Portions of the Epilogue first appeared in "Translating Prewar Culture into Film: The Double Vision of Suzuki Seijun's *Zigeunerweisen*," *Journal of Japanese Studies* 30, no. 1 (2004): 35–63, reprinted here with permission of the editors. Portions of the translations of Hyakken's fiction first appeared in Uchida Hyakken, *Realm of the Dead* (Normal: Dalkey Archive Press, 2006), reproduced courtesy of Okuno Kikumi, the Japanese Literature Publishing and Promotion Center, ACE Japan, and Dalkey Archive Press. I am thankful for the financial support of the Agency for Cultural Affairs of Japan (Bunkachō) and the guidance of the Japanese Literature Publishing and Promotion Center in publishing my translation as part of their Japanese Literature Publishing Project. I would also like to thank Elmer Luke for the copyediting.

Last, I would like to thank my family for their support and patience over the many long years of writing. I could not have done it without Niels Miller, who kept me going with good companionship and humor, put up with the nonstop working hours, answered pesky grammatical questions, and provided critical technical support. My life would not be complete without Elias, who has brought me so much joy and love.

This book is dedicated to the memory of my father, Raymond DiNitto, who inspired me to pursue my studies. I deeply regret that he did not live to see this project appear in print.

# *Contents*

# *Figures*

# Uchida Hyakken

## A Critique of Modernity and Militarism in Prewar Japan

# INTRODUCTION

In an aesthetically moving montage in his 1993 film *Madadayo,* Kurosawa Akira depicts his protagonist observing the passing of the seasons from his ramshackle hut as the Second World War comes to an end around him. The film is based on the life and writings of short story writer and essayist Uchida Hyakken (1889–1971), who despite having lost everything in the air raids that ravaged Tokyo, remained in the city for three years in a small shack next to the burnt-out ruins of his neighbor's house. Hyakken had experienced the cultural flowering of modernization following the Great Kantō Earthquake in 1923, only to see the capital in ruins once again as American B-29s firebombed the city in 1945.

Hyakken's life, like the cultural production of Japan's prewar era of the 1920s and 1930s, was fundamentally shaped by the experience of the modern (*modan*) and of war. These two historical moments of modernity and militarism have traditionally been understood as separate, with the shift happening in the early 1930s, as a decadent Western lifestyle gave way to fascism.[1] The modern celebrated the cosmopolitan, consumerism of the metropolitan dweller, while the war muted and eventually silenced artistic expression. Recently there has been a revival of interest in the cultural production of Japan's modern era, with works of both high art and mass culture receiving overdue critical attention. With regard to the Asia-Pacific War, however, Japanese scholars continue to decry the lack of a literary response, and are quick to take writers to task for not speaking out against the government.[2] Such paradigms have structured our understanding of modern Japanese cultural history, but they have also negated the work of writers who sought a literary path over the ideological one of nationalism. The separation of these two eras prevents us from seeing connections between the cultural and political responses to a prewar modernity that stretched from the 1920s into the total war of the early 1940s. Uchida Hyakken is one such writer who, in always opting for the literary, successfully critiqued the discourse of both modernization and of the war. His writing provides a counter-narrative to this story of modern Japanese literature by complicating the history told within.

This book seeks to move beyond analytical structures that rendered Hyakken's literature insignificant, in order to examine his writing as a means for establishing a critical language not couched in the strident vocabulary of prewar politics. Critics have traditionally applied a measuring stick of war responsibility, which credits only those leftists who served as ideological counterparts to the vehement rhetoric of the extreme right. But, in a writer like Hyakken, we see how an articulation of modernity took on political overtones as the modernity project became militarized in Japan's interwar years. The fleeting experience of modernity in the 1920s provided Hyakken with a literary language for critiquing the rhetoric of immutability of the 1930s, which was used to fuel Japan's war in Asia. Hyakken honed his critical language on cultural modernism, but since he did not adopt the openly ideological position of the left, his work does not merit recognition in the paradigm noted above. Yet, in his focus on both the extraordinary and the quotidian everyday, Hyakken countered the harsh realities of modernization and imperialism. He crafted an apt tool for critiquing Japan's modernity project, while at the same time protecting literariness from the invasive dictates of ideology.

The analysis in this book is in no way meant to devalue the important role played by leftist writers who were imprisoned, tortured, and killed during the war years, nor to exculpate those who collaborated with the imperial project. Rather, it is a vehicle to appreciate the various literary reactions to the modernization of the 1920s, while at the same time, open up a literary space of protest, an alternate intellectual response to the era of militarism. In the process, we can come to recognize the literary contributions of a writer such as Uchida Hyakken, and the difficulty of the path negotiated by authors who sought to continue writing in the dangerous climate of the prewar. As an active writer in this era, Hyakken had to find a vehicle for expression to attend to the cultural and political changes around him. As David Harvey notes about such changes, the artist could "contest them, embrace them, try to dominate them, or simply swim within them, but the artist could never ignore them."[3] The options open to Hyakken were the unreservedly political language of the proletarian movement, the realism of Naturalism, the solipsistic narratives of the I-novel, and the experimental poetics of modernist movements such as the Surrealists. Hyakken, however, found an alternative idiom for creating a critique of modernity in its cultural and military forms, namely the language of the everyday. Like German theorists Georg Simmel and Walter Benjamin, Hyakken was able to "fabricate an 'alternative' aesthetic for attending to the experience of modern everyday life."[4] Like his modernist counterparts, he accomplished this by awakening an "acute consciousness of language."[5] Hyakken began experimenting with critical language as he responded to the new material realities and the crisis of representation that rendered prewar everyday life fleeting and ephemeral. Within his mundane, everyday linguistic settings, he makes the familiar unfamiliar, and returns to a time when modernity still retained an aura and the possibility for transformation and critique.

This book takes up Hyakken's fiction and essays written during Japan's prewar years, namely the imperial eras Taishō

(1912–26) and the first fifteen years of Shōwa (1926–89).[6] I take a cultural studies approach in order to insert Hyakken's writing into the prewar context and to describe the intersection of his literature with the material and discursive surroundings of the time: a consumer-oriented print culture; the popular entertainment of film; the capitalist and cultural force of an emergent middle class; a planned, yet sprawling metropolis; and the war machine of an expanding Japanese empire. In doing so, I am consciously breaking with a line of criticism that emphasizes the autobiographical aspects of Hyakken's writing, an approach that has long been prevalent in Japanese literary studies. These critics laid the groundwork for future analyses by illuminating important connections between the author's personal life and his literature, but an unfortunate side effect has been the circumscription of Hyakken to an individual, private realm detached from the era in which he wrote.[7] Due to the biographical focus of this approach, Hyakken appears disengaged from the changes of modernity and occupying an apolitical position during the prewar; however, given the encompassing nature of the rising tide of militarism, such a position ceased to exist. As the government cracked down on the dangerous ideologies of modernism and liberalism, the personal became political.

In the following chapters, I seek to open up Hyakken's work, and to find an alternate means for figuring prewar cultural history, especially with regards to the literary community's critique of the war. Chapter 1 of the present study highlights his acute sensitivity to the forces of modernization that erased the unique voice of the author and permanently disabled our ability to communicate experience. Chapter 2 examines Hyakken's turn to the *zuihitsu*, and the quotidian, ephemeral nature of this essay-like prose form. Through this genre, Hyakken questions the viability of the highly individual experience in an age when literature became subject to market forces. In Hyakken's critique of the unique authorial voice, we can see a means for moving toward a critique of the war and the challenges encountered by writers no longer able to speak an auratic text. Amidst the suppression of thought and speech in the 1930s, many authors sought and were granted cover from censorship in the chatty, unstructured *zuihitsu*.

Over the course of the 1930s, Hyakken moved from the literary to the national, as he used the discourse of the fleeting to critique the immutable rhetoric of the war machine. Set against the backdrop of rising militarism, Hyakken comments on modernity as an ideological movement supporting Japan's military incursions on the continent. Chapter 3 discusses the ways in which his short stories—one about an old actuality film from the Russo-Japanese War era and another about the Yūshūkan war museum at the Yasukuni Shrine—reveal the shifting nature of this discourse. In Chapter 4, Hyakken turns to the constantly changing landscape of the city, *the* physical manifestation of modernity itself. Hyakken finds history buried in the city's recesses, where time is discontinuous and echoes of the past intrude uninvited. Hyakken purposely returns to metropolitan sites of rupture to critique the myth of the eternal and the homogeneous national.

## Uchida Hyakken and Modern Japanese Literature

Since Uchida Hyakken is little known in the English-speaking West—the first translations of his work were published in 2006—I include here a biographical sketch, which also serves to locate Hyakken within modern literary history.[8] The sections that follow this biography examine Hyakken's relationship to modernity and the conceptualization of the everyday in prewar Japan.

Hyakken has long enjoyed a cult following in Japan for his eclectic writing, both during his career and after his death in 1971. He is best known for the mysterious, dark fiction of his early short story collections and for his entertaining, lighthearted *zuihitsu*, but his writing is difficult to summarize under any one theme. The richness of his work is found in the wide variety of styles, genres, and venues encompassed over the course of his fifty-year career.[9] This includes fiction, *zuihitsu*, war diaries, poetry, travelogues, and children's stories. Stylistically speaking, he established a simple, modern idiom in his debut book *Realm of the Dead* (*Meido*, 1922) upon which he would continue to draw throughout his career. His work has been described as embodying a "Japaneseness," and certainly the reedy riverbanks of his first book call to mind the landscapes of his native Okayama, as well as the eerie settings of the kabuki theater;[10] however, the short sentences and overemphasis on the first person pronoun indicate the influence of Western literature. Hyakken's play with language and fragmentary narrative echoes the trends of modernism, but his work does not begin to enter the highly experimental realm of the, at times, tortuous prose of some of his contemporaries. Hyakken exhibits characteristics of the avant-garde who sought to establish entirely new literary modes, while at the same time he is reactionary in his desire to return to a purity of language untainted by mass culture. It would be a mischaracterization to claim a central position in the literary canon for Hyakken, but an equal mistake to dismiss his writing as insignificant. From his position on the margins of elite literature, Hyakken eschewed unified narrative and used his fragmentary, brief, simple style as a means to critique the modern world around him and to express sentiments contrary to the mainstream rhetoric of the time.

Uchida Hyakken (see Figure 1) was born on May 29, 1889 in Okayama City to Uchida Hisayoshi and Mine, the proprietors of a family *sake* business. Named after his maternal grandfather, Eizō, he did not begin using the pen name Hyakken until his high school years (1908). Hyakken's childhood memories of growing up in Okayama provide a backdrop for many of his early stories, and he took his pseudonym from the name of a local, seasonal river, along the banks of which he passed time as a youth.[11] It was in Okayama that he also met his future wife Kiyoko, the younger sister of his high school friend Horino Yutaka. His memories of Okayama, however, are not all pleasant. His father died suddenly of beriberi heart disease when Hyakken was sixteen, and the family business folded. Yutaka also passed away at the age of twenty.

Fig. 1 "Hyakkien [Uchida Hyakken] at the Shōhinken." By Koishi Kiyoshi. From *Uchida Hyakken*, vol. 42 of *Shinchō Nihon bungaku arubamu*. Courtesy of Koishi Yasuo and the Okayama Culture Foundation (Zaidan hōjin Okayama-ken kyōdo bunka zaidan).

In addition to forming an Ur landscape for Hyakken, Okayama was also the site of his budding interest in literature.[12] While still a middle and high school student, Hyakken contributed prose and poetry to the youth journal *Chūgaku sekai* and its spin-off *Bunshō sekai*, as well as to newspapers and local publications, under a variety of pen names.[13] He began reading Natsume Sōseki the same year his father died, starting with *I Am a Cat* (*Wagahai wa neko de aru*, 1905-07) in 1905 and *Drifting in Space* (*Yōkyoshū*) in 1906. On the suggestion of his teacher, Hyakken sent his story "The Tale of an Old Cat" ("Rōbyō monogatari," 1908) to this great modern writer in 1909, and much to his delight received a favorable reply.

This epistolary exchange would be followed up with a face-to-face interview when Hyakken moved to the capital in 1910 to study German literature at Tokyo Imperial University. Hyakken was a product of the modern schooling system instituted in the Meiji era (1868–1912), the Tokyo-centered model that brought graduates of the prestigious provincial higher schools into the capital for further education at the elite national universities. Like many of the aspiring writers of his generation, Hyakken would remain in Tokyo to seek his literary fortunes. He began attending the Thursday gatherings (Mokuyōkai) at Sōseki's house where he met other disciples, many of whom went on to become well-known figures in Japanese literature, and he formed important literary friendships with writers Akutagawa Ryūnosuke and Morita Sōhei.[14]

Sōseki passed away in 1916, but he continued to exert influence over Hyakken's personal and professional life. Both Sōseki's dark and mysterious "Ten Nights of Dreams" ("Yume jūya," 1908) and *Drifting in Space*, as well as his humorous *The Young Master* (*Botchan*, 1906) and *I Am a Cat*, are considered models upon which Hyakken based such works as *Realm of the Dead* and *I Am a Cat: The Fake Version* (*Gansaku wagahai wa neko de aru*, 1950).[15] Sōseki also posthumously provided Hyakken with employment as an editor and compiler of his collected works.[16] After graduating in 1914, Hyakken needed a steady source of income to support his wife Kiyoko, whom he married in 1912, their two children, and his own mother and grandmother who had moved up from Okayama in 1915.[17] Hyakken took on three jobs teaching German. His first was in 1916 at the prestigious Military Academy (Rikugun Shikan Gakkō), which produced elite officers for the Imperial Army.[18] In 1918, Akutagawa recommended Hyakken for a job at the Yokosuka Naval Engineers Academy (Kaigun Kikan Gakkō), where Akutagawa himself was teaching English. Their relationship teaching together is portrayed in Hyakken's poignant and amusing story "The Bowler Hat" ("Yamataka bōshi"). Hyakken's last academic post was at Hōsei University in 1920, the year his grandmother passed away.

Among Sōseki's disciples, Hyakken was a literary late bloomer. His debut work *Realm of the Dead* did not appear until twelve years after he moved to the capital, when he was already age 33.[19] The collection comprises eighteen stories, some as short as two pages, centering on an unnamed male protagonist.[20] This character travels through eerie, disconnected landscapes inhabited by seemingly familiar faces from an inaccessible past. Try as he might, the protagonist is usually unable to retrieve his memories, but this does not keep him from following these guides to sideshows, abandoned riverbanks, mysterious towns, seashores, and temples. He stands by as the other characters fall prey to smallpox, get eaten by leopards, steal his wife, and undergo physical transformations. He himself is chased by a large turkey, reborn as a mythical beast, strangled by former lovers, and tricked by a fox. In the course of these encounters, he kills innocent children, meets an unborn brother, and nearly reunites with a dead father.

Postwar critics would later identify *Realm of the Dead* as the essence of Hyakken's literature; however, fortune was not originally on Hyakken's side.[21] The work was published in February of 1922, but the foundry or pre-press proofs for *Realm of the Dead* burned in the fires of the Great Kantō Earthquake of 1923. This disaster destroyed Tokyo and neighboring Yokohama, killing and injuring close to 250,000 people, and dealt a tremendous set-back to the publishing industry. Hyakken's book had gone through an initial small-run printing of 500 volumes and had appeared on bookstore shelves.[22] But with the destruction of the proofs, a reprint would not be possible until 1934, despite the efforts of well-known writers such as Akutagawa and Satō Haruo. In an oft-repeated sentiment, Uchida Michio laments that Hyakken missed his opportunity to have an impact on the Taishō literary scene because the book was not reprinted earlier, and hence failed to circulate among important writers and critics.[23]

Lack of exposure due to the limited copies of the initial print run was only part of Hyakken's problem. The work had in fact been available to the reading public in more than one format; sixteen of the eighteen stories appeared in *Shinshōsetsu*, an established literary magazine in 1921, and Akutagawa and Morita Sōhei had published articles on Hyakken's stories in the January issue, urging the literary community to read his work. According to Akutagawa, the real problem lay elsewhere. The stories had been read by some, but were not well received. Akutagawa indicates that, based on the reviews he has seen, the critics did not know what to make of Hyakken's fiction. Akutagawa finds Hyakken's stories interesting because Hyakken is not held prisoner to the trends of the literary establishment. However, this freedom may have been an important factor in the work's demise. Akutagawa explains that the literary elite could not appreciate Hyakken's originality because they were unable to think outside of superficial stylistics.[24] Akutagawa was most likely referring to the fact that upon reading *Realm of the Dead*, Hyakken's contemporaries would have found neither a familiar realist narrative nor a thinly veiled biographical framework, dominant literary trends that had begun in the early years of the twentieth century.[25] Two questions then arise: what was Hyakken writing and how should he be situated within the literary context of early Taishō?

When Hyakken began writing his short stories in the 1910s, he stood witness to the disintegration of the Naturalist movement with its spare literary style that eschewed fabrication and technique. Naturalism, however, did not completely disappear; it gave way to the realistic, intensely personal, quotidian narratives of the I-novel. However, as the cataclysmic changes of modernity ruptured the cultural and physical landscape of the 1920s, realist narratives became arguably ill suited to represent the shifting perspectives of space, time, and cognition. New writers began to challenge the everyday reality represented in the transparent prose of Naturalism. Modernism's preoccupation with language brought a resurgence of interest in literary creation.[26] Modernist writers questioned the reality of the everyday, the constants of time and space, the logical unfolding of a linear narrative, and the convergence of writing and thought.

Any attempt to locate Hyakken within modernism is complicated by the fact that the process of defining the movement in Japan is fraught with difficulties. Despite the fact that the Japanese experienced similar disruptions on the level of material culture as did Europe and America, critics limit the aesthetic response to small avant-garde movements. Writers who experimented in this vein, such as Satō Haruo, are usually not included under this rubric, and other clearly modernist movements are excluded.[27] Take, for example, the following observation by Miryam Sas: "Surrealism in Japan is written into literary history as a movement that never was, or trivialized as a movement that hardly was, invisible to the canonical, educated eye. . . . It never coalesced."[28] The designation of two other groups illustrates the varying definitions of modernism circulating in prewar Japan: the Newly Arisen Artistic School (Shinkōgeijutsu-ha) modernism is often equated with the appearance of modern life, or "attention to certain distilling [modern] objects" in fiction, while the writing of the New Sensationalist School (Shinkankaku-ha) is defined less by the appearance of this modern life, than by the linguistic and narrative strategies employed to react to and represent it.[29] Such distinctions further complicate the definition of modernism and identification of its writers.

Hyakken does not fit within any of these camps, and it would be a misrepresentation to imply that he was associated even loosely with these self-proclaimed modernist groups. However, Japanese critics have hinted at Hyakken's modernist tendencies. Itō Sei, known for his translations of James Joyce, wondered if the European modernist movements of Symbolism, Dadaism, and Surrealism were any newer or more experimental than Hyakken.[30] Acclaimed writer Mishima Yukio also remarked that Hyakken's story "Kudan" brings to mind Franz Kafka's famous *Metamorphosis*.[31] As Chapter 1 examines,

Hyakken certainly joined the modernists in questioning everyday reality, time, space, and linear narrative, and he used these and other means to attempt to return aura to his text.

Hyakken did not successfully produce an auratic text, and his failure to achieve literary distinction with *Realm of the Dead* irrevocably changed the course of his career, gradually turning him away from fiction. Despite his prodigious output—some 64 works—over the course of the 1920s, in journals such as the respected *Chūō kōron* and *Shinshōsetsu*, Hyakken would not establish himself as a writer until the publication of his second book in 1933, *Hyakkien's Miscellany* (*Hyakkien zuihitsu*).[32] The first of many volumes of *zuihitsu*, this collection of 34 short works ranges in topic from childhood reminiscences to musings on airplanes, yo-yos, and facial hair; memories of the protagonist's first and last meeting with his mentor, the great novelist, Natsume Sōseki; and seemingly more fictional stories about loan sharks and a life of poverty.[33] The reader is hard pressed to find a central theme or character to unify the collection. Some stories are written in the first person, while others are in the third. The protagonist, often a bumbling intellectual, is referred to by a variety of names including Uchida and Hyakken, as well as the (Fujita) Hyakkien of the title, but he is equally as often unnamed or assigned seemingly unrelated names. There is no consistency in length or tone. Many of the *zuihitsu* are a scant few pages of essays or fragments, while others easily number in the double digits. The mood runs the gamut from the lighthearted and comic to the poignantly serious. The varied and disparate nature of the collection is indicative of the range of the genre itself. The lack of a strict narrative definition allowed for Hyakken to experiment with the *zuihitsu* and create a new form, a "novelistic *zuihitsu*" (*shōsetsuteki zuihitsu*) that offered new narrative possibilities in the 1930s with which Hyakken could critique elite fiction.

The formless, essay style of the *zuihitsu* had long been a part of Japanese premodern literature, with origins stretching back into the thirteenth century and earlier.[34] *Zuihitsu* again came to prominence in the 1920s and 1930s as an alternate to the narrative restrictions of the novel, and flourished as a literary mode and a cultural commodity. However the genre never acquired the distinct status of the novel. In 1935, writer and entrepreneur Kikuchi Kan excluded it from his influential literary award for "pure literature" (*junbungaku*), the Akutagawa Prize, and postwar critics wrote it out of the history books. A consideration of the *zuihitsu*'s status outside the literary system of distinction also allows for a brief, yet important, discussion of Hyakken's place in the literary hierarchy and the relationship between high art and mass culture.

Prewar literature is often described as the battle between the highbrow *junbungaku* and the lowbrow "popular" or "mass literature" (*taishū bungaku*). This distinction between high art and mass culture, what Andreas Huyssen has termed the "Great Divide," is one way to think about Hyakken's position within modern literature.[35] Hyakken's writing secured him a place in the modern canon—but not a central one, as illustrated from his placement in anthologies of modern literature, sharing volumes with other lesser-known authors.[36] Yet, the notion of canonization masks issues that fall between this great divide, especially in relation to the *zuihitsu*. Hyakken is most comfortably placed on the side of the elite, along with writers such as Akutagawa Ryūnosuke and others of Sōseki's circle. His decision to specialize in *zuihitsu* excluded him from the distinction of the Akutagawa Prize, but many elite authors wrote and profited from the *zuihitsu*. Akutagawa's *zuihitsu* headlined *Bungei shunjū* from its inception in 1923 until his death in 1927. The *zuihitsu* sold better and paid higher manuscript fees than elite fiction, and it challenged seemingly impenetrable distinctions between highbrow and lowbrow literature.

Despite the appreciation of the genre in Japan—*zuihitsu* are still being written—the mechanisms of pure literature did not allow it to be granted recognition. The canonization process is one that defines literature as *shōsetsu* (fiction), and effectively marginalizes other generic forms. Chapter 2 argues that the *zuihitsu* was too close to market forces to be included in any definition of elite writing. Its distance from fiction (elite writing) can be seen in both the layout and advertising strategies of prewar journals. *Zuihitsu* headlined *Bungei shunjū*, which consequently meant that they were not included in the *sōsaku* (creative writing/fiction) section, and Kikuchi Kan marketed the writing as a side course to the regular, more intellectual, fare found in other magazines.

Hyakken's engagement with the *zuihitsu* negatively affected his chance of acquiring literary distinction, but it put him in a position to publish in both elite and mass venues, as was common for writers in an era defined by market forces.[37] But his contact with mass culture was not limited to writing. His semi-fictional essays were adapted for the cinema in the late 1930s, when the film industry was mining literature for screenplays in an attempt to raise the level of this relatively new genre. The resulting art film (*bungei eiga*) *Roppa's The Pale Faced Professor* (*Roppa no Hoojiro sensei*, 1939) was marketed on the star power of Furukawa Roppa, a famous actor from the popular vaudevillian theatre. This film is one such hybrid which crosses the great divide by combining the high art of literature with the mass culture of film. Although Hyakken consented to the project, this brush with mass culture left him disappointed. The film was a success, but he felt his writing had been cheapened by the transfer to this mass medium. He decided to rededicate himself to achieving a level of pure expression (*junsui bunshō*) that can only be captured through the act of reading. In a move characteristic of modernism, Hyakken's retreat to the realm of pure language exhibits the elite's "anxiety of contamination."[38] Unlike others who actively and willingly engaged with mass culture, such as Tanizaki Jun'ichirō's ventures into the film industry, Hyakken was ultimately unwilling to give up control over the word and his unique authorial voice, even though he realized it was something he had already lost.

Hyakken did not, however, abandon fiction, as seen in his publishing record from the 1930s. The success of *Hyakkien's Miscellany* secured a reprint of *Realm of the Dead* with Iwanami, an established publishing house. The rate of publication for these years is impressive: *Triumphant March into Port Arthur*

(*Ryojun nyūjōshiki*, February 1934), *Hyakkien's Miscellany Continued* (*Zoku Hyakkien zuihitsu*, May 1934), *The King's Back* (*Ōsama no senaka*, May 1934), *Hyakkien's Book of Haiku* (*Hyakkien haiku chō*, June 1934), *The Stringless Koto* (*Mugenkin*, October 1934), *The Crane* (*Tsuru*, February 1935), *Hyakkien's Diary* (*Hyakkien nikki chō*, April 1935), *The Bumpy Road* (*Dekoboko michi*, October 1935), *Hyakkien's Diary Continued* (*Zoku Hyakkien nikki chō*, February 1936), *Rapture* (*Uchōten*, July 1936), *A Busy Houseboy* (*Isōrō sōsō*, June 1937), *New Rain Miscellany* (*Zuihitsu shin'u*, October 1937), *The Northern Sea* (*Hokumei*, December 1937), *Bridge on the Hill* (*Oka no hashi*, June 1938), Kien's Chatter (*Kien ōdan*, February 1939), and *Chrysanthemum Rain* (*Kiku no ame*, October 1939). This list encompasses a wide variety of fiction, including eleven collections of *zuihitsu*, a book of poetry, two diaries, one collection of fictional short stories, one novel, and even a book of illustrated fairy tales. The various collections of *zuihitsu* and fictional works include upwards of 30 to 40 stories apiece.

The great upswing in Hyakken's market value between the 1920s and 1930s is evident in the following advertisement for an anthology titled *The Banquet* (*Daienkai*), which appeared in the front page of the August 1935 issue of the journal *Arabesuku*, a special edition featuring ten essays on Hyakken:

> One of a kind, a writer without rival in all of Japanese literature—Who can compare to Uchida Hyakken? Parallels can be drawn with [Edgar Allan] Poe and [E. T. A.] Hoffmann, but can Hyakken be so readily summed up? Certainly not! For isn't Hyakken more than just literature? One who eludes even the conceptual grasp of criticism—This is Uchida Hyakken!

This may appear to be overblown copy, but the existence of the advertisement and the reference it makes to the Western authors speak to Hyakken's status.[39] Poe and Hoffman were well known to the literate prewar reader, and any favorable comparison with these great authors was a recognizable commercial and literary seal of approval. The copy language was supported by publishing statistics. By the 1940s, Hyakken's work was being printed in runs of 9,000 to 10,000 copies, quite a change from the limited 500 edition runs of his early collections.

In terms of Hyakken's personal life, however, the decade of the 1930s held some upsets. In 1934, Hyakken left his teaching job at Hōsei University, along with fellow Sōseki disciple Nogami Toyoichirō, as a result of the well-publicized "Hōsei Disturbance" (Hōsei *sōdō*).[40] This incident has been described as "one of the most disturbing examples of campus unrest in Japanese university history."[41] It would end both Hyakken's academic career and his friendship with Morita Sōhei, another Sōseki acquaintance who had also entered Hōsei's employment in 1920. Sōhei and Hyakken never spoke after this falling out, and Hyakken only broke the silence after Sōhei's death on December 14, 1949 with *The True Story of Sōhei* (*Jissetsu Sōheiki*, 1950). Although the disturbance strained Hyakken's personal life, it was not without its positive aspects: namely, freeing him to pursue his writing.

The same year Hyakken resigned from Hōsei, his second short story collection, *Triumphant March into Port Arthur*, was published. In many ways, the collection is a continuation of *Realm of the Dead*, as Hyakken noted in his preface:

> Of the twenty-nine stories in this collection, the first seven have a story-telling quality to them, while the remaining twenty-two are short pieces similar in tone to those in my previous book *Realm of the Dead*. After ten long years, I finally finished *Realm of the Dead*. The book was ready to be published, but in that year Tokyo was struck by terrible misfortune. The great earthquake and accompanying fires completely destroyed the foundry plates, causing the book to suffer the unfortunate fate of going out of print. For the next ten years, I gnawed at my pen and ripped through paper, and somehow after piecing together this mere collection, I was lucky enough to receive the favor of a publisher. When the book was finally about to be printed, I reflected back on the path of writing and found it to be far too long and precipitous.[42]

Over a decade later, the influence of Hyakken's misfortune with *Realm of the Dead* is apparent, as is the new direction of his *zuihitsu*. The preface is signed: "From the House of Hyakkien." The similarity to the earlier collection that Hyakken refers to can be found in themes like doubling and vision that Hyakken began to experiment with in *Realm of the Dead*. These are reprised in a number of stories, including "The Tiny Double" ("Waijin"), in which a miniature version of the protagonist appears. This use of doubling is most notable in "The Reflection" ("Eizō"), which describes the protagonist's nightly encounters with his own reflection outside the glass door to his bedroom. The face appears repeatedly, and as it becomes bruised and discolored, so does that of the protagonist, who tries desperately to find a means of escape. Afraid of his own reflection, the protagonist avoids mirrors and glass, only to meet his doppelganger again at night. In the last scene, this "reflection" enters the room, and the protagonist, frozen in fear, is unable to speak or escape as his double leans over him as if to say something. Other stories include a lament for an old lover who dies, a colleague who commits suicide, and various others with human-animal transformations. However the content is so varied as to be difficult to capture under any one theme. Two of the most noteworthy stories reference the war, and are discussed in the next section.

Hyakken continued to write and acquire recognition for his fiction and *zuihitsu*. A six volume collected works titled *The Complete Hyakken Miscellany* (*Zenshū Hyakken zuihitsu*) was published between November 1936 and April 1937. Although this is primarily a *zuihitsu* series, it included stories from the fictional *Realm of the Dead* and *Triumphant March into Port Arthur*, testifying to the importance of these works in his oeuvre.

In 1939 Hyakken took a commission with the Japan Mail Steamer Corporation (Nippon Yūsen Kaisha) as a consultant on mail correspondence, records, declarations, and the like. He would work there for the next six and a half years, and through this job would travel to Taiwan in November 1939 on a journey that formed the basis for his *Ship Dreams* (*Fune no yume*, 1941). Although he no longer held a formal affiliation with Hōsei University, he continued to meet with students, in a fashion somewhat reminiscent of Sōseki's Mokuyōkai. Two of his disciples, Hirayama Saburō and Nakamura Takeshi, would visit him from their jobs with the Japanese Government Railways, and his friendship and future train trips with Hirayama form the central narrative in the *Idiot Train* (*Ahō ressha*) series.

Travel also features in *Lightning at Sea* (*Oki no inazuma*, 1942) and *The Road Back* (*Modori michi*, 1944). Yet despite his propensity for excursions both abroad and within Japan, Hyakken chose not to pull up his roots at a time when many were fleeing the aerial bombardment of Tokyo; he remained in the city for the duration of the war. Hyakken's house burned down in the B-29 air raids of May 26, 1945, the second of two strikes staged two days apart that turned the city to ashes. He moved into a three-mat hut on his neighbor's property, and would spend the next three-odd years living there with his companion Satō Koi until a new house was built in May 1948. His memories of life in these Spartan, cramped quarters would be published after the war in the form of a *zuihitsu* collection entitled *The New Account of My Hut* (*Shinhōjōki*, 1947)—a play on Kamo no Chōmei's thirteenth-century classic—and in two diaries, *Tokyo Burning* (*Tōkyō shōjin*, 1955), and the posthumously edited *Hyakkien's Postwar Diary* (*Hyakkien sengo nikki*, 1982).[43]

Acting as a counterpoint to these somber diaries, Hyakken began serializing his humorous parody *I Am a Cat: The Fake Version* in the April 1949 issue of the journal *Shōsetsu shinchō*.[44] The following year he celebrated his 61st birthday with the inaugural "Maada kai," Hyakken's annual birthday party later made famous through Kurosawa Akira's film *Madadayo* (1993).[45] The year 1951 saw the first installment of his popular *Idiot Train* series, entitled "The Idiot Special Express" ("Tokubetsu ahō ressha"), also printed in *Shōsetsu shinchō*.[46] The book *The Idiot Train* would appear in three volumes in 1952, 1953, and 1956, the first of these coinciding with celebrations for the eightieth anniversary of the Japanese National Railways, during which Hyakken was made honorary head of Tokyo Station for a day.

Other highlights from the 1950s and 1960s include his *zuihitsu* collection *Nora* (*Nora ya*, 1957) named after his beloved runaway cat. Appended to this diary style story are copies of the reward signs Hyakken posted when the cat disappeared. Hyakken's affection for animals featured in a number of works, notably the cats in *Nora* and *Kuru, Is That You?* (*Kuru ya omae ka*, 1963), and the birds in the *Hyakkien's Miscellany* essays. As testimony to Hyakken's postwar fame, his 1933 *Hyakkien's Miscellany* was reprinted in *Shōsetsu shinchō* in monthly installments from January 1959 through September 1970. Hyakken continued writing *zuihitsu*, producing individual pieces and collections up until his death in 1971. He wrote a total of 32 volumes of *zuihitsu*, including his last book, *Gates Close at Dusk* (*Nichibotsu heimon*, 1971), which was published on April 15, five days before he died at the age of 81.

In recognition of Hyakken's contribution to literature, the Japan Art Academy (Nihon Geijutsuin) nominated him for membership in 1967. Hyakken, however, declined via a short memo basically stating that he did not feel like joining. His curmudgeonly declaration was featured on television and in the press, where his words were shortened to the now famous quotation, "iya dakara, iya da!" or roughly translated, "I said no and I meant it!"[47]

Hyakken published roughly a volume a year over his fifty-year career, and at times he was even more prolific. He fulfilled many of the prerequisites for a modern author: as a youth he contributed to influential literary journals such as *Bunshō sekai*; he allied himself with one of the giants of modern literature, Natsume Sōseki; as a member of Sōseki's circle he mixed with well-known contemporaries such as Akutagawa Ryūnosuke; he held a prestigious university position; he had a special issue of a literary journal dedicated to him; he had his fiction reprinted and anthologized numerous times; and finally, he was recognized toward the end of his life for his literary achievements by the Art Academy.

## Prewar Modernity: Hyakken Responds

Baudelaire famously characterized the experience of modernity as one of "the transient, the fleeting, the contingent; it is the one half of art, the other being the eternal and the immutable."[48] Baudelaire's observations have been echoed in the works of modern writers and thinkers, as well as in scholarship on the experience of modernity in the West.[49] In the case of Japan, the temporal compression of the modernization process does not allow for ready comparison with movements in pre- and interwar Europe. Consider, for example, the accelerated evolutionary schema in which modern Japanese literature originates in the late 1890s and is followed by the appearance of modernism a mere two decades after modern literature itself took root.[50] However, Japan did indeed experience the transient and fleeting, most markedly in the interwar years of the 1920s and 1930s. This sense of contingency manifested itself in material change on a scale not seen in the first era of modernity, the Meiji period: industrialization, mechanization, urbanization, demographic shifts, urban restructuring, commercialization of the cultural market, emergence of the middle class and the masses, bourgeois consumerism, and rapid growth in systems of communication and transportation.[51] Unlike in the Meiji era, this societal modernization, the phenomenon of "modern life" (*modan raifu*), which in many senses meant a modern, Western life, reached beyond the elite and filtered into the daily activities of the average urban dweller. The Great Kantō Earthquake of 1923 provided a physical equivalent to the philosophical break with history, and allowed for new perceptions of reality. These material and representational shifts wrought changes in the cultural responses of artists in this era. Writers reacted to the tremendous fragmentation, chaos, and fleeting sense of the present, a part and parcel of the rupture with history. It was against this ever-shifting basis of everyday modern life, this crisis of representation and language, that artists formed their aesthetic.

For a writer such as Uchida Hyakken, modernization meant first and foremost a change in the very nature of writing itself. Indeed, the first two chapters of this book are primarily concerned with literary issues. Any discussion of prewar literature must address the modern printing system and its impact on literature and culture at large. But there is an earlier, and perhaps more significant, event that defined literature for Hyakken: the replacement of woodblock printing with movable type as the new standard around 1890. Kōno Kensuke describes the appeal of the printed word and the fetishistic attachment that young boys had for early printing sets.[52] However, the novelty of the printed word soon disappeared as the sheer volume of printed works increased. Reading patterns also changed from detailed and discriminate to shallow and indiscriminate. Movable-type texts were no longer such objects of fascination, nor could they recreate the particularistic relationship between reader and text found in block-printed works. Hyakken was one such boy with an attachment to early printing sets, and this nostalgia would inform his concept of the auratic text.

As discussed in Chapter 1, Hyakken longed to reproduce the unique manuscript qualities of the block-printed word. He attempted to return to the aura of such early texts through the use of unusual formatting and other literary devices in his first book, *Realm of the Dead*. However, he was not able to make such a return, and his textual experiments were not understood or appreciated by the arbiters of literature. This is not surprising given the qualitative changes in the "capital-intensive publishing industry of the twentieth century"; namely, an increase in the volume of printed texts, a shift to indiscriminate reading patterns, and a commodification of literature.[53] As Miriam Silverberg notes, this was "most definitely the dawn of the era of mechanical reproduction."[54] With the rapid development and expansion of the industry after the Great Kantō Earthquake, writing became a cultural commodity and writers had to respond to the market forces of print capitalism.[55] This scale of commodification increased dramatically with the *enpon* or one-yen book, starting with Kaizōsha's 1926 subscription series, *Complete Works of Contemporary Japanese Literature* (*Gendai Nihon bungaku zenshū*). This and other series, based on the idea of the Harvard Classics, made literature available to the nonspecialist, who could not afford to purchase the collected works of individual authors.[56] This new commodity—a multivolume, affordable, subscription series—revolutionized and modernized the print industry, bringing it into the age of mass production and full-fledged advertising. It also allowed writers to profit handsomely from their craft. Writing had become a lucrative venture, but the production of auratic texts became difficult in this new system. The artist had to produce a unique work for purchase by a bourgeois reader whom he often held in contempt. Hyakken reacted negatively to the commodification of literature in which aura was lost in the mass production of textual material, now reduced to an ephemeral consumer product.

If Hyakken was lamenting these effects in the early 1920s, any hope of returning to a previous system was dashed by the end of the decade. Middlebrow readers were purchasing books as accoutrements to their new modern lives, and the myth of authorial control had finally been shattered in the face of undeniable market forces. Hyakken was not successful in restoring aura to his text, but he did recreate the disorienting experience of modernity in *Realm of the Dead*. As discussed in Chapter 1, Hyakken's protagonist is caught in the eternal repetition of the present, and without recourse to historical narrative, cannot make sense of his experience. Without access to the past, neither can he accumulate that experience in order to translate it into meaning; hence the act of remembering is traumatic. This nostalgia for a lost past intrudes onto the present, creating doubles and fluxes in time, further blurring the line between reality and illusion, original and copy. The character's search for the unity of narrative leads him to folklore, but the certainty of tradition remains beyond his grasp. Living in a distracted mode of perception, he is unable to see and interpret his own actions. Like his characters, Hyakken's anxiety as a modern writer is palpable in *Realm of the Dead*. Just as his protagonist is overwhelmed and silenced, Hyakken at this stage of his career was unable to see the possibility for a critical articulation of modernity that could lead to a transformation of the world around him. The darkness of this vision resonates with the tone of his stories.

In a shift away from the bleakness of *Realm of the Dead*, Hyakken began writing *zuihitsu*. This new genre provided him with a light-hearted literary mode unfettered by the narrative restrictions of the novel, but more importantly, with a new idea of literature itself. In his *zuihitsu,* Hyakken plays with the concept of an auratic text by mocking the very seriousness of the I-novel authors who clung to their unique identity in an age of endless copies. On one level, Hyakken's *zuihitsu* can be seen as his reconciliation with the new role of literature, one that celebrated the materiality of modern life, much like the modernism of the Newly Arisen Artistic School.

It would not be an overstatement to argue that Hyakken's success with the *zuihitsu* was predicated upon print culture and its role in the creation of a "modern life" for the emergent, middle-class, middlebrow reader. Print culture became one means of selling a modern cultured lifestyle characterized by Western middle-class glamour and efficiency. The *zuihitsu* was in many ways defined by this material side of modernism, or as it was termed in Japan, *seikatsu.*[57] Modern life was sold in department stores and films, in everyday products such as fountain pens and cosmetics, and in the print culture of advertisements, journals, and books. Kikuchi Kan, editor and creator of *Bungei shunjū,* intentionally marketed the light, easy-to-read *zuihitsu* to on-the-go readers seeking to live this modern lifestyle. *Zuihitsu* was the quintessentially modern form of print culture, providing a sense of both shock and intimacy for the reader. These chatty unstructured texts fit perfectly the life of the modern urban dweller, who could consume his magazine on the train while commuting into work or while relaxing at home with the family in their new culture house (*bunka jūtaku*).

In these *zuihitsu,* Hyakken questions our ability as modern subjects to speak from an individual, auratic position not tied to a fleeting present. If such a position was difficult in the 1920s, as authorial voice was lost to the machine of capitalism, it would become impossible over the course of the 1930s, as modern consumer subjects became imperial subjects and authorial voice was silenced by the dictates of propaganda. Despite these forces and his initial disheartenment by the failure of *Realm of the Dead,* Hyakken discovered the potential of writing and truly developed his critical language in his writings on the war. Chapters 3 and 4 examine his turn from the literary to the national as the once ephemeral nature of discourse became immutable.

Government censorship in the prewar attempted to reestablish control over the discursive to serve the militarizing state. The war itself can be seen as another crisis of representation and language. The rhetoric of the war that dominated life in 1930s Japan is often seen as a rejection of the decadent, Western-inspired, materialist modernism captured in the catch phrase "erotic grotesque nonsense."[58] However, we need not see the war machine as a rejection of modernity; in fact, the discourse of war represents the second half of Baudelaire's equation, namely the eternal and immutable. From intellectual movements to the culture industry to political rulers, there was a visible attempt to create historical continuity to mask the rupture with the past rendered by modernity.[59] The Return to Japan (Nihon Kaiki) movement advocated a return to a timeless past of ethnic Japanese values, a fatherland of ancient memory.[60] The government sought to erase the era of 1920s modernity, as they recycled discourse of the Russo-Japanese War (1904–05) to rally support for the Manchurian Incident (1931) and Japan's subsequent incursions into Asia. The relativism of modernism—a reaction to the tremendous fragmentation of space, place, time, and language—became dangerous, both politically and intellectually, to the myth of nationalism and its immutable "Japanese" character.[61]

The force that had the greatest impact on daily life in the 1930s was undoubtedly the war. Although the era is often labeled the "prewar" or alternately "interwar," these are misleading since Japan's Fifteen Years War (Jūgonen sensō), which climaxed in World War II, began in 1931 with the invasion of Manchuria. The concept of nationhood reached beyond Japan's geographical borders to create an empire in a physical and imaginative sense. Empire became ever-present in everyday life in the 1930s, as Japan cast its imperialist net wider and wider over China and its other Asian neighbors. The average Japanese citizen's contact with the war was not limited to draftees and returning soldiers. War permeated popular culture in the form of theme products: food, toys, books, films, theater productions, music, exhibits, and lecture series. War became both a tool of government propaganda and a lucrative cultural product. Literature was not immune; anything referencing wars and militarism, past or present, was either censored or read against this new context of 1930s empire.

Hyakken's second book, *Triumphant March into Port Arthur,* was one such item read against the imperial context. The title of this collection is a slogan from the Russo-Japanese War that had been rehabilitated by the Japanese state to justify its takeover of Manchuria in 1931. Revamped, heroic images of this old battle, and of a valiant General Nogi Maresuke, became new tools of government propaganda and media sensationalism. The Yūshūkan war museum at Yasukuni Shrine, the central shrine for commemorating Japanese war dead, was being rebuilt, and in a nod to the new rhetoric of pan-Asianism, the new building was constructed in a traditional Japanese gable-roof style. This was an erasure of the Western symbolism found in the architecture of the Meiji era structure built to commemorate those who died in the Restoration. The museum received new attention as soldiers lost in service to the Emperor's new war on the Asian continent were returned home over the course of the 1930s. Government propaganda was successful in suturing the ruptures of modernity so as to create an unbroken historical memory stretching beyond earlier battles in Asia back to an essential Japanese identity.

Hyakken shared his private grief over the war in a *zuihitsu* titled "The Nose" ("Hana," 1938), that he wrote for the *Tōkyō Asahi shinbun.* In the essay he recalls hearing of his former student's death: "When I heard the report of second lieutenant Ōhashi Chōichirō's death in battle, I remembered the evening twilight at the Yasukuni Shrine some fifteen or sixteen years ago. Chō had come back to Yasukuni, now a spirit of the fatherland. I imagine him wandering out to the sumo ring toward the back of the shrine, searching for fragments of his childhood dreams" (4: 85).

Hyakken refers to the time when he walked home through the shrine with two students (Chō and another boy) who played in the sumo ring while he watched. It was dusk and the ring faintly glowed amidst the approaching darkness. Hyakken watched the boys until they were told to leave by the military police. In remembering his former student, Hyakken calls him a *gokoku no oni* (the spirit of a person who died defending the fatherland), a patriotic term bereft of the ambiguity in his other stories. Critics have argued that Hyakken never engages the ideological side of his student's death or of the shrine, and reminisces only on a personal level.[62]

Hyakken was, however, well aware of the rising militarism and the concurrent discourse of the eternal; he taught at the prestigious Military Academy, and his job at Hōsei University located him just behind Yasukuni Shrine. Hyakken was also one of the few writers who refused to join the Japanese Literature Patriotic Association (Nihon Bungaku Hōkokukai) founded in May 1942. This was the most successful of the government's organizations to mobilize writers for the imperial cause, as noted in the group's charter: the goal was to "establish our world view as writers of the Empire."[63] Although, as Jay Rubin notes, one had to be a member in order to write and publish during these years, Hyakken was able to put out three books between 1942 and 1945: *Lightning at Sea, The Road Back,* and a book of poetry titled *Hyakkien's Haiku* (*Hyakkien haiku,* 1943). This may have been due to Hyakken's use of the *zuihitsu,* a form that was not seen to possess the critical potential of literature. The suppression of thought and speech in wartime Japan led many authors to seek out the *zuihitsu,* and critics such as Tosaka Jun and Miki Kiyoshi debated the value of the form in the 1930s.[64]

Hyakken addresses the issue of national and personal memory in his short stories, where he critiques the rhetoric of war as a discourse of shifting symbols and an erasure of the history of modernization. Chapter 3 of the present study examines two stories that reference the war. The first takes up the issue of memory through an actuality film from the Russo-Japanese

War. The real General Nogi is replaced by his blurry, celluloid, commodified image in this film that lacks a cohesive, heroic narrative. The second story describes a nightmarish visit to the Yūshūkan, now rendered a fleeting specter haunted by dead soldiers with eerie yellow skin. Unlike Hyakken's earlier works in which characters were unable to access the past, this story shows the reader how that past has been recreated and recast to meet new and different needs. He demonstrates that those memories are malleable, subjective, and ambiguous—a message that would have been dangerous in wartime Japan, where the government had little tolerance for indeterminacy. Hyakken's use of the fragmentary and ephemeral may have allowed him to evade the censors, but looking beyond the lack of openly political language, his antiwar message is clear.[65]

In 1938, as the war raged and Japan expanded its empire in Asia, Hyakken published a collection of vignettes on the city titled "Tokyo Diary" ("Tōkyō nikki"). What may seem like an unusual topic given the national context turned out to be another opportunity for Hyakken to counter the increasingly vehement rhetoric of the war. In focusing on the city, Hyakken returns to *the* site of prewar modernity. Tokyo underwent fundamental changes that shaped it into a prototype of the present day metropolis, integrating monuments, buildings, and plazas into the city design. The cities were modernizing so rapidly that they were quickly leaving behind the traditional ways of the countryside. Taishō was the age of the city and the era of urban planning that wrought the largest changes on the local landscape, specifically on Tokyo, the cultural, literary, and political capital. New concepts entered the local language as urban planning (*toshi keikaku*) transformed everyday urban spaces. The 1920s were also the era of the "city story" (*toshi shōsetsu*), in which well-known landmarks, neighborhoods, and prominent features of Tokyo's new urban reality commonly appeared, as the city became an oft-used setting.[66] This urban literature, however, was lost to the canon as writers turned away from the city in the 1930s and denounced their earlier fiction, some even deleting these stories from their collected works.[67] As military concerns took over, the national focus shifted from the local to the war overseas, and the city largely disappeared as an idea in Japan.[68]

Hyakken's "Tokyo Diary" must be placed within the context of rising militarism and nationalism. As argued in Chapter 4, Hyakken's return to the city is working against the backdrop of the conservative discourse of the Return to Japan movement that denied the national identity found in the modern city and promoted a return to an immutable, often rural, Japanese past. Hyakken refutes the ideology of this movement as his protagonist visits important sites of modernity, capitalism, and imperialism concentrated in the high city: Tokyo Station, the Marunouchi Building, the Imperial Palace. He conducts a literary archeology to uncover alternate histories and strata of memory buried within the urban. Like his conservative counterparts in the Return to Japan movement, Hyakken is also engaging in the production of memory. However, for Hyakken, this memory is temporary and multivalent; it does not offer the unambiguous rhetoric of a return to a Japanese past somehow untainted by Western modernity. Hyakken demonstrates time and again that such an immutability does not exist. Rather, Hyakken's memory leads us back to the city, the locus of Western modernity and an important center for the modernization reforms that brought the nation into the new century. He leads us back to the very site that the Return to Japan intellectuals assailed as a site of loss of traditional identity.

As the war intensified, the government became more and more successful at bringing public discourse under its control, and literature and literary journalism were grinding to a halt. The government succeeded in shutting down the major liberal magazines *Chūō kōron* and *Kaizō*, and although literature in all forms continued to be written, literary concerns were forced to serve the militarist agenda. After Japan's defeat, writers struggled to come to terms with their complicity with the war.[69] Hyakken escaped these debates, due to a number of factors. Unlike well-known writers such as Tanizaki Jun'ichirō and Nagai Kafū, who opted for silence or a "literature of nostalgia," Hyakken did publish during the war.[70] His decision to write *zuihitsu* may have spared him censorship, given the lightweight, non-intellectual (apolitical) reputation of the genre. However, his work from the 1930s does carry a clear critique of the state—a critique through a return to a past that neither endorsed the national rhetoric nor posed an immediately recognizable threat to it.

## Critical Possibilities in the Modern Everyday

Hyakken's language of protest is couched within a mundane, everyday reality that references the past through outmoded images such as old newsreels, magic lanterns, and monuments from the early days of modern urban planning. He takes the reader back to a time when these objects had an aura, a sense of novelty and awe. In doing so, Hyakken returns a magic to his texts and creates an environment in which the familiar becomes unfamiliar, therefore allowing for the possibility of transformation or critique. This possibility of finding the extraordinary with the ordinary happens within the context of the everyday.

The uncontrollable disruption of the present by the spectral past, seen in Hyakken's texts, takes the forms of memories, ghosts, and doubles. Lost history returns in a disturbingly fragmented, uninvited form. This characteristic of Hyakken's fiction, concentrated in *Realm of the Dead*, has been read as the evocation of a dreamlike state emanating from the author's diaries. The failed reunion of the protagonist with his father in the story "Realm of the Dead" is indicative of Hyakken's losing his own father, or metaphorically, his mentor Sōseki. This rubric of dreams weds an autobiographical reading of Hyakken's work with aspects of the fantastic.

The focus on the dreamlike quality of Hyakken's work began as early as 1921 when Akutagawa Ryūnosuke extolled the virtues of Hyakken's writing through a favorable comparison with their mentor: "Unlike Natsume Sōseki's 'Ten Nights of Dreams,' these stories don't merely pretend to be dreams, but are written exactly as if they were dreamt."[71] Postwar critics continued this line of analysis, describing Hyakken's fiction as a "dream novel" (*mugen shōsetsu*) and a "series of dreams" (*yume no keiretsu*) from which the protagonist can never awaken.[72] Certainly the nonlinear narratives, sudden scene changes, and appearance of unexplainable phenomena, such as the return of the dead or of the unborn, doppelgangers, and mythical beasts, could fit a dream pattern. The literary inheritance of texts such as Sōseki's "Ten Nights of Dreams" inclined critics to interpret the events in Hyakken's short stories as emanating from the realm of nocturnal visions.[73]

But to confine the analysis to the dreamlike is to disconnect Hyakken's work from the realities of the prewar era, and to prevent the emergence of a critique of modernity and the state. Rather than discuss Hyakken's stories in terms of real and unreal, fantasy and dreams, we can utilize the idea of the everyday, specifically focusing on the dialectical nature of the term, which signifies both the quotidian existence of daily life regulated by capitalist modernity, and "the everyday as Other—as that which is outside, that which is omitted or escapes from the regimentation of the modern world."[74] This paradigm illuminates the significance of Hyakken's temporal disruptions, his focus on the present, and the irretrievability of the past. It also accounts for his use of doubles, repetition, and fragmentation. We can see the unusual in Hyakken's texts emerging from a mundane linguistic world.

The concept of the everyday allows for connections to be made across Hyakken's literary styles that have traditionally been regarded as disconnected and unrelated. Hyakken's fiction and *zuihitsu* exemplify the double nature of the everyday; they are representations of the everyday as quotidian, and at the same time are unregimented, heterogeneous narrative developments outside of standard literary modes. It also creates a bridge between Hyakken's writing and prewar culture; both literary and public discourse in the 1920s and 1930s characterized the everyday or "everydayness" (*nichijōsei*) as a shifting notion, a doubleness created through the experience of living in multiple modernities, multiple realities. For prewar Japanese, the everyday represented both halves of Baudelaire's equation: a constantly shifting lived reality and an idealized immutable that only existed in the past or in some unforeseen future. Hyakken represents this duality in the textual fabric of his work. The following chapters examine these transformative possibilities of the everyday in Hyakken via the local Japanese context of the prewar and the lens of Western theory.

The prewar period was characterized by an "overwhelming, almost overdetermined, interest in and enthusiasm for everydayness."[75] The use of the term "everyday," however, was paradoxical. It represented the site of modernity, as well as a means of apprehending and critiquing modernity and culture itself. It was the key term in prewar debates over the content of daily life and the need to identify cultural purpose and meaning. The concern for it was shared by modernist avant-garde and modern consumer alike.[76] The meaning of the everyday was tightly bound to the notion of culture, and remained an open site of contestation. The term was used by a range of critical and commercial voices without any agreement on its meaning. It was within this very ambiguity that the discourse was formed.

From the viewpoint of material culture, everyday modern life was marketed to the public through Hollywood films and print culture, in the department stores and on the city streets. Citizens negotiated the modernity of daily life at their jobs, at home, and in their leisure activities. Ethnographers Kon Wajirō and Gonda Yasunosuke envisioned culture as a series of creative everyday practices. They located potential in the everyday consumer culture rather than in an unchanging national character. These men sought to reunite the everyday with the reality of daily life.[77] Along with Kon and Gonda, other critics examined the "primacy of the performative present."[78] Tosaka Jun saw the potential for critical thinking in the *zuihitsu* as thought itself became "quotidianized." Hirabayshi Hatsunosuke studied the relationship between new technology and the experience of everyday life, looking at the ways in which science mediated mass culture.

In contrast, philosophers Watsuji Tetsurō, Kuki Shūzō, folklorist Yanagita Kunio, and the Japan Romantic School (Nihon Roman-ha) did not see the everyday as an ever-changing present, the now of immediate experience, the lived moment. Rather, they desired to place the everyday outside of "contemporary phenomenal life" or to reject the experience of modernity all together.[79] For these conservative thinkers, the everyday was a past of tradition that could be stabilizing or binding, but that had fixed conceptions of community and culture used to check the consumptive production of the present.

As this modern life clashed with traditional practices and values, thinkers began to question its authenticity as "Japanese culture." Amidst the militarist climate of the 1930s, culture took on the dangerous connotations of liberalism, and the state sought to control its harmful influence. Various attempts were made to rein in culture and control its excesses. Debates raged in the 1920s and 1930s over the meaning of culture and its use as both a philosophical concept and a consumer marketing device to sell everything from houses and lifestyles to fountain pens. Everydayness was the key term in prewar culture debates. It is not an overstatement to say that in Japan, daily life became the site of ideological contestation attempting to define cultural purpose.

The discourse of modernity upon which Hyakken comments converges around this notion of the everyday. In Hyakken's debut text, *Realm of the Dead,* he struggles with the shifting nature of reality and with the notion of doubleness. The stories are set in the pastoral, but Hyakken's protagonist is subject to the "ever-fluctuating stimulus field of constant immediacy" characteristic of the metropolis.[80] In his work, Hyakken reproduces the patterns of modern urban life: the quick, chaotic, and fragmentary experiences that lead to a nervous restlessness. Like the city dweller, Hyakken's protagonist develops a distracted mode of attention to survive in this new environment.[81] The modern everyday forces a constant reaction to the new, but also an adjustment to the relentless repetition of capitalist modernity: the routine of the factories, of a regimented, segmented time. The doubleness created through this experience has been discussed in terms of a "cultural code switching" between the old and new, the Japanese and Western.[82] But as a writer, Hyakken reacts to the doubles produced via the simulated realities of modernity. The modern, capitalist system exchanged the unique experience for a plurality of copies found in film, photography, print culture, and the mass media.

This endless, shifting process remained hidden by a capitalist progress which presented itself as a homogeneous experience. In order to reveal the unevenness and discontinuity of the capitalist urban everyday, Hyakken returns to a time when the changes of modernity and our means of interacting with the world—visual, textual, oral—were still new. In *Realm of the Dead* Hyakken uncovers the psychological state of the urban dweller not yet indifferent to the shocks of modern spaces, media, technologies, and interactions.[83] Hyakken's return is to a time of aura. The old actuality film in "Triumphant March into Port Arthur" recalls the alienating and emotion-filled reactions of Japanese viewers seeing celluloid images of their dead countrymen on foreign soil for the first time. The wandering in "Tokyo Diary" evokes the disorientation produced by new urban spaces, and grants Hyakken's protagonist access to lost histories and mysterious happenings hidden in the fabric of the modern city. Hyakken's attempt to return aura to the text relies on his ability to infuse a magic into his language. It is within this linguistic realm of aura that Hyakken finds the extraordinary necessary for transforming the everyday.

The everyday provided a means of escaping, undermining, and subverting the simultaneously disorienting and homogenizing forces of modernity. "Japanese thinkers envisaged an everyday world filled with alienation brought on by routine yet still filled with possibility, the different in the same: the place of transformation."[84] The everyday is a site of resistance to the alienation and oppression of modernity, and a place to find the extraordinary within the ordinary. Hyakken focuses on the spaces of everyday life (*nichijō kūkan*): the modern city—museums, buildings, plazas—and the urban experience; the cinema and the new subjectivities and spaces it created; and the media spaces of journalism and literature.[85] Within these spaces he introduces alternate temporalities by focusing on the outmoded, which has the power to disrupt the homogenizing effects of capitalist modernity, as it did for contemporary European Modernists.[86] He employs techniques common to Western theorists of the everyday who critiqued capitalist commodity culture, such as the defamiliarization of Surrealism and the wandering or *dérive* of the Situationists. This methodological similarity allows Hyakken, like his Western counterparts, to reveal the discontinuity of capitalist modernity.

Writing *Realm of the Dead* at the beginning of his career, Hyakken could not see the everyday as a site of resistance. He did not share the optimism of Walter Benjamin, who envisioned the distracted mode of modernity as a means for critical articulation. Moving into the *zuihitsu*, Hyakken honed his critical voice, but it was not until his stories referencing the war that Hyakken truly found the potential for transformation. Unlike Western theorists Simmel, Benjamin, Henri Lefebvre, and Michel de Certeau, who saw transformation at the level of everyday practice, for Hyakken, possibility lay in the language of writing.[87] His return to aura happened at a point when the nation's intellectuals were searching for a timeless past of cultural tradition. By focusing on discontinuity, Hyakken was able to turn his language of cultural modernism into a critique of the war rhetoric, which had erased earlier moments and voices that existed outside the narrative of an ahistorical, homogeneous national. Amidst the rapidly militarizing world around him, Hyakken found his own means of protest within the language of the literary.

ONE

# *Resisting Modernity in* Realm of the Dead

> I walked down a long embankment toward Ushimado harbor, between the vast ocean and a shallow inlet. The reeds in the inlet stood tall, peeking over my path. In the distance they had grown even taller, finally engulfing the embankment.
>
> —Uchida Hyakken, "Fireworks" ("Hanabi")

*Realm of the Dead* opens as Hyakken's unnamed protagonist looks into the distance and sees his path disappear. The extreme disorientation associated with this experience characterizes the protagonist's predicament throughout the collection, the author's attempt to navigate the modern literary world, and the reaction of an elite literary audience baffled by a collection of bizarre stories in a book with no page numbers. *Realm of the Dead* met with a cold critical reception, and Hyakken's anxiety was acute. Writing his debut book after the loss of his mentor, Hyakken was seeking entry into the literary world, all the while recognizing that the very distinction he sought meant little in the modern representational system. *Realm of the Dead* is a metaphor for the writing process, and Hyakken's book is an act of resistance to the new consumptive patterns of modern print culture. But this act, the book itself, was a failure. Hyakken successfully recreated the experience of modernity, but did not find a means to critically apprehend it. This attempt to return to an earlier relationship between author, text, and reader was misunderstood by his peers. Time, however, worked in his favor. *Realm of the Dead* came to occupy a central place in his oeuvre, as postwar critics lauded the book as the essence of Hyakken's writing.

The bewildering changes of modernity are readily seen in the collection's eighteen short stories. Hyakken's protagonist moves through unsettling landscapes where he meets seemingly familiar faces from an intrusive yet inaccessible past. These pastoral settings are infused with fear and loss, as the protagonist encounters dead family members, menacing women, and mythical animals. The rural locale does not insulate him from the afflictions of the modern urbanite—the unease of open spaces, loneliness of the crowd, disassociation from any concrete historical experience, neurasthenia, and social isolation—for the countryside home is now also a foreign space.[1] Within this setting, Hyakken's protagonist attempts to make sense of his encounters and to understand his past and himself. He is haunted by his past, but is unable to articulate it as memory, and hence control it. Unmoored from history, he is rendered mute by the modern experience. Trapped in the present, he is doomed to a life of repetition without meaning. Hyakken leaves his protagonist paralyzed, speechless, and alone. This alienating, unsettling landscape is clearly one of modernity. *Realm of the Dead* is a response "to the new complexities of a social existence passed among strangers in an atmosphere of intensified nervous and psychic stimulation."[2] Hyakken depicts the very historical moment in which he is living.

Modernity is also represented in the writing experience. Hyakken traversed a new literary landscape with *Realm of the Dead*, one characterized by a capitalist system of representation. He was part of the market-oriented, technologically sophisticated industry, which facilitated the spread of literature and the creation of a nationally read canon. Hyakken's writing demonstrates how the modern capitalist system "makes exchangeable what is singular" by replacing the unique experience with a plurality of copies.[3] This plurality denies Hyakken a voice—namely, the unique voice of the author. Like his characters, Hyakken is rendered mute by modernity, and ultimately the trauma experienced in the book is a loss of distinction and of the aura. Hyakken realizes that the prophetic text no longer exists and he writes his own elegy.

In evoking the language and symbols of cultural modernism, Hyakken created a text that was difficult to read, and *Realm of the Dead* was not received well at the time of its debut. Hyakken's use of defamiliarization—casting the outmoded, the fragmentary, and the everyday as Other—represents his attempt to find forms for interacting with and capturing the experience of living in the modern world. The critical failure of the text further confirms Hyakken's message about the impossibility of creating shared meaning in the modern representational system. Although he did create a form suited to represent this distracted modern experience, in the end, he did not find a viable means of effectively communicating and productively engaging it. Hyakken was not able to critically articulate the modernity he experienced, and he did not see the possibility of transformation and positive change. Ultimately this failure took on importance in the late 1930s, when Hyakken's return to *Realm of the Dead* served as a rejection of conservative calls for a return to a national past.

## Suspect Vision and Failed Reunions

In "Realm of the Dead," the title story of Hyakken's collection, the protagonist encounters his father in a ramshackle, dimly lit chophouse by the river:

> On this moonless and starless night, it was only the top of the embankment that shone with a dim, gray light. At some point the men had climbed the hill, and I could still see their figures trailing off in the faint glow. I tried to make out my father, but the shapes of the men blurred together into an undistinguishable mass. (77)

The story overflows with a painful nostalgia, and the protagonist's missed opportunity to reunite with his father represents one of the many failures in Hyakken's text. The failure not only involves the familial connection, but the possibility for the protagonist to better know himself. Set in a darkened borderland, the protagonist attempts to come to terms with his past; in actuality, his father is dead. But "Realm of the Dead" ends as Hyakken's protagonist turns his back on the embankment, and on his father, and heads home, bringing the collection to a close. Through these actions, he effectively turns his back on the past and on his attempts to create meaning out of this encounter.[4]

The protagonist's lack of success is due to his impaired vision; the darkness of the setting exacerbates the difficulty he has in seeing his father and accessing his own memories. The ability to see has traditionally been associated with the ability to know; the power of vision is the power of knowledge and self-knowledge. However, in "Realm of the Dead" vision does not lead to knowledge of the past or of the self. In everyday modernity, the link between the two has been broken. The reliability of the eye decreases along with that of the objects being viewed. The communicative power of a stable, objective vision is lost with the viewing itself. Traditional forms of seeing can no longer be used to represent modern experience.

Hyakken addresses these issues through an obvious attention to visuality, the position of the observer, and light and darkness.

> Atop the steep embankment a dark path stretched silently and coldly into the night. Inside the dingy chophouse below, old tin lanterns cast a faint glow out into the blackness of the mounded earth. I was sitting in one of the worn-out seats, not eating, but filled with a longing for company. The table was bare, and the lonely reflection off the surface chilled my face. (1: 65)

The glow inside the chophouse comes from the *kantera*, a Japanese loan word from the Portuguese for portable tin lanterns lit by oil or candles.[5] These lanterns create the dim lighting that provides not only atmosphere, but also an integral element to the plot. Seated in this dimly lit restaurant, the protagonist's "lonely reflection" off the bare tabletop chills his face as he looks over at and listens in on a group of older men gathered next to him. But he is not able to see or hear clearly; figures appear as shadows and sounds are muted. A barrier separates the protagonist from his surroundings, but it is not completely impermeable, and certain images and sounds do penetrate.[6] These range from the disappointingly murky to the shockingly clear.

The protagonist's difficulty seeing comes not solely from the dim lighting of the *kantera* and the objects he seeks to view. It is a function of shifts in the concept of vision itself introduced into Japan in the later part of the eighteenth century. Western viewing devices such as peep boxes, optiques, and magic lanterns brought about changes in the "systems of visual awareness."[7] Such devices offered access to a view of the real through the transformative powers of the objective "Western scientific gaze," but this reality was mechanically produced. These objects transformed the nature of viewing and spurred debates over the truth or falsity of this new form of visuality.[8] Hyakken references one of these old viewing devices, and the debates themselves, when describing the way in which his protagonist sees a man (his father) in the restaurant.

> The man with the loud voice was older, a little over fifty. His singular image reflected off my eye like a shadow picture from a magic lantern. I could see him gesture as he spoke to the others obscured in the darkness. Although his silhouette was visible to me, I couldn't tell what was going on. I couldn't make out his words, and his voice wasn't as clear as it had been just moments ago. (1: 65)

Hyakken describes the man as a shadow picture (*kage-e*) from the magic lantern, or as it was called in the mid-eighteenth century, the "devil lantern" (*oni tōrō*).[9] This older technology originally came from Dutch projections of images drawn on glass. Images could be cast inside a room and onto different screens. Magic lanterns were still popular at the turn of the twentieth century, during Hyakken's childhood. This seeming anachronism was due to the time compression of accelerated modernization in Japan that resulted in the overlapping of technologies, the coexistence of magic lanterns and commercial films.[10] These lanterns were also a common literary device. Uno Kōji's "The Dream Viewing Room" ("Yume miru heya," 1923), features a magic lantern as a beloved object from childhood and a metaphor for the imagination.[11] Whereas Uno delights in seeing that which is not really there, Hyakken describes the frustration and fear of a subjective and sometimes false vision.

Hyakken uses devices from the late Edo period, but his is not the powerful, dissecting "Western scientific gaze." Rather, Hyakken reveals the stunted power of the visual, the broken link between vision and knowledge. This is not the rupture caused by photography, but an earlier shift that Jonathan Crary locates in the nineteenth century, specifically in the nexus of new viewing devices, the physicality of the observer, and philosophical, scientific, and social discourses. These forces worked to displace the stable and fixed relations of vision and knowledge that were exemplified in the camera obscura. This led to the production of a new kind of observer and the subjectivization of vision. The reliability of the eye decreased, a result of the shift from objective to subjective, and was challenged by other optical devices. The vision of the eye no longer predicated a "real world."[12]

In Hyakken's time, issues of reality and truth came to the fore most obviously in the area of film, as viewers in Japan quickly came to demand realism and truthfulness less than a decade after the introduction of the medium in 1897.[13] At the same time, consumer culture was creating simulated realities of modernity. Hyakken's "Realm of the Dead" is tinged with nostalgia for a slightly earlier time. A reader in the 1920s would have seen Hyakken's *kantera*-generated magic lantern as outdated, especially when compared to the fast-paced illuminations of the silver screen. The magic lantern pictures would recall a lost childhood, making them perfect for the story of a reunion between a father and son.

Hyakken's antiquated magic lantern, however, is not pure nostalgia; rather, it is a conscious use of the outmoded to defamiliarize the viewing experience and return an aura to the process through this temporal distance.[14] This allows Hyakken to play with the position of the observer in order to demonstrate how modern vision is subjective and suspect. Hyakken's protagonist looks across the dark restaurant, and the image of his father is cast into silhouette by the light of the *kantera,* which serves as the light source for the magic lantern. The object of the viewing, the man, appears as a silhouette against the darkness, a one-dimensional image. Although this image moves and speaks, the protagonist is unable to see or hear him well. The protagonist is placed in the position of observer, but is simultaneously made part of the viewing apparatus, namely the screen onto which the images are projected and made visible. The images are literally cast onto his eye: "His singular image *reflected off my eye* like a shadow picture from a magic lantern" (watashi no *me ni,* kage-e no yō ni *utsutte ite*). The Sino-Japanese character for the verb *utsuru* connotes a sense of light, reflection, and vividness.[15] The connection between darkness and visuality is manifest in the language itself. As both observer and viewing apparatus, the protagonist lacks the objective distance necessary to see his father.

The reference to shadow pictures also provides an important clue to the familial relation between the protagonist and this man. The magic lantern is related to another important lantern in Hyakken's story, a votive lantern (*chōchin*) used at the Festival of the Dead (*obon*), a summer festival for remembering one's ancestors, which is also known as the Feast of Lanterns (*chōchin no matsuri*).[16] Lanterns are lit to guide and welcome home the spirits of the dead. Earlier in Hyakken's story, one of the men complains about the protagonist, "He couldn't be bothered to light a lantern and come greet you" (1: 65). The man is referring to a custom observed in the countryside, where family members light lanterns, proceed to the gravesite to meet the spirits of their ancestors, and guide them back to the ancestral home. The son (protagonist) in Hyakken's story does not observe these customs in remembering his father, and, in fact, this authentic, premodern light source is no longer an option for a modern viewing. Without the light of the lantern, his father is unable to make the return trip. This initial failure to reunite has repercussions for the end of the story. It also means that the father will only appear to the son as a one-dimensional image; he is a ghost visible only through shadow pictures.

The men leave the restaurant and ascend the embankment. The protagonist tries to follow, but can no longer find his father as the blurry mass of men moves into the distance. The story ends as the protagonist is also transformed into a shadow image: "I cast my teary eyes to the ground. In the light of the lantern, my shadow loomed large against the black embankment. Watching it, I cried for a long time. With the embankment at my back, I returned on the dark road through the fields" (77).

His form literally becomes a shadow created by the *kantera* light, projected and enlarged on the embankment. Rather than his eye, the embankment that he failed to climb now serves as the screen, allowing him to view himself. This screen (the embankment) is a barrier separating the protagonist from his father. The men's images are projected onto different screens and hence they never meet. The protagonist returns home, presumably leaving the realm of the dead to return to the world of the living. However, this final image of the protagonist as shadow also raises the prospect that he, too, is a ghost. It is possible that both men are dead and that even in death they are denied a reunion.

The modernity of magic lanterns created a new visuality, but Hyakken argues that this new vision is not a path to self-knowledge. We have become incorporated into the machinery of the visual, and become part of the viewing devices, but in this process we have lost the objective view of the eye. Hyakken's protagonist is given a mechanically generated view of himself on the embankment screen, but this view hinders not only his ability to reunite with his father, but his ability to see into himself. With self-knowledge, the protagonist would have been able to piece together his memories and recognize his father at some point earlier in the story. This knowledge would have penetrated the dimness that characterizes "Realm of the Dead." But, unable to perceive the real and, hence, understand the self, Hyakken's characters are left alone in the shadows with no possibility to create meaning out of these chance encounters with memory.

## Textual Doubles and Echoes of the Past

The protagonist continues to be haunted by the past in "The Companion" ("Michizure"). While crossing a dark mountain pass, he encounters a strange man:

> A cold wind blew down the hillside, and dead leaves rustled as I descended the dark mountain pass. I heard the sound of running water around me, but whether it was far or near I couldn't tell. In the recess of a distant mountain, two or three lights flickered in the wind. Then I was surprised to see another appear much closer, glimmering like a raindrop. But those lights were no use to me. They shone back indifferently. The warmth spreading across my back soon turned to a chill.
>
> I trudged on. A man walked beside me. I didn't know when we had joined up, but he never strayed from my side. He only broke his silence to call out my name, "Ei-*san*." He wouldn't respond to my questions, leaving only the cold echo of his footsteps as we walked together. At times I noticed him, but kept on as if he wasn't there. The only thing I knew for sure was that I had crossed the pass alone. (1: 34)

The protagonist has trouble overcoming his disbelief when the man claims to be his unborn brother, but even after he has been convinced, he finds himself unable to form a connection with him. He cannot make sense of this encounter because he cannot access the past. The key to decoding both the unusual landscape and his personal history lies in intertextual links that have been severed. The preexisting textual context, an earlier version of the story, has not only been lost, but is no longer a valid means of transmitting meaning. Without access to this information, the protagonist cannot move beyond the present to acknowledge his brother, and hence, his experience in this story is characterized as déjà vu. Not only does the protagonist feel he is traveling in circles, but he begins to resemble other characters he meets. In the process, he loses his singular identity and becomes a function of the modern, capitalist, repetitive text.

Although they are walking together, the protagonist cannot remember when this man first appeared at his side. In addition to the existence of this unexplained visitor, the road they walk along, the lights in the distance, and the sounds of nature signal to the protagonist that something is amiss. The protagonist wonders if they are walking along a riverbank, but he is unable to find any water nearby. Yet somehow, despite the withered landscape, he keeps hearing running water at an indistinguishable place in the distance. These inexplicable sounds and features act to defamiliarize the landscape. This is not the nostalgic space of a pastoral home. Hyakken removes that familiarity in order to introduce this unusual familial connection.

As readers, we have the sense that the existence of an actual riverbank would be a welcome sight to the protagonist; it would provide him recourse to traditional narratives that would help explain his circumstances. The riverbank is a site of liminality, a locale for ghosts from the kabuki theater and the spirits of dead children, who congregate at the riverbed of judgment to grieve for their parents in the other world.[17] Although traditional narratives of the riverbank might help Hyakken's protagonist make sense of his situation, confirming the spectral nature of his guide would make for rather cold comfort. Even this certainty, however, is not allowed. The road is so dark the protagonist is unable to see where he is going and at times he wonders if he has wandered off the path. The blackness of the night also defies explanation; he cannot see his own feet, yet he is able to distinguish features of the distant landscape, which is somehow visible even though the lights in the far hills are gone. The protagonist's vision is again compromised by the murky setting.

As he walks with this companion, the protagonist relies on the sound of this man's footsteps to guide him along the path.[18] He is unfamiliar with the lay of the land and begins to fear he is traveling in circles when he keeps hearing the sound of running water. This spatial déjà vu and the increasing familiarity, both of the landscape and his companion's voice, work together to produce the sense that the protagonist is repeating actions of some time in the past, without necessarily being fully aware of what they were then or what the repercussions are now.

The protagonist may in fact be repeating his actions from other stories in the collection. The reader can find a clue to the identity of this strange companion in "The Echo" ("Kodama"). At one point in this earlier story, the protagonist and a woman pass by a statue of Jizō, the Buddhist guardian of pregnant women and children, born and unborn. In front of the statue is a votive candle that appears to the protagonist to have been recently lit. This candle may have been lit for the protagonist's guide in "The Companion."

Hyakken utilizes the effect of spatial and temporal déjà vu to identify this companion. As the author plays with the flow of time, the protagonist experiences a coexistence of the present and past, as time advances and retreats, repeating itself. This is not the regimented, segmented time of the modern rational, but a circular time, one that folds back on itself. The companion exists outside of the homogeneous modern time, residing in the everyday as Other. His true identity as the protagonist's unborn brother is revealed here in the cyclical time of karma and rebirth. Hence the significance of the votive candle in "The Echo."

As the protagonist (Ei-*san*) walks with this strange companion who claims to be his unborn brother, the man pleads for recognition, begging the protagonist to address him as "brother." The protagonist is reluctant to comply, and in his verbal exchange with the companion their identities begin to overlap.

> "Ei-*san,* I want to hear Father's voice. Is it like yours?"
>
> "How would I know?" I snapped back at him. And then it hit me with the chill of icy water. His voice—it was the same as mine!

"That's it, that's the voice!" he said, almost choking on his tears. I wavered between dread and sorrow.

"Ei-*san*, please say it."

"Uuuhh," I said, filled with sadness at the thought of calling out to my unborn brother.

"Are you going to say it? You don't know how happy it would make me. Please, hurry up," he said.

As I listened to his pleas, I was losing the ability to tell our voices apart. Where did his end and mine begin? My eyes overflowed with tears. (1: 36–37)

The doubling or repetition works on multiple levels in this text. The protagonist recognizes that his voice is the same as his brother's, and the brother hears the father's voice in the protagonist. Identity is both plural and singular, floating and fixed. The protagonist comes closer to understanding this encounter in the conclusion of the story, when he suddenly realizes his role in past events.

Listening to him speak, I had the flash realization that somewhere, sometime, I had spoken those same words. The sound of that water—I'd heard it before, too. It was all so familiar to me now.

"If I leave now, who knows if we'll meet again," he said tearfully.

I struggled, but the sounds stuck in my throat. I listened to him speak in my own voice, and as I heard those unforgettable words, I longed for that painful time in the past. I was calling out to him, reaching for my brother, but in that instant this companion of mine was gone. My body suddenly felt heavy and I couldn't walk another step. (1: 37)

The sound of the companion's voice, coupled with that of the water, triggers a forgotten memory deep within the protagonist. Filtered through the experience of spatial and temporal déjà vu, the protagonist is placing himself in the same location, but in his brother's position, at some time in the past. Events from long ago repeat themselves; the roles have reversed, but the voice remains the same. The protagonist remembers speaking the same words as his unborn brother, but this act of memory retrieval leads to a physical paralysis. Having confirmed the existence of his brother, the protagonist is immobilized in the act of self-identification. He is unable to fully access this fragmentary memory, and hence he is unable to confirm his singular identity. Are he and the brother separate people, or is he reliving a moment from his own past?

This doubling effect is not limited to these two men.[19] The text of "The Companion," is riddled with doubles. One is Hyakken himself, whose given name is mentioned in the story. The protagonist is called "Ei-*san*," which is an affectionate abbreviation of both the protagonist's name and of Eizō, Hyakken's given name.[20] By giving the protagonist in "The Companion" a name, Hyakken distinguishes him from all the other protagonists in *Realm of the Dead*, who remain unnamed. By naming the protagonist after himself, Hyakken clues the reader into the significance of the doubling. However, the connection to Hyakken is not personal but textual, taking the form of two stories, which serve as pretexts for "The Companion." Like his unborn brother, these textual histories have the power to reveal the source of the protagonist's repeated actions, his déjà vu, but they are forever lost to him.

The first textual double is Natsume Sōseki's "Ten Nights of Dreams" ("Yume jūya," 1908). This short work by Sōseki is thought to have inspired the content and style of a number of the stories in *Realm of the Dead*.[21] The similarity to his mentor's work is apparent, but the significance of Hyakken's story lay in the element of uncertainty that he brings to Sōseki's themes. Sōseki's dream of the third night is thematically closest to "The Companion." This dream opens with the protagonist carrying a six-year-old child on his back, a child he later realizes is his own. The child is blind, yet he is able to guide the protagonist into the woods to the root of a cedar tree. Along the way, the child anticipates the protagonist's thoughts and fears, and is able to see into the past and the future.

> "A little further and you'll see what I mean. It was on a night just like this," he said from up on my back, as though speaking to himself.
>
> "What was?" I asked, all the while hoping to dodge the issue.
>
> "Come now, you know what I mean," his answer tinged with scorn.[22]

The protagonist begins to remember, but is afraid of what his memories will bring and hopes to abandon the child first. But once they approach the cedar, he is confronted with the truth about his past.

> "Father, it was at the base of that cedar, right?"
> "Yes, it was," I answered without thinking.
> "It was the fifth year of the Bunka era, the year of the dragon, was it not?"
> Yes, of course, it *was* the fifth year of Bunka, the year of the dragon.
> "You killed me exactly one hundred years ago."
> As soon as I heard the words, the realization suddenly hit me. On a dark night like this, at the root of a cedar, I had killed a blind man a hundred years ago in the fifth year of the Bunka era. The instant I became aware that I was a murderer, the boy on my back became as heavy as a statue of Jizō.[23]

The connection between the two stories is clear. The blindness of the child in Sōseki is represented by a different type of vision loss in Hyakken's story. Despite the child's inability to see, he serves as a guide for Sōseki's protagonist. In "The Companion" the darkness of the landscape keeps the protagonist from discerning his location, yet his companion has no trouble seeing or leading the way. The statue of Jizō in "The Echo" appears in Sōseki in the form of the child at the end of the story. But the key events linking the two stories are in the conclusions. Both protagonists have a flash realization of their role in past events, one that is triggered by the voice or words of their companions. In Sōseki, the protagonist realizes his past and the child turns to stone. In Hyakken, the protagonist's body becomes so heavy he can no longer move. Hyakken's protagonist is essentially transformed into the Jizō statue, in effect commemorating his unborn brother's death, and perhaps his own in another lifetime.

There are important differences here as well. Sōseki's protagonist is able to fully access his past and realize his role as murderer one hundred years ago. The cyclical nature of the hundred years adds a level of surety and coincidence more suited to a folktale. Hyakken's protagonist is not granted this level of certainty. He mentions a painful yet nostalgic time in the past, but he does not know the details of that past event or his relationship to his unborn brother during this time. Unlike in Sōseki's story, Hyakken's protagonist cannot fully explain the existence of this man via the karmic cycle of rebirth, because Hyakken elides important details regarding the past event and the relationship between the two actors. Neither can Hyakken's protagonist (or the reader) be certain the companion is strictly a doppelganger. The answers lie in another text that has been lost to both subject and reader: the original version of "The Companion," titled "The Embankment" ("Dote," 1917).[24] Although the setting and the existence of the companion remain the same, Hyakken significantly revised the story for publication in *Realm of the Dead*. "The Embankment" describes an eerie encounter in the mountains, but the visitor never identifies himself as the protagonist's unborn brother. Rather, he leads the protagonist to a well in the mountains and tells a story about an illicit affair between a Buddhist nun and priest. A horse happened upon the couple during a secret rendezvous, and became possessed by some unknown spirit. It cried out in a humanlike voice. The nun fled and the horse pursued. She was unable to outrun the horse and jumped into a well. When the priest finally caught up, the horse was wildly circling the well, and he could not approach. The priest killed himself in the woods. After relating this story, the companion turns to look at the protagonist, who finally understands: "Now I understand, I thought, crouched down as though struck by a cold bolt of lightening. In that instant, my companion bellowed in a voice so loud and frightening as to split open the earth, 'I am that priest!' And then this man, the scene before me, and the sound of the water all disappeared."[25]

This early version is more traditional in its storytelling techniques. It reads like a *nō* play, in which the protagonist encounters a ghost from the past. In such ghost *nō* plays as "Atsumori" or "Nonomiya," the narrator/protagonist is a traveling monk who meets a person with connections to a specific locale.[26] This local person tells a story about somebody from the past, and seems to be privy to unusually detailed information. The local bids farewell to the monk, only to return as his or her true self, the spirit of a great warrior or court lady with ties to the present location. The monk listens to the spirit's story and often assists in releasing the ghost from the karmic cycle that traps it in this state of eternal haunting.

"The Embankment" has clear similarities to this dramatic tradition. The companion/ghost of Hyakken's story leads the protagonist to the well, a specific geographical location. He sits on the large, stone wall out of which grows a strange grass that resembles women's hair. The protagonist approaches and looks in the well. He sees the reflection of the small circle of water and hears the sound of a vortex churning inside. The companion then begins his tale. After revealing his true identity, the companion fades away, confirming his spiritual nature. The sound of the water disappears, as do the images of which the companion spoke. The protagonist is released from the haunting.

When Hyakken rewrote the story, he recast the companion as the protagonist's unborn brother and added a significant amount of dialogue regarding the companion's desire to have his brother acknowledge him. Hyakken purposely created a deeper connection between the two men, implying that the companion may also be a previous incarnation of the protagonist, who remembers words spoken in his own voice at some unspecified time in the past. However, Hyakken does not completely erase the earlier story. The protagonist in "The Companion" continues to hear water out in the distance, but without the accompanying explanation of the original version.

> We walked side by side on a long road that might have been a riverbank, but as my eyes wandered in the darkness they found no water, only the black surface of the withered, harvested fields sucking in the wind. Still I kept hearing that sound, as if someone were trying to churn up a deep, stagnant pool. Much to my relief, my companion's footsteps occasionally drowned out this noise, but the reprieve was short, and the sound of running water soon echoed in my ears again. (34)

The sound of this water is troubling because the protagonist cannot locate it. He keeps hearing it and starts to think he is walking in circles. It is further troubling because it is an echo of the tragedy told in the earlier text. Hyakken superimposed "The Companion" onto "The Embankment," but then removed enough of the original text to leave the references ungrounded and disjointed. The protagonist in "The Companion" keeps searching for the water, but he will never find it, because its source, the original text, has been lost in the process of reproduction. The doubling effect in "The Companion" is a comment not only on Hyakken's rewriting of "The Embankment," but on the loss of meaning inherent in the reproduction of texts in a modern capitalist system. The original (text, self, authorial voice) is lost in a plurality of copies. Hence the protagonist's interaction with these lost histories and texts takes the form of déjà vu. He keeps re-experiencing a moment of the present, but one that he does not have the means to understand. He cannot access the past because the intertextual links have been severed. But even if they were accessible, such references, such textual forms, no longer serve as a means to represent the modern experience.

## Rewriting Folklore

The shock of defamiliarization continues in "Kudan," a story of physical transformation, named for a monster of regional Japanese mythology. The story is reminiscent of the traditional narratives of kabuki and *nō* that are referenced in "The Companion," and of Franz Kafka's *The Metamorphosis*, but the surprise in Hyakken's tale is intensified by the intimacy of the first person narration. The story is based on memories of a tale from the protagonist's youth. However, once reborn as this legendary beast, the protagonist's memory, or perhaps the legend itself, goes awry:

> A large yellow moon hung in the sky, its flat color void of luminescence. I thought it was twilight but couldn't be sure. Was the bluish light filling the sky behind me from a setting sun or a rising sun? A dragonfly appeared against the moon's surface, but when its shadow

disappeared, I lost sight of it. The field around me extended as far as the eye could see. I stood soaking wet, water dripping from the end of my tail. As a child, I'd heard stories about the *kudan*, never thinking that this would be my fate. But now I was the bogeyman, a monstrous half-breed, a cow with a human face. In this vast, shadowless field, I had nowhere to turn. Why was I here? What had become of the creature that spawned me? (17)

Folklore provides a textual source for this and other stories in *Realm of the Dead,* but the comfortable familiarity of these tales from the past, whose endings are known in advance to the reader/listener, is beyond the protagonist's grasp.[27] The mapping of the world offered by folklore, one which runs counter to the rational explanations of modernity, is no longer a viable means to represent modern reality. Unlike in Meiji when science and mystery coexisted, in Taishō the mysterious has been relegated to the realm of nostalgia. In this modern world of information, the art of storytelling has come to an end.[28]

"Kudan" opens as the protagonist awakens, reborn a mythical creature. In this legendary landscape, he encounters family and friends, notably his son, as he tries to make sense of his new life. The wetness of the protagonist's body implies a recent exit from the womb. As he slowly dries off, he begins to remember his human life, but cannot figure out when it came to an end. Alone in this open field, he ponders his new existence, which according to legend will last only three days. Even more frightening to him is the realization that before he dies he must relate a prophecy. He takes comfort in the fact that he is alone. But no sooner does he hear the sound of human voices carried on the wind, when a crowd forms on the horizon and the situation becomes desperate.

The *kudan* is penned in by the masses awaiting his words, but as time passes they grow uneasy and every movement or lack of movement on his part is taken as a sign. At one point he is brought a bowl of water. Once he drinks from it, the crowd takes it as a sign that he will make the prophecy, but in actuality, he has nothing to say. He looks around and recognizes faces in the crowd, friends, relatives, old teachers, and students, all desperately trying to get a look at him, at the *kudan*. Although the protagonist has been reborn in this strange "underwater-like field" (1: 22), this other world is peopled with familiar faces from his human past.

The crowd comments that the beast looks familiar. The voices the protagonist hears are also familiar but he cannot place them, except one. At the end of the story, the crowd grows fearful of what the protagonist might say and decides maybe it is best not to hear the prophecy, but to kill the *kudan* before he speaks. This last suggestion is made by the *kudan*'s human son. Recognizing his son's voice, the *kudan* rises to see him and the crowd flees in fear. This is not the nostalgic reunion hoped for in "Realm of the Dead," but neither is it a source of trauma. Rather than lament a missed opportunity to reunite with his son, the protagonist, now left alone, stretches his forelegs, yawns, and feels confident that despite the legend, he will not die.

Hyakken's story is based on a local tale familiar from his childhood in Okayama, but his retelling diverges significantly from the original *kudan* story.[29] According to Hyakken's contemporary Toyoshima Yoshio, the mythical *kudan* of western Japan is a godlike beast born once every hundred years. The *kudan* lives for three years without eating, drinking, or speaking, foretells changes that will happen in the world, and then dies.[30] His muteness over the three years adds special value to the prophecy once it is made. Hyakken's *kudan* is most concerned about having to make this prophecy, about having to foretell the future. But the crowd flees and the beast is left alone. In fact, the only word he speaks is out of frustration that the crowd is trying to force him to drink more water.

> The man in the white kimono kept bringing me water. The crowd fell silent each time he offered me the vessel, but as soon as they saw I wasn't drinking from it, they'd roar back to life. He brought water more frequently, putting it closer to me each time. I found this annoying and got angry. Then another man, carrying another vessel, walked up to me and stared at me. He shoved the vessel up under my face. I recognized him. I couldn't say exactly who he was, but the sight of him riled me.

When he saw that I had no intention of drinking the water, he clicked his tongue in disgust. "Not going to drink it, huh?"

"No," I replied in anger.

The crowd went crazy. I looked around and saw to my shock that the stands had emptied and the onlookers were climbing over the fence. They ran toward me, cursing and raising their voices. I was terrified.

"He spoke."

"He finally said something."

"What'd he say?"

"Who cares? It's what he's *going* to say." (21)

This is hardly the lofty prophecy the crowd awaited, but it is the only word the *kudan* speaks in the entire story. The crowd's response is an indication of Hyakken's mocking attitude. In the end, the actual content of the long-awaited prophecy seems to matter little. In addition to this comic scene, Hyakken changed other details in the original myth: he collapsed the timeline from three years to three days, had the *kudan* drink water during his brief lifetime, and most importantly, allowed the *kudan* to live.

Hyakken took liberties with this piece of folklore. He used the *kudan* tale as a textual backdrop against which he crafted his own version of the events and created his own monster. This rewriting of the original tale works in such a way as to surprise the protagonist himself. The protagonist mentions having heard the story of the *kudan* as a child, but the tale, this story of local origin, does not turn out the way he remembers. Hyakken departs from the folkloric tradition.

Kawamura Jirō concludes that unlike the story of the Minotaur in Greek mythology, Hyakken's "Kudan" provides neither a powerful, awe-inspiring monster, nor a rich, allusive literary text. The *kudan* is not only a pathetic worldly creature, but worse, he is also a fake. If, indeed, the protagonist had been reborn as this unique being, then he would easily be able to fulfill the prophecy and tell the crowd what they want to hear. Hyakken's *kudan,* who retains his human face, is ashamed of his wretched appearance and fearful of being recognized. Kawamura interprets this fear of recognition as based not in shame over his physical form, but as a fear of what will happen when the crowd finds out he is not the real McCoy.[31] Hyakken frustrates the critics because "Kudan" resists the heavy mythical overtones of the Minotaur, the fate-driven coincidence of Sōseki, and the intense alienation of Kafka. Takahashi Hideo decried the *kudan* as a monster which "has no ties to tradition, imparts no meaning, allows for no interpretation."[32]

Takahashi is correct. Hyakken's *kudan* is not the *kudan* of folklore, but an anachronistic beast of modernity. The masses demand something from the *kudan* that he cannot provide. This *kudan* does not deliver the prophetic text expected of him, for such a text no longer exists. The *kudan* is no longer bound by the narratives of folklore, the "local ways of mapping the world" that were "dismantled and reorganized" by the scientific, ideology-driven Meiji powers.[33] By the time Hyakken was writing his story, these fantastic intrusions into the modern had been suppressed by reason and science, and supplanted by the accelerated exchange of information.[34] In the modern age, storytelling had become a mundane act of disseminating such information, although the *kudan* is incapable of even that.

"Kudan" is not a nostalgic lament for local ways of the past. Hyakken purposely rewrote the original tale to demonstrate that the narratives of folklore are no longer viable in the modern world. The experience of the modern everyday cannot be apprehended by traditional forms of communication, such as this local legend. The meaning of stories such as "Kudan" can be found precisely in the resistance to meaning, in the rejection of traditional overtones, and in the interpretational void Hyakken presents to the reader. The reader's inability to make sense of *Realm of the Dead* parallels the crowd's unsuccessful attempts to attribute meaning to the *kudan*'s behavior. "Kudan" serves as a metaphor for the interpretative process, but one that is short-circuited. Hyakken leaves the reader, like the protagonist, at the mercy of the story.

## The Fragment as Narrative Mode

Hyakken's protagonist attempts to engage with his past through the various means discussed above, but these traditional forms are dead ends. In personal terms, the protagonist does not reunite with his lost family members. In geographical terms, he never arrives at his intended destination.[35] Trapped in the present moment, he catches glimpses of the past and of the meaning behind his actions in the present. He longs for understanding, but the past intrudes in a form stripped of its narrative significance.

His experience is symptomatic of modernity; it is not only the case that traditional forms can no longer represent the modern experience, but that experience itself no longer accumulates to the point where it can become a meaningful vehicle for communication. Hence we see Hyakken's protagonist unable to move beyond the fragments of the past (his experience) to an articulation of the whole. This experience of the fragmentary occurs both on the level of the plot and narrative construction. Hyakken utilizes the fragment as a narrative mode to represent his character's disorienting encounters living in the modern world, and as a means to comment on the inability of the author to create a meaningful narrative. These forms the protagonist uses to access the past are the very forms the author uses to craft his stories, but they have been stripped of their meaning. Fragmentation of the protagonist's experience results in a fragmentation of the storytelling itself. The cohesive narrative is a thing of the past.[36]

This experience of the fragmentary comes into play in "Realm of the Dead" as the protagonist listens to his father tell a story. After seeing his father as a shadow picture, the protagonist's attention is drawn to a bee in the restaurant. Out of the murkiness, the insect comes into sharp focus, and the voice of the man (his father) acquires a newfound clarity. The man comments on the size of the bee and compares it to his thumb, which also stands in sharp contrast to the background. As he recounts a story about a bee, his voice becomes clearer, and the images he speaks of appear before the protagonist's eyes.

> "I once caught a bee in a glass pipe and sealed the ends with paper. The buzzing of the bee moving around inside made the paper vibrate like an organ." As his voice became clearer and clearer to me, I was overwhelmed with an unendurable longing, but for what I didn't know. Something weighed heavily on my heart as I listened.
>
> "I set the pipe on my desk and my son begged me to give it to him. Kind of a stubborn kid, you see, and once he got started, there was no telling him otherwise. Losing my temper, I grabbed the pipe and marched out to the verandah. The sun was shining on the rocks in the garden."
>
> I felt I could see that boat-shaped rock in the garden, shining in the sun. The image was so clear to me.
>
> "The bee got away when the glass smashed on the rocks. What a goddamn shame."
>
> "Father!" I cried out. But my voice didn't seem to reach him. The men quietly got up and left. (1: 66)

As the father retells the story, the protagonist senses a longing, but for what, he cannot say. The past begins to come into focus; his father's voice becomes clearer and the protagonist sees images that in their clarity stand in stark contrast to the murky setting of "Realm of the Dead." The father sketches an outline of the story, but for the protagonist it remains in fragments—a bee, the thumb, a rock in the sun. His vision is no longer obscured, but he lacks the ability to incorporate these pieces of his past into a narrative which would allow him to reunite with his father. These fragments are part of a larger narrative about his past that remains inaccessible. Without an articulation of the whole, the protagonist is unable to make the connection he so desperately wants. His cry at the end never reaches the other side. The men climb the embankment and walk away.

A similar incident happens in "Fireworks," involving the mysterious woman the protagonist meets while walking along the embanked path quoted at the beginning of this chapter. She approaches from the distance and politely bows. Since she looks familiar, he returns the greeting and starts walking with her, following her lead. At one point they descend from the embankment, walk along a shallow stream cut in the sand, and mysteriously arrive at the entry to a long passageway.

After entering with some reluctance, he starts to remember why she is leading him into the house, but unable to separate himself, he follows her. When he finally resolves to leave, she cries out and falls to the ground exposing her neck.

> I was about to return to the corridor, but was stopped by the sight of her as she lay there on the verandah. The nape of her white neck—young, fresh and beautiful—stood out against the drabness of her appearance. My legs froze in shock. I'd seen her before! Was it ten years ago? Perhaps twenty? We'd met at a crossroads, where I'd seen her neck. In that instant of remembrance, the woman came up behind me and grabbed me by the throat.
>
> "You cheat! You unfaithful good-for-nothing cheat!" she screamed.
>
> My legs felt weak. I couldn't move. Twisting around, I turned to look at her, but there was no one there. She was gone, but something beyond my vision kept strangling me from behind. Paralyzed, I tried calling for help, but the words stuck in my throat. (5)

The sight of the woman's neck triggers the protagonist's memory. He is able to remember her neckline as they passed at a crossroads, but he cannot see what is strangling him. The unseeable (*me ni mienai mono*) represents the narrative core of his memory, the details which would reveal the nature of his relationship with this woman. But here, as in "Realm of the Dead," the memory is fragmentary, as is its visual representation: the neck of the woman, the thumb of the protagonist's father. The protagonist is confined to these bits and pieces, while the whole remains literally obscured from view.

The protagonist is again left searching for his past in "The Echo," another story in which he follows a woman who seems to be no more than a distant memory. Like "Realm of the Dead," "The Echo" is cast in darkness, a darkness that deepens as the story progresses. The protagonist follows a woman carrying a small child on her back. As night falls, she becomes even more shadowy, to the point where he can no longer see her. He is led forward by the sound of her crying. Even though his sense of sight fails him, the sound remains clear. There is something familiar, not about her, but about the sound of her crying. Again, his memory of her is restricted to fragments: "I wanted to remember the circumstances of this sobbing and so I followed her, but even though parts of the picture were coming back to me, the whole was still elusive" (23). He tries to remember his connection to her but cannot, or at times is afraid to. There are various points in the story when the protagonist decides to leave her and return home to his family, but the possibility of remembering her keeps him following behind.

Unlike the two previous stories, the memories in "The Echo" are triggered by auditory or physical stimuli. At one point in the story, the protagonist passes by houses that are shuttered closed.

> When I passed them and heard the echo of my footsteps, I remembered that I'd been on this road before. I recalled the sound of my footsteps seeming to chase me.
>
> "No, those are *my* footsteps you hear," she had said as we walked along together that day. The realization of where we were hit me with the shock of icy water. (24)

The sound of the footsteps grants the protagonist partial access to this memory, namely, the location of the event, but not the woman's identity.[37] Further complicating his attempts to recall the past is the possibility that the woman in the memory is not the same woman he is currently following. Clues in the language lead the reader to believe she is, in fact, someone else. In his memory, they are walking together, beside each other, whereas the protagonist makes a point to mention that he is following behind the woman in "The Echo." Secondly, he mentions that this happened "on that day," or more literally, "at that time" (*sono toki*) which is a reference to another time in the past. The protagonist is not able to retrieve the past, and neither is he able to fix his memories to a specific point in time, further evidence that he is stuck in an endless cycle of repetition.

A second instance of memory retrieval happens in connection to a physical echo.

> The road bent out onto an embankment. We descended to a rocky riverbank and began crossing a bridge. It was very narrow, barely the width of my outstretched arms. The swaying of the planks made

> me uneasy. She continued to cry. Her movements rippled back to me, intensifying my fear with each step. As I moved uncertainly across the planks, I realized this was not the first time I'd crossed this bridge. Again, I thought I might remember why the woman cried, but the thought of remembering was terrifying.
>
> I stopped mid-bridge, resolving to go home. The children were waiting for me. The wind blew, and the area under the bridge rustled like a field of tall grass. When the wind stopped, the child started crying. He sounded even weaker than before. The boards under me undulated with the echo of her footsteps. As the bridge slowly steadied, I realized she was gaining distance on me. The thought of losing her filled me with an unbearable loneliness, and I hurried to catch up, frantic. (24)

Here again the protagonist is left with fragments of his memory. The swaying planks allow him to recall the bridge from a previous crossing, and the possibility of remembering the source of the woman's cries keeps him in pursuit. However, since he is unable to synthesize these fragments into whole pictures (whole sentences), he is denied access to their significance and meaning. The source of his loneliness is obscured, as is the full memory of this woman's identity and his role in past events.

The protagonist in *Realm of the Dead* is unable to convert these images (experiences) into a communicable form—visual or otherwise—which would hold meaning. He cannot place the image of a woman's neck or the sound of another's crying into the larger context of memory. In his interactions with these various men and women, the protagonist never reaches the point of meaningful articulation. This is not due to a lack of effort on his part. The protagonist's difficulties result from the fact that in modern life experience no longer accumulates to the point it can be reflected upon and communicated. This phenomenon was observed by German thinkers such as Walter Benjamin and Georg Simmel who conceived of experience as twofold: the individual, lived-through, moment-by-moment "sensate registering of the world" (*Erlebnis*), and a separate level of "shared discourse" which comes from a concrete historical experience (*Erfahrung*). The trauma of everyday modernity is that "*Erlebnis* is no longer registered as *Erfahrung*."[38]

This latter concept is no longer viable in the modern everyday, hence there is no means for reflecting upon and bringing collective meaning to the shocking nature of daily experience. As though modeling Benjamin's experience of modern life, Hyakken's characters never reach the level of shared discourse because they are trapped in the present. As Benjamin notes, "the man who loses his capacity for experiencing feels as though he is dropped from the calendar," trapped in a passing moment of *Erlebnis*.[39] Hyakken privileges the *Erlebnis*, the passing moment, and hence his characters are "locked into an eternal repetition of the same."[40] They are unable to move beyond the fragmentary experience of the now, or the individual experience of the moment, in order to reach the context of a larger narrative or a community.

This fragmentation results in a repetition, which occurs not only within a single story, but across the collection as a whole. As the reader progresses through *Realm of the Dead*, the characters grow increasingly familiar. The same protagonist seems to populate all the stories, and his travels along similar paths lead him to hauntingly familiar faces. As he repeats his actions, the reader will tend to see connections emerge. Critic Yamaguchi Tōru, for example, reads the disconnected tales of *Realm of the Dead* as a single narrative: the journey into and eventually out of the depths of hell.[41] Hyakken's first-person, unnamed protagonist begins his journey along the seaside path in "Fireworks." The mysterious woman he meets serves to guide the protagonist into hell, where he travels into a past constructed of false memories. The protagonist's journey, and the collection, ends as he turns his back on the embankment and returns home in the final story, "Realm of the Dead."

Yamaguchi's metanarrative hinges on recurring settings and locations that crop up in the individual stories, such as the bald mountain (*hageyama*) that appears in "The Companion," "The Chinaman" ("Shinajin") and "The Short Night" ("Mijikayo").[42] This repetition of location, which occurs at the level of the text, frightens the protagonist, as if he is aware of the textual context, the linguistic fabric of the world in which he resides.

Yamaguchi compares *Realm of the Dead* to a mosaic, a composition of multiple, fragmentary pieces that requires a distance on the part of the observer in order to come into view. This distance is not simply spatial, but is created on the semantic level; one of the primary keys revolves around the word *ushi* meaning "cow." Yamaguchi connects the sound *ushi* in Ushimado, the port toward which the protagonist is traveling in "Fireworks" with the cow-man in the story "Kudan." He also connects this to the Sino-Japanese character for *kudan,* which is composed of the characters for "person" and "cow." The meaning and pronunciation for the Sino-Japanese components of the word *kudan* ("person and cow," *jin to ushi*) also provide a clue to the protagonist's strange name in "Jintōshi" (Jin-to-ushi). Yamaguchi argues that the protagonist's experience with the mysterious horse doctor in "Jintōshi" is frightening because he knows that he, too, will undergo a transformation, namely his rebirth as the cow-man of "Kudan."[43]

Although connections build across the stories as the reader progresses through *Realm of the Dead,* they do not resolve the fragmentary nature of the collection, nor are they meant to. These similarities are instances of repetition, but one used as a particular mode of the fragmentary, a narrative suited to represent the modern world. Hyakken purposely leaves gaps, taunting his protagonist and reader with glimpses, but not allowing them the critical distance necessary to see the design in the mosaic. The protagonist's experience of the lived-through, in the present tense of each story, never accumulates to the point of reflection or communication. His predicament is repeated, and he is not able to draw on situations in earlier stories in order to break the cycle.

Critics have commented on this fragmentary aspect of Hyakken's work. In 1921, fellow writer and friend Morita Sōhei noted Hyakken's abbreviated style and his tendency to leave important sections unclear.[44] This ambiguity is also addressed by Tanemura Suehiro, who imagines Hyakken's stories as fragments of some larger text which has since been lost. If the reader had access to this lost context, the stories would not be so perplexing.[45] Waki Teruko similarly views Hyakken's characters and settings as stripped of their narrative fabric or *monogatari*.[46] Hyakken makes reference to this narrative whole in "Fireworks": "In a room a little farther on a book lay open on a stand, its pages old and tattered. I glanced at the book, and my companion seemed to suggest that if I would only read it, everything would make sense. But I averted my gaze and hurried on past. This left me agitated, unable to calm down" (5).

We can imagine this old book as Waki's *monogatari,* Tanemura's lost text, or Benjamin's shared discourse. The loss of context, narrative fabric, accumulated experience leaves Hyakken's protagonist trapped in this moment of time, stuck in this endless cycle of the present. The protagonist's difficulties are compounded by the restrictions of the text, a text which does not yield history. *Realm of the Dead* demonstrates that the fragmentary nature of everyday existence does not allow for critical engagement with modern life to take place. It only yields the trauma of the lived-through.

Hyakken's characters are unable to make sense of the fragmentary world in which they live. The stories are filled with a sense of the incomplete. The protagonist's actions are never realized, never completed. Hence his memories remain fragmentary. If in fact he is part of a narrative whole describing his journey into hell, that whole is comprised of incomplete pieces of something larger, and it is these lost texts that remain beyond his ken. Hyakken offers no solutions, resolutions, or neat endings. He does not explain. The action takes its course and remains unresolved. In lieu of the traditional storytelling tools, this fragmentary mode of narrative construction served as Hyakken's means to represent modernity. However, the downfall of such a narrative mode is that it did not allow for a critical articulation of that very condition.

## Trapped in the Everyday Language of the Text

Hyakken further denies his characters context—historical, personal, or narrative—by confining them to the level of the text. His characters are not merely trapped in the present, but in the printed present (tense) of the text. They live purely within its linguistic fabric. Hyakken creates this world through the use of a simple, commonplace style, which is deceptive in its simplicity.[47] Hyakken renders his textual world mundane, while at the same time, creating a background against which he highlights the power of language itself. The extraordinary experiences of the protagonist are all the more shocking because they rise out of these everyday circumstances. Although Hyakken's simple language does not provide his protagonist the means to escape his predicament, *Realm of the Dead* offers glimpses of the power of the word lurking within the homogenized language of the modern representational system.

Hyakken initially confines his characters to the textual level by severing the link between author and subject. The text functions autonomously; there are no viable references to anything outside of it, which would provide context for the reader or the protagonist.[48] Kōno Kensuke argues that Hyakken is able to achieve this because he separates the "I of the text" (*bunshōjō no watashi*) from the "author himself" (*hissha jishin*).[49] Hyakken clearly delineates the "I of the text" through his reliance on the first person pronoun, something considered unnatural in Japanese.[50] This emphasis is apparent in the opening lines of many of the stories in *Realm of the Dead*.[51]

I walked down a long embankment toward the Ushimado harbor. ("Fireworks," 1: 11)

I embarked on a long pilgrimage. ("The Crow" ["Karasu"], 14)

I took her to see the sideshow. ("The Lizard" ["Tokage"], 29)

I descended the dark mountain pass. ("The Companion," 1: 34)

These simple subject-verb sentences are reminiscent of writing from the prewar era, ranging from the prose of the I-novelists to that of Akutagawa Ryūnosuke. However, this is not a feature of Hyakken's work previous to *Realm of the Dead*, and hence it marks an intentional shift in style.[52] Although there are similarities to the I-novel style, Hyakken's writing is functioning differently.[53] The I-novelists created a deep connection between author and subject, a central feature of their semi-autobiographical stories. Hyakken, by stripping the author from the text, leaves his first-person protagonist cast adrift in a sea of words. His relationship to the author, or anyone else in the story, is unclear at best, and often nonexistent.

It is not simply that Hyakken's characters have no connection to the author, but that they have no connection to anything except the action that happens within the confines of the story. The characters may have a past in the form of familial relations, but this past cannot be accessed or is forgotten as the protagonist progresses further into the individual stories.[54] Hyakken does not develop characters in order to give the reader a fuller sense of who they are. We are not provided with the context to imagine their lives outside the story, and it seems neither are they. Hyakken's characters exist only at the level of the word—there is no other reality for them.[55] Within this textual reality, Hyakken creates a world where language is all powerful. The characters are at the mercy of the words that form the world around them. Language acts as a force in Hyakken's texts, directing the protagonist's plight.

This supremacy of language manifests itself in the extreme degree of indeterminacy that characterizes *Realm of the Dead*. The text emphasizes the speculative nature of the protagonist's observations, as well as his vague emotional and perceptual states.[56] The protagonist is constantly remarking that things appear a certain way, since he cannot be completely sure of his own judgments. This is indicated in Japanese by expressions such as *rashii, yō da, yō/sō na ki ga suru, nantonaku, hakkiri shinai,* and *bon'yari shite iru*. Hyakken relies on this indeterminate language to deny his protagonist a sense of surety and an understanding of the world around him. Hyakken's language recreates the loss of perceptual acuity and conscious awareness experienced by the modern urban dweller.[57]

Hyakken uses this to effect in "Realm of the Dead" when the protagonist's father is telling the story about the bee. The protagonist cannot determine the origins of the longing (*natsukashisa*) he feels, nor can he say with precision what is weighing on his heart. These descriptive passages are filled with indeterminate expressions, as though language itself hinders self-knowledge. At one point, the protagonist is able to overcome this and clearly identify the man as his father. However, Hyakken soon casts the story back into the realm of uncertainty when the protagonist recalls the sound of his father's voice urging the men to leave the restaurant: "'Yes! Of course. It's him,' I thought as I followed them. I wasn't far behind, but they were long gone. As I searched, a voice like my father's sounded in my ears. 'Shouldn't we be heading out again soon?'" (1: 65).

The protagonist is again put at a distance from his father through the use of these indeterminate expressions. It is not the father's voice the protagonist heard, but the voice of somebody who sounds like his father (*chichi rashii hito no koe*).[58] This distancing effect works in conjunction with the fragmentation to further isolate the protagonist from the certainty of knowing the whole story. This linguistic distance is akin to the personal "dissociation" experienced in the modern metropolis.[59]

Language continues to play a powerful role, trapping the protagonist in a world created by his own thoughts and words. An example of this can be found in "Driftwood" ("Ryūboku"), in which the protagonist finds a wallet and decides to turn it in.[60] Hurrying to the police station, he worries that he will run into a policeman along the way and have difficulty explaining why he is in possession of somebody else's wallet. He begins to regret having picked up the wallet, and just as he pulls it out of his coat, so as not to look suspicious, a man appears. The protagonist is sure he is a detective. Later in the story the protagonist is approached by another man. Upon seeing the wallet in the protagonist's hand he says, "Found some money, huh? How much you got?" (27). He tells the protagonist to spend it, and soon the protagonist is thinking of the money as his own. The protagonist tries to leave, but is pursued by this man who starts calling out "Thief! Thief!" The protagonist flees on a path by the river, but it turns into loose rocks and he begins slipping into the water.

> The ground was giving way beneath me, even if I stayed still, and I could hardly stand up. I tried to retrace my steps, but if I went back I might meet that man. I couldn't possibly go back the way I'd come, but I was too scared to go ahead. As I worried about what to do, I slid further and further toward the river. I tried to take a few steps back, but I slid even further than before, and then further still. I thrashed about with abandon. At last I came to a stop. My leg had caught on a stump of driftwood. I couldn't move an inch. Tears welled in my eyes. Now I was the thief. I thought about my wife and children at home, and a loud cry came from my mouth. Tears streaming down my face, I opened the wallet and snuck a last look inside. (28)

The event of finding a lost wallet is drawn from the realm of the mundane, but the protagonist's experience is overly coincidental. His fears of being mistaken for a thief come true. It is not simply that the protagonist cannot act of his own accord or that he has an overactive imagination. Rather, his imagination, verbalized on the printed page, gives rise to the very experience he dreads. The pursuer need only call out the word "thief" for the protagonist to be transformed into that which he feared most. The ground beneath him literally disappears along with his former identity, and he is paralyzed. The suggestion is all powerful, and the protagonist is trapped in a linguistic world created by his own thoughts. The only explanation offered in the story for the protagonist's actions is at the literal, textual level.

The verbalization of the protagonist's thoughts and fears creates a menacing situation on the level of the narrative. Another such instance occurs in a story titled "Jintōshi," a reference to a word written on a piece of red paper and handed to the protagonist. The protagonist does not understand this word, but he reads it aloud in the text. As he later finds out, "Jintōshi" is a name given him by a strange doctor of herbal horse medicine, a name that signifies the protagonist's new status as a disciple to this doctor. The act of renaming creates a new identity for the protagonist, but his old identity remains unstated and unclear. The story starts mid-action, yet it is told as a reminiscence from some time in the future: "Someone had offered to introduce me to her, so I slipped out of the house unnoticed. Along the way, I figured she was somebody else's mistress. I walked alone for a long time on a strange, abandoned road until I arrived at the house" (9).

The protagonist never explains why he goes to this house to meet this woman. He finds her attractive but is troubled by her white hands. There is something strange about the way she rubs her nose with the back of her hand that makes the protagonist think she is a fox. The fox lore refers to a Japanese folk belief that foxes can bewitch humans, often by taking the form of women. At one point in the story when the protagonist decides to leave, she stops him by asking, "You haven't forgotten me, have you?" (12). Once she says this, the protagonist has the feeling that he was involved with her in the past, but he cannot remember anything about her or their relationship. Up to this point in the story, there was nothing familiar about the woman at all, but the mere suggestion that the protagonist could have forgotten her creates a hazy memory in his mind. Hyakken again makes use of indeterminate language to create this effect.[61]

The story ends as the protagonist is taken on a medical call with the doctor and his younger brother, who is also his assistant. The protagonist lights the way along a dark path, and when he enters the designated building, his lantern illuminates hundreds of small glowing objects in the room, objects which turn out to be the eyes of horses. As he looks closer he sees the assistant amidst the animals.

> I watched him, not knowing what he was doing. There was another gust of wind. The huge eyes of the horses glared back from the darkness as the image of the brother in their midst floated into view, illuminated by the burning light in the horses' eyes. At the sight of him, I screamed, delirious. I threw the lantern aside and fled down that endless, unknown road. The woman was the last thing on my mind. The brother's face had been that of a horse. (13)

The simple act of writing a name on a piece of paper irrevocably changes the protagonist's life. If the doctor's brother can transform into a horse, then the protagonist, "Jintōshi," could meet a similar fate. As we have seen, the protagonist of *Realm of the Dead* has just such an experience later in the collection in "Kudan."

Hyakken creates this mundane yet unpredictable fictional world through the use of a "curt" and "commonplace" language.[62] This everyday linguistic (*nichijō gengo*) space is that of a familiar world, yet there is "something extraordinary in its very ordinariness."[63] The unusual words and images of Hyakken's text sink into this layer of the ordinary, until they are brought to life, or surface to the level of the protagonist's attention. There is no clear border in the storytelling of *Realm of the Dead* between the mundane everyday and this experience of the extraordinary, in other words, the everyday as Other. The line is always slipping in small, hidden places. Geographical features, strange perceptual abilities, weather conditions, glances and sounds, even a single word can initiate this shift, revealing the connection between these two faces of the everyday. Masugi Hideki and Shōji Hajime describe these slippage points in the text as hinges (*chōtsugai*) or joints (*jointo*), or to use the words of Mishima Yukio, they serve as "a bridge connecting the real and the surreal."[64] Hyakken accesses the power of the word, which although it is locked away in the "crevices and recesses of the quotidian," has not been fully expunged by modernity.[65]

The extraordinary in *Realm of the Dead* acquires its shock power specifically because it occurs within an ordinary, everyday context. For it is here at the level of the everyday that Hyakken locates his critique and documents the traumatic shifts occurring in modernity. This is not the realm of fantasy, but the means for Hyakken to find a mode of representation to articulate the changes he sees. Hyakken unmoors his characters from their narrative history, but at the same time recreates the historical conditions of that modernity. Despite the transformative power Hyakken invests in the word, in *Realm of the Dead*, this linguistic everyday is not a site of resistance. Hyakken's conceptualization of the everyday lacks the critical and liberatory potential envisioned by other observers of modernity.[66] Just as Hyakken's protagonist is unable to escape his predicament, Hyakken himself tried to escape this capitalist system of representation and return to a time when the heterogeneous nature of language held a certain power, but ultimately he realized this was no longer possible.

## Longing for the Aura of the Printed Word

Through his emphasis on language, Hyakken returned a sense of magic to the printed word, a sense that had been lost in the modern system of movable-type texts.[67] This is also the effect Hyakken was trying to achieve with the peculiar formatting of the original 1922 edition of *Realm of the Dead,* a series of features that added an extra layer of the unusual to the reading experience.[68] Through these gestures, Hyakken sought to undermine the new mode of consuming literature. He ended up producing a physical text that confounded readers.

The cover design of the original edition was remarkably plain, especially when compared to some of the beautifully jacketed books by Hyakken's contemporaries. Set off against a dark gray background, Hyakken's name appears along with the names of the publisher and the designer. Above the title is a picture of a fox—a replica of an image from the Yakushiji Buddhist temple in the ancient capital Nara—in the style of a woodblock print. There are no other images or patterns on the exterior cover. Given the long-standing practice of decorating book covers, often lavishly, Hyakken's cover can be read as an act of conscious minimalism that gives away no clues about the content.[69]

Upon opening the book, the reader found a table of contents listing the individual stories, but nothing else. There was no indication of the pages on which the stories started, no link between the table of contents and the text. In fact, the book had no page numbers at all, and neither were there running heads used to indicate the title of the book or the individual sections. *Realm of the Dead* is an unparsed collection of words.

In many ways, this unorthodox formatting is well suited to the content: both the layout and narrative progress like a path without signposts. Since there are no guides, the reader must follow the protagonist through a series of fragmentary, eerie, disconnected experiences set in a landscape constructed from distant, partial memories that are never fully revealed. Like the protagonist, the reader is trapped within the stories without recourse to clearly marked exit or entry points, reliant upon the traversing narrative to navigate the text.

In a conversation recalled by Hyakken's disciple Hirayama Saburō, Hyakken attributes the decision to delete the page numbers to the publisher, Tōmondō, who felt it necessary to give the book a new feel, something simple yet refreshing.[70] Yet in a separate conversation also recorded by Hirayama, Hyakken himself takes credit for the formatting decision: "If someone was going to read my work, I didn't want them reading halfway then finishing the rest some other time. In order to stop the skipping around and haphazard reading from this page to that, I took the page numbers away."[71]

Regardless of who made the decision, this act can be read not only as a playful experimentation with the conventions of the modern printing (movable-type) system, but also as a rejection of those very conventions toward standardization and mass production.

Kōno Kensuke places Hyakken in the latter group; *Realm of the Dead* is a rejection of the print culture of the age, a culture of standardized, mass-produced, movable-type texts. The onset of movable-type printing resolved ambiguities inherent in more decorative cursive styles, which had emphasized the aesthetics of calligraphy over clarity. Movable type eliminated occurrences of similar looking calligraphic Sino-Japanese characters being mistaken for one another. The difficulty inherent in the act of reading *Realm of the Dead* is a rejection of the ease of reading facilitated by modern printing.[72] Kono sees Hyakken attempting to dislocate this mass-produced system, a system built to enable information transfer and reading efficiency.[73]

The ease of reading that Kōno discusses is difficult to gauge; a modern day reader of movable-type print cannot comment retrospectively on the difficulty of woodblock-printed texts for earlier readers, who were accustomed to calligraphic woodblock texts. It is more productive to recast Kōno's argument about ease of reading in terms of standardization and the relationship between reader and text. Unlike typeface where every font constitutes a standard, in woodblock-printed books, "a given character or syllabic sign will not be identical throughout the text but is subject to the infinite variety of handwriting."[74] Since these blocks were carved based on handwritten manuscripts, the texts each had a different style and personality, or stated otherwise, an aura. This was closely related to the cultural and literary associations attached to calligraphy. These books could also bring the presence of the author into the text with a preface written in his or her own hand. Even though multiple copies were printed from these blocks, the texts retained aura via "traces of the practiced hand."[75] More than leading to any difficulty in reading, these block-printed books "enforce a more particularistic relationship between reader and text than was possible with movable type."[76]

Hyakken would have been introduced to movable-type texts in his youth, since they replaced woodblock printing as the standard around 1890. Kōno describes the fetishistic attachment of young boys and aspiring writers to early printing sets. The printed word had tremendous appeal.[77] However, such a system necessitated the mechanisms of mass production, and soon the novelty of the printed word was diminished by the sheer volume of printed texts. It was not only novelty that was lost. Once widely produced and distributed, printed texts experienced a "decay of the aura." In this modern system, a plurality of copies is substituted for a unique experience.[78] The relationship between reader and text, the "unique experience" of woodblock-printed calligraphic books, and later of early movable-type books, was lost in the plurality of mass culture. Although only 500 copies of *Realm of the Dead* were printed, the book was part of the new system of printed texts, and for Hyakken, aura had been lost.

Working within this modern, mass-produced print system, Hyakken could not reproduce the unique manuscript qualities of block-printed texts, nor could he recreate this special relationship with the reader. But this was exactly what he was trying to do. Hyakken teases his reader with a table of contents page; he lists the titles of the individual stories, but does not provide any means for locating them in the collection. He thereby forces his audience to react and read in a certain way. With movable type, reading speed and volume had increased, and critics and writers such as Takayama Chogyū complained about the shift from detailed, discriminate, repetitive reading to more shallow, indiscriminate patterns.[79] Hyakken was trying to counter the consumptive trends in the reading process by forcing his reader to slow down and read from beginning to end.

The typological difficulty of navigating *Realm of the Dead* did not escape the reader's notice; Hyakken's disciples commented on the unusual nature of the book.[80] As Gérard Genette argues, "no reader should be indifferent to the appropriateness of particular typographical choices, even if modern publishing tends to neutralize these choices by a perhaps irreversible tendency toward standardization."[81] The format of *Realm of the Dead* purposely countered this trend toward standardization—the homogenizing, flattening forces of modernity. On the surface, Hyakken's formatting and design choice lend the book a sense of the playful and new, but they are a clear rejection of the conventions of the modern print system of mass-produced, movable-type texts. Hyakken attempted to return to an older model of reading where he could control the relationship among author, reader, and text. In the process, he demanded concentration from a distracted modern reader (including the literary elite), who was ultimately incapable of providing it. The modern print system may not have neutralized Hyakken's typographical choices, but the modern reader was in no position to make sense of them.

## Silenced by the Feminine Modern

Hyakken attempted to subvert this modern system by means of a fragmented narrative mode, an everyday language, and an unusual book format. Although Hyakken successfully produced a text that accurately reflects the disorienting experience of living in this modern world, he discovered the limits of the author's power. The collection speaks of trauma, and Hyakken's anxiety is palpable in *Realm of the Dead*. The protagonist suffers a fear-inducing paralysis, a loss of voice, a loss of self. Hyakken was similarly unable to find his voice within the literary world; he was not granted distinction by the literary elite (*bundan*). The book may be an act of resistance to modernity, but ultimately Hyakken, like his protagonist, was unsuccessful in finding a means to create shared meaning.

This sense of loss as an overwhelming, uncontrollable aspect of modernity is figured in Hyakken's text as woman. That which is feared is codified as female, particularly the silencing power of the modern everyday experience. The protagonist is rendered mute at critical points in *Realm of the Dead*, and he loses opportunities for shared discourse because he cannot engage with the past, be it in the form of textual histories, visible memories, auditory fragments, or oral tales. But in order to come to terms with his past, he must convert his experiences to memory. Therefore, his attempts at engagement are in fact attempts at articulation, for "the past must be articulated to become memory."[82] However, these attempts are thwarted by the women in the book.

In contrast, as seen in his interactions with the men in the book, the protagonist's articulations come too late to be effective, such as those in "The Companion," "Realm of the Dead," and "Kudan." The protagonist calls out to his unborn brother, but in that very instant his companion disappears. When he finally recognizes his father, his voice never reaches the man with whom he hopes to reunite. The protagonist is similarly unable to communicate with his son in the last story. These instances of failed communication with male characters in the book—fathers, brothers, sons—produce a strong emotional response in the protagonist. This is usually one of nostalgia and regret over lost opportunities, lost chances to better know the self. However, his encounters with women produce a dramatically different response. These women are not versions of the self, but represent the radical Other. They induce fear in the protagonist and render him speechless. Hyakken's protagonist finds himself mute and unable to free himself from his trauma by narrating his past.[83]

The consistently negative portrayals of women in the book leave the reader wondering as to Hyakken's misogynistic tendencies, however, this is better attributed to a figuring of modernity as feminine. The negative aspects of modernity are projected onto the female characters in the book. A brief survey reveals the negative characterization typical of women in *Realm of the Dead*. The protagonist's wife in both "The Pier" ("Hatoba") and "The Smallpox Demon" ("Hōsōshin") are under suspicion of adultery. More menacing are the tricksters found in "The Short Night" and "Seaweed" ("Ryūsō"). In "The Short Night" the protagonist falls under the spell of a fox who changes into a beautiful young wife. The fox makes a baby from dry leaves, and the protagonist attempts to expose the fox by holding the baby over a fire. The fox woman resists at first, then threatens him: "'I'm going to burn it like you say,' the young wife said defiantly. 'And if the baby turns out to be a baby, I'll make you pay'" (48). In the latter story, the protagonist chases after a beautiful girl who is following an old woman. The old woman has eyes that spin like whirlpools and pierce deep into the protagonist, throwing him into a state of confusion (38). The protagonist kills this woman in order to get to the girl. He runs away with the girl to a strange beach, but when she sings in the voice of the old woman, he starts to suspect something is wrong. "I feared what was in her heart, but I resolved not to think about it. I squeezed her hand with all my strength. Her hand was cold and broke with a snap. In shock I turned to face her, but she was not the girl. She was the old woman I'd killed back in the field" (40).

The protagonist's fearful and paralyzing encounters with these women begin in "Fireworks," the opening story to the collection. He meets a strange woman along the embankment and follows her into a mysterious house. "Fireworks" ends as the protagonist is strangled by an invisible assailant. He is unable to move or speak: "Paralyzed, I tried calling for help, but the words stuck in my throat" (5). This verbal and physical paralysis is troubling, but it is noteworthy that the protagonist never attempts to speak at any point previous to this in the entire story. He has thoughts, but they are never verbalized on the page. He has no voice. The protagonist's unspoken intentions and memories are overpowered by the woman's verbalizations, rendering him mute. Throughout the story she answers his unasked questions, as seen in the scenes below.[84]

> The reeds became taller and taller, and above me I could hear their flowery tops brushing up against one another. Darkness surrounded us as the embankment crept into the night. The sky burned crimson. A pale red tinged the darkening crests of the waves, reflecting back an unusual color. I looked at the waves, and then back at my companion.
>
> She pointed toward the offing and said, "It's getting dark out there, too. We'd better hurry." (3–4)
>
> The fireworks had faded into the surrounding sky, but the embers must have fallen into the reeds. Lost in thought, I admired the beauty of the vision before me.
>
> "Yes. The whole area will burn. Let's hurry," she said. (1: 12)

This dynamic between the protagonist and a female character is repeated in "The Echo," where the protagonist is similarly speechless, and in "The Lizard" ("Tokage").[85] In the latter story, the protagonist takes a woman to a sideshow. During the performance, a bear gets loose, kills a performer, and then lunges for a cow on stage. Frightened, the protagonist tries to flee.

> I ran down the stairs in a panic. I looked at the stage and watched as the bear leaped forward and wrapped its front paws around the cow's head. It was too horrifying to watch, but as I stood frozen the woman came flying towards me. She wrapped both her arms around my neck and held it fast. I writhed in pain. I was afraid the bear would reach us at any moment and tried to shake her loose, but she tightened her grip and would not let go. In fear and pain, I struggled, feeling strength drain from my body. A cold sweat covered me, and I felt profoundly tired. She put her mouth to my ear and whispered, "You don't know the truth yet, do you?"

I did not care and did not respond. I just wanted to know who she was.

"I'll tell you," she said, her voice kindly, as she effortlessly lifted me in her arms and descended the stairs rapidly. As she carried me toward the stage, I screamed as my arms and legs flailed about. Each step she took toward the stage sent waves of horror through me. I could not speak. I went numb. I could not move. The face of this woman who was carrying me flashed before my eyes, and nothing made sense. (1: 33–34)

The story ends as the protagonist is carried toward his death by a woman more monstrous than the wild animals on stage. Again he is physically paralyzed and unable to speak. He is also unable to identify the woman despite the fact that he already knows her. He opens the story by saying: "I took her to see the sideshow" (29). However, this woman has transformed into something beyond the protagonist's ability to recognize or understand.

This woman has a strange power over the protagonist. Like other women in the collection, she is able to respond to his thoughts and answer his unasked questions. The woman's prescience terrifies and shocks the protagonist.

Up on the large banner was a picture of a bear biting the side of a cow. Blood flowed from the cow's flank, which seemed to soak the banner bright red. After seeing this picture, I no longer wanted to see the sideshow, but when I was about to tell her this and head home, she squeezed my hand hard and said, "This looks interesting. Let's go in!" I was shocked, unable to express my reservations. (29)

He is further frightened by the hotness of her hand, and her desire to stay for the show and see the kill. He comments: "I was getting more and more disturbed by the woman I'd come with, . . . I found her excitement not only incomprehensible but also abhorrent, . . . I wanted to get free of her and flee" (32).

The most distressing aspect of this story is the uncontrollable power the woman wields. Not only is the protagonist immobilized and speechless, he is rendered unable to make sense of his surroundings. Because the protagonist is powerless in the face of these women, he is led to his death (or so the reader supposes) in "The Lizard," and to a place of no return in both "Fireworks" and "The Echo." In the former it is geographical, as the woman warns the protagonist: "The embankment's been washed away. There's no way back" (5). Even more troubling is the mental space into which the woman in "The Echo" leads the protagonist at the end of the story.

> It seemed to grow even darker. The sky yielded not even the faintest light. We'd crossed the bridge, but I couldn't tell the road from the fields. I was guided by the sound of her crying, even as the blackness of earth and sky pressed in with each step. The wind was still. The grass was silent. All that was left was the weeping voice of this woman carrying her baby, walking in front of me, pulling me along into nowhere. In the end I forgot about my family. But I couldn't stop searching in the terrifying darkness for things from my past. (24–25)

The protagonist is led by the sound of this woman's voice, and the physical reverberations of her footsteps, into the space of his own mind, into his memories. But here, too, he is left searching in the dark. His present life drops away as he forgets about his family and his home, but his identity is not fortified by his past. His inability to see the whole picture and to understand his relationship to the past, and by extension, to these women, is a function of his muteness. Trapped within the present world of the text, Hyakken's protagonist cannot escape, because he lacks the ability to speak, the power of the word, which would grant a fuller access to the past and allow him to accumulate his experiences to the point of meaningful articulation.

There has been much speculation in the scholarly literature on Hyakken about what or who is strangling the protagonist at the end of "Fireworks." It could be the woman in an altered, invisible form or some unspoken memory from his past. These are, in fact, the same thing. The muteness of not being a coherent historical subject keeps Hyakken's protagonist from creating memory, and the fear induced by this condition is codified as feminine. The woman in "The Lizard" is the most threatening of the collection, but the women in *Realm of the*

*Dead* are variations on a theme. They are an amalgamation of the feminine, or stated otherwise, they are the uncontrolled and uncontrollable feminine, the entity upon which the author projects his fears of modernity.

Such a depiction of women is not unique to Hyakken. In late nineteenth-century Europe, the "image of woman served as a receptacle for all kinds of projections, displaced fears, and anxieties (both personal and political) which were brought about by modernization and the new social conflicts."[86] In Japanese literature from the Meiji period onward, women were used to represent the alluring yet dangerously powerful aspects of modernity.[87] More than any commentary on women, this use of the feminine is a means for Hyakken to exemplify his frustrations and anxieties as a writer who has lost the power of the word in the modern representational system. The protagonist of *Realm of the Dead* cannot speak and so he cannot overcome his trauma. Similarly, Hyakken lacks the ability to speak the prophetic text, to critically articulate modern life. In *Realm of the Dead*, we see the author's fear of losing aura and individual voice. Hyakken lamented the fact that he could not recreate the particular relationship between reader and text found in woodblock or early movable-type texts. He tried to recapture the unique, creative voice of the author, but, like his fictional characters, his text was lost in the plurality of copies. The aura had decayed through the process of mechanical reproduction.[88]

*Realm of the Dead* is Hyakken's attempt to find a form to articulate this new modernity, to move beyond the experience of it as a lived moment to the point of a shared discourse. Hyakken experiments with the physical and linguistic contours of his book, but ultimately *Realm of the Dead* is a failure of articulation. The book effectively describes the experience of the lived-through, but does not move beyond it. Unlike other theorists of modernity, Hyakken did not, at this point in his career, see the possibility of creating a means to critically articulate modernity. Walter Benjamin hints at the possibility that the distracted modern state of perception could act as a means to communicate experience.[89] But Hyakken's characters never reach this state of critical perception and articulation. They remain blind and mute in the face of everyday modernity.

Hyakken's own muteness, his inability to speak modernity at the level of shared meaning, is indicative of the limits of the modern condition. This appears throughout *Realm of the Dead,* but it is most clearly represented in "Kudan." In rewriting the folktale in his own idiom, Hyakken allowed the beast to live, but he produced something that was not recognized as a prophecy. Similarly, Hyakken's *Realm of the Dead* was not recognized as literature by the *bundan,* the keepers of literary capital and the only group able to grant legitimacy to the text. However, Hyakken's "Kudan" ends as the beast shrugs off this experience. "Kudan" is a recognition that aura and distinction are being lost, but also an indication that Hyakken realized the limited value of literary authority in the new capitalist system of representation. Hyakken is the *kudan,* and he was laughing, but the literary establishment did not get the joke. In fact, it backfired, and Hyakken's literary debut was a critical failure.

The fact that Hyakken was not granted distinction should not lessen the value of the text as a comment on modernity. His characters experience the trauma of the modern everyday, unable to build up experience in order to find meaning. They are disconnected and fated to repeat and reproduce experience without recourse to the anchor of memory, identity, tradition, or history. *Realm of the Dead* was produced out of this quintessentially modern experience. This struggle with modernity—the inability to critically articulate modern life—is embedded in the textual fabric of the stories themselves. Hyakken's *kudan* may laugh, but this is the only moment of lightness and humor in a text filled with trauma and loss. As the title warns, we are in the realm of the dead—the modern market that does not recognize intellectual distinction—into which Hyakken traverses deeply.

*Realm of the Dead* opens as Hyakken's protagonist loses his way, and indeed, he wanders throughout the collection. The road may have been lost in modernity, but Hyakken ends *Realm of the Dead* with the possibility of an exit, an alternate path: "With the embankment at my back, I returned on the dark road through the fields" (77). The protagonist of "Realm of the Dead" is allowed to leave this borderland, but he leaves it alone, stripped of family, home, identity, and voice. Over the course of the 1920s, Hyakken also found an exit from this traumatic experience of modernity. He left the realm of fiction and turned to the *zuihitsu*.[90] This choice would irrevocably alter the direction of his career. Hyakken would go on to make his name with this essay form, but in doing so he would exempt himself from recognition in a modern literary system based on fiction. Ironically, his resistance guaranteed that he would never receive the distinction he originally sought.

Hyakken's discontent with modernity and the bleakness of *Realm of the Dead* notwithstanding, the inability to return to earlier modes of writing and reading signals an important recognition on Hyakken's part that any return to a past predating the changes of modernity was impossible, an idea that would run counter to the conservative voices of the decade that followed. Hyakken continued to refine this language of cultural modernism and would, in the intervening years, turn this disorienting experience into a critical voice.

# TWO

# *A Critique of Elite Fiction: Professor Fujita Hyakkien and the Prewar* Zuihitsu

> There are currently so many *zuihitsu* being published and read that it is no exaggeration to say we are living in the age of the *zuihitsu*. I'm even more shocked by the fact that *zuihitsu* are being published in anthologies. The person responsible for making *zuihitsu* known to the world today is undoubtedly Uchida Hyakken. His collections never fail to sell less than 10,000 to 12,000 copies.
>
> —Tosaka Jun, "Shisō to shite no bungaku"

Over the course of the late 1920s and early 1930s, Hyakken turned his attention to the *zuihitsu* and found commercial success with this lighter mode of writing.[1] As Marxist critic Tosaka Jun confirmed, Hyakken had become by 1936 the leading writer of this essay-style, catch-all genre, the roots of which date to Japan's classical period.[2] The radical difference in tone between the dark, contemplative *Realm of the Dead* and Hyakken's comic *zuihitsu* masks the fact that he continued to address many of his previous concerns. Hyakken's earlier discontent with modernity, primarily a literary one over the loss of authorial voice and distinction, was now voiced through the light-hearted, mocking tone of the *zuihitsu*. No longer seeking the distinction associated with writing pure fiction, Hyakken took a playful tone in addressing capitalist modernity by confounding his reader with a plurality of copies in the form of multiple voices and alter egos. This made for an effective critique of elite fiction and its emphasis on the unique authorial voice. Hyakken continued to refine his use of the language and symbols of cultural modernism, in the process questioning the existence of an auratic individual voice outside the fleeting experience of the present, where previously stable notions such as identity were in flux.

Hyakken found in the modern *zuihitsu* a more accommodating space for his literary experiments and his critique. The *zuihitsu*, which had enjoyed a resurgence during the one-yen book boom of the late 1920s and early 1930s, was well suited to addressing Hyakken's concerns. Modern *zuihitsu* captured the quotidian and transient nature of everyday life and its emphasis on the present moment. This ephemeral writing proved to be highly marketable as it was consumed by new professionals living the modern life. The *zuihitsu* is notorious for its slippery nature and its tendency to defy definition or categorization, and in the prewar era, the rubric encompassed a wide variety of content and styles. The flexible nature of this undefined genre is akin to that of the term culture itself, which was heavily debated in the prewar years. Like culture, the *zuihitsu* had strong ties to a national past, but the prewar version embraced modern (Western) life. The mixed nature of modern culture, which has been characterized as code-switching, montage, and intermedic, is readily seen in the hybrid *zuihitsu*.[3]

Hyakken's decision to write *zuihitsu* had positive and negative repercussions for his career: he established himself as a writer, but exempted himself from recognition. The loose generic definition of the *zuihitsu* allowed Hyakken to create his own version by crossing over into the territory of the I-novel (*shishōsetsu*), the premiere form for serious literature. He combined the *zuihitsu* and the novel to produce fragmentary, touching yet often comic, semi-autobiographical essays, many with traces of plot and narrative structure common to the novel. Yet, as much as the *zuihitsu* was an established form and a central component of mass, consumer, and literary culture, it never claimed the authority of the novel. Hyakken realized in *Realm of the Dead* that literary authority meant little in the new capitalist system of representation, but things had changed in the 1930s. With the establishment of the Akutagawa Prize for pure literature (*junbungaku*) in 1935, writers created a system of national recognition and regained a foothold on cultural capital.[4] By choosing to write *zuihitsu*, a genre not eligible for the prize, Hyakken exempted himself from recognition by these literary authorities. This is not to say that there exists in Japan no means for appreciating *zuihitsu* — they are still written and published — but that the genre tends to defy literary critical analysis.[5] Yet in its separation from "literature," the *zuihitsu* proved useful in providing a forum for criticism, which also allowed writers to evade censorship.[6]

Within the context of the early 1930s, the decadence of modern life shared newspaper pages with the tensions of encroaching militarism.[7] In this time of tremendous social and cultural flux, Hyakken crossed traditional boundaries separating literary genres, elite and mass culture, and writing and film, but he did not cross these lines without reservation. Despite his play with authorial voice, ultimately Hyakken was unwilling to relinquish control over his work. When his *zuihitsu* were translated into film, he rejected this modern creation and reverted to the conservative realm of pure language. In seeking refuge in the high modernist side of the "Great Divide," Hyakken asserts his claim as an author to control meaning, a right that was slipping away in the propagandistic climate of the 1930s.[8]

## Hyakken, the *Zuihitsu*, and the Birth of Professor Fujita Hyakkien

Hyakken had been publishing *zuihitsu* in a variety of magazines and newspapers over the course of the late 1920s and early 1930s, and originally had a difficult time getting his work published as a single volume. Once released, however, his first collection *Hyakkien's Miscellany* (*Hyakkien zuihitsu*, 1933) received a glowing review in one of the leading dailies by Murō Saisei, an author who had openly criticized the genre in the late 1920s. The collection is named for Professor Fujita Hyakkien, one of Hyakken's many literary alter egos.[9] *Hyakkien's Miscellany* sold extremely well and was reprinted more than ten times.[10] Hyakken became the representative *zuihitsu* writer within a mere three years of the book's debut.[11] His popularity is further evidenced by cinematic and theatrical adaptations of his *zuihitsu* in the late 1930s. Japan was again in the grip of *zuihitsu* fever, and Hyakken made his name as a master of the form (*zuihitsuka*).[12]

Hyakken's *zuihitsu* production far outweighs that of his fiction, but unlike the latter, his *zuihitsu* have received little in the way of critical attention.[13] This stems from a number of reasons, but one factor lies in the uncategorizable nature of the *zuihitsu* itself. The term was widely used in the 1920s and 1930s by writers and publishers alike, but it remained undefined, or was defined so broadly as to encompass a bewildering range of forms: travelogues, semi-fictional stories, critical reviews, diary entries, poetry, essays, and racy literati gossip.[14] A survey of *zuihitsu* compilations from the era demonstrates how widely used and seemingly misapplied the term was in the prewar years.[15] Hyakken's literature was no exception. His *zuihitsu* compilations resist the taming influence of a unitary theme. Variation occurs not only in terms of thematics, but also in content, tone, style, length, and narrative voice. *Hyakkien's Miscellany*, one of his most famous collections, comprises 34 pieces ranging widely in all of these areas.

The following pages will consider excerpts from *Hyakkien's Miscellany* in order to better appreciate the varied nature of the writing and Hyakken's status as a master of the form. We should note that Hyakken's *zuihitsu*, and modern *zuihitsu* in general, remain virtually untranslated and unknown to the English-language reader.[16] This is partly a function of the relationship between translation and canonization, but is also due to the lack of critical standards in Western literature for analyzing such varied, and at times unstructured, writing. Through these examples, we can see how Hyakken's understanding of the genre took shape and why his version of the *zuihitsu* is worthy of critical attention.

The majority of Hyakken's *zuihitsu* are written in the first person, both as fiction and nonfiction, and ranging stylistically from flat editorial comments to intimate autobiography. Some *zuihitsu* have a clear narrative thread while others are collections of seemingly random remarks. A number of the more fictional pieces first appeared in the *sōsaku* or creative writing column in journals only to be later incorporated into a *zuihitsu* volume.[17] Such cross-categorization is understandable for the more emplotted of Hyakken's works; the rationale for their later inclusion in a *zuihitsu* compilation seems unclear, but this serves to highlight the looseness of the *zuihitsu*'s generic boundaries. In fact, the range we see in Hyakken's work is typical of *zuihitsu* in the leading journals of the day, many of which had a *zuihitsu* column. Given the degree of crossover, distinctions made between Hyakken's fiction and *zuihitsu* may appear artificial or forced; however, his works were marketed separately, as seen in their placement in literary journals. Hence a distinction between fiction and *zuihitsu* clearly existed in the minds of prewar publishers, critics, and readers. They may not have been able to define the term *zuihitsu*, but they knew what it was not.

A number of Hyakken's *zuihitsu* are best described as essays, meaning they lean toward the editorial rather than the fictional. However, the term "essay" should be understood not as a structured, argumentative form, but as a personal musing more in line with the literal definition of the term *zuihitsu*, namely writing that "follows the brush." An example of such writing by Hyakken can be seen in a playful two-page selection titled "The Magic Carpet" ("Ukatōsen").[18]

Humans have long desired to soar through the skies. Deep in sleep, they dream of becoming birds, their bodies coursing through the heavens and floating around overhead. This desire manifests itself in common expressions like "I'm in seventh heaven," [*ten ni noboru kokochi*] "My heart leapt with joy" [*tobitatsu omoi*], or "I feel as if I were flying on a magic carpet" [*ukatōsen*]. Playing with yo-yos is no doubt a silly and childish thing, but I remember similar toys from my childhood going in and out of fashion. And now I've heard that just such a pastime existed in ancient Greece as well. (1: 200–201)

In this light-hearted *zuihitsu*, Hyakken discusses the pleasure of playing with a yo-yo, and he compares it to the sensation of intoxication or dreaming. The author discusses his own preferences, and admits the difficulty of trying to relate, in writing, the common appeal of flying and yo-yos. In another short (two-page) *zuihitsu* titled "First Class Coach" ("Ittōsha") the narrator's likes and dislikes are placed in the context of trains.

Having never ridden first class, I indulged on a train ticket from Ueno to Sendai. Since I was teaching at the Army and Navy academies, I got the civil servant half-price discount. The ticket was even less than second-class coach, but with no discount for the express portion, it ended up costing quite a bit. I boarded the one o'clock express. (1: 191)

Despite his initial excitement, the narrator ends up being the only person in the first class car and is overcome with loneliness. The attentiveness of the train staff only serves to accentuate his unease.

Once we reached Sendai, I was ready to get off when the attendant grabbed my canvas bag and carried it away. He jumped onto the platform before the train had even stopped and ran my bag over to the ticket window. He then spoke to the train employee working the gate saying: "There's this strange man on the train, so be sure to check his ticket closely," or so I feared. The attendant returned to where I was milling about. "I've delivered your bag to the wicket sir," he said, leaving me no alternative but to give him 50 *sen*. As I passed through the gate, I couldn't stop yawning and tears spilled down my cheeks. (1: 192)

The tone in this latter selection is less playful and reads more like the reminiscence of some personal experience. As mentioned above, both of these are well within the range of material regularly found in prewar *zuihitsu* columns. However, the question remains as to the appeal of such writing. These short essays can seem frivolous and overly personal, but the light nature, the frivolity itself, may have been what appealed to the reader of the day. As journalist-critic Chiba Kameo noted in 1926, "torturous editorials and ponderous novels" were not effective at relieving the stress of modern life.[19] In contrast, the *zuihitsu* required little focus and its very ephemerality delivered a quick, pleasurable, often humorous, read. Chiba expressed his confidence that the *zuihitsu* would "relax, comfort, and set free the troubled mind," and this was certainly one of the functions of *zuihitsu* in the prewar era.[20] However, literary critics evaluated Hyakken's *zuihitsu* on different terms, praising the narrative qualities in his work, qualities not readily found in *zuihitsu* such as those excerpted above. For a taste of these qualities, we must turn to works such as Hyakken's short (five-page) "Tale of Owl Woods" ("Kyōrinki").

The events of last fall, specifically the night of September 20, are still fresh in my mind. I was chatting up on the second floor with Kikushima, who'd stopped by for a visit. After he left, I wandered around the quiet back streets of town. The wind gusted as I approached the wide road in front of the hospital. Up ahead where the hill began its rise, the road darkened in the twilit shadows of large tree branches. A prematurely old moon hung hazily over the hill.

I went home and climbed upstairs. Before entering my room, I leaned on the veranda railing and looked at the sky. A long, thin, ashen cloud flowed low over the neighbor's roof, just clearing the ridge poles running north to south. Hidden in its midst was the moon I'd seen earlier. Despite the narrowness of the snakelike cloud, the moon never emerged from its cover.

My wife came running upstairs on the evening of November 10.

"It's too horrible for words. There was a murder next door," she said. "The husband, wife, and that college student were all killed, right there, in a pile by the kitchen door. I can't believe it."

I was unable to fully process her words.

"They say you can see them from outside the house," she said.

The usual evening hush had settled over the neighborhood. The beautiful glow of the electric lights spilled out from behind the storm doors that had been shuttered early to keep out the wind. For some unknown reason, as I started to listen to my wife's terrifying story, I thought of the cloud from that night in September. (1: 334)

In the remainder of the *zuihitsu*, the protagonist recounts his day at work on November 10. He teaches at a school in Yokosuka, and during a break he walked out to the schoolyard facing the sea. On the abandoned seashore he saw an unusually large bird that seemed to be chasing him. He also remembers crying, but can't recall the reason why. All he can say is that he experienced feelings akin to those of September 20, when he was waiting for the moon to appear. He is shaken by the realization that while the horrible events were going on next door—the student killed the old couple and then committed suicide—he and his family were going about their business completely unaware. The rest of the story details the protagonist's discussions with policemen and reporters who provide him with more information on the killings.

This piece is classified as a *zuihitsu*, but stylistically speaking, the description of the landscape and the cloud-hidden moon are reminiscent of the short stories in Hyakken's second fictional collection, *Triumphant March into Port Arthur* (1934). Like the two prior examples, this *zuihitsu* is written in the first person, but there is a tangible layer of fictionality that is not present in the more editorial works. One of the most common and notable ways in which Hyakken crosses into the fictional is by weaving autobiographical elements into both his stories and his *zuihitsu*. He accomplishes this by incorporating the following: narrators and fictional characters who resemble him in name, age, profession, and demeanor; characters named after his pen names; titles that refer to these fictional alter egos; historical figures of literary fame; reminiscences from his childhood; and episodes from his published diaries. The autobiographical nature of these *zuihitsu* is characteristic of his work in the genre, and is significant in light of the I-novel and its emphasis on authorial voice and a close author-subject connection.

One group of *zuihitsu* that fits within this autobiographical category mentions Natsume Sōseki, Hyakken's mentor. In "The Farewell" ("Miokuri"), the narrator talks of going to Kobe to wish farewell to Sōseki's son, who is traveling to Europe. But most of this two-page entry is dedicated to a fire that delays the narrator. It is only in the last lines of the story that the reader finds out the narrator arrived in Kobe and met with Sōseki's son before his overseas journey. Like the narrator, the narrative here is sidetracked by seemingly unrelated details and incidents, and the reader's expectations of the "story"—namely the contents of a meeting between the narrator and Sōseki's son—are never met. This intentional sidetracking is also at work in the slightly longer (five-page) "Frock Coat" ("Furokku kōto"), in which the protagonist begins with the events on the day of Sōseki's death.

> I was on night duty at Sōseki's home on the evening of December 8, 1916. The doctor and I huddled around the fire and passed a sleepless night in the room next to my ailing teacher.
>
> Around daybreak, the master's pulse exceeded 140. The 50-year-old head nurse who'd been sent over from the university hospital had been promptly reporting on Sōseki's condition every hour or so as the night wore on.
>
> Sōseki passed away at dusk on the ninth. We disciples had taken shifts on sick watch, but the rotation ended with me. (1: 282)

The opening to this *zuihitsu* raises the reader's expectations about Sōseki, a popular and well-known writer, but in fact, the story has little to do with Hyakken's mentor. There is hardly any discussion of Sōseki beyond what is mentioned above. On the morning of the ninth, the protagonist has to go to the Military Academy to attend a ceremony for incoming students. Before leaving, he receives the doctor's assurance there will not be any sudden changes in Sōseki's condition. After the orientation, the protagonist enters a room to address his class of students. While climbing the podium, he trips and falls on his behind, and barely restrains himself from losing his composure: "In that instant my defenses gave way under the stress and pain of a sleepless night. I felt myself losing control, ready to break down in tears, but I got a hold of myself. When I got up I realized the strange black object rolling around by the students' feet was my hat" (1: 283–84).

The second part of the story switches to 1924, the year after the Great Kantō Earthquake and to another embarrassing incident in which the protagonist falls down on a visit to the rebuilt Naval Academy. In these stories, we see Hyakken's talent for taking the reader somewhere he didn't expect, and involving him in a story that would, if presented on its own, hold less interest. This is certainly part of the appeal of these *zuihitsu* for the average reader of the era. The enticement of a story about a famous literary figure leads unexpectedly to a light, yet personal story about Hyakken or his alter ego. Readers would have known the details of Sōseki's death and the fact that Hyakken was his disciple. Regardless of whether or not the protagonist's story is based in fact, the opening sets up the reader to believe it is a true account of the events in Hyakken's life on the day his mentor died, therefore strengthening the tie between author and protagonist.

Another group of Hyakken's *zuihitsu* that can be loosely categorized under such an autobiographical heading includes what would appear to be childhood reminiscences like those found in "Amber" ("Kohaku") and "Cholera" ("Korera"). In both works, the protagonist talks about being the son of a *sake* brewer, as was Hyakken himself. In the former, he buries some pine sap used to seal *sake* barrels in the hopes of making amber. In the latter, his family flees a cholera outbreak at a seaside inn, only to have it follow them back to their hometown. These appear to be stories from Hyakken's childhood, but he casts doubt on their factual, autobiographical nature with comments like those in the conclusion to "The Narrow Straw Mat" ("Samushiro"), a story about the protagonist's childhood experience with a strange beast trapped in a neighboring storehouse and a visit from a fox shaman. Although this story is in the fictional collection *Triumphant March into Port Arthur*, it originally appeared in 1933 in the *zuihitsu* column of the *zuihitsu*-economics magazine *Keizai ōrai*. The work ends: "As to whether this all really happened, or whether improbable delusions have crept into my already hazy memories, I no longer know myself" (163). In making such remarks, the protagonist reinforces the truthful aspects of the story, while at the same time makes the reader question the factuality of the account. The lines between author and subject, truth and fiction are not clear, nor are they meant to be clear. Hyakken is playing games and is making the reader decide.

The game-playing continues as Hyakken appears in a variety of guises in his *zuihitsu*—as the narrator/protagonist identified as Uchida, as Hyakken, as Fujita Hyakkien, and as Aochi Toyojirō, one of Hyakken's pen names and a recurring fictional character—undermining the singular connection between author and subject and countering the belief in a unique authorial voice. This narrator/protagonist also describes himself as a German professor at the Military Academy, and as a writer, mentioning the titles of stories Hyakken himself published. He talks about other events closely associated with Hyakken, such as meetings with Sōseki and with loan sharks. This narrator/protagonist matches a description of the author, and Hyakken is encouraging the reader to take his own life as the subtext for reading the miscellany. This is most prominent in a set of six stories, written in both the first and third person, which feature a character named Professor Hyakkien. These stories, along with some of his "poverty tales" (*binbō monogatari*), form a core of works that Hyakken uses to locate his *zuihitsu* in an indeterminate space between fiction and autobiography. The earliest of the Professor Hyakkien stories, "The Memoirs of Professor Hyakkien" ("Hyakkien sensei genkōroku"), is also the longest *zuihitsu* in the *Hyakkien's Miscellany* collection, at 25 pages. This rambling tale centers on the comic mishaps of Professor Fujita Hyakkien, a middle-aged German instructor at a private university in Tokyo. It opens with a description of our surly protagonist.

A little after the rundown clock at the Yanagiya inn struck noon, Mr. Hyakkien, lying under the north facing window in room number twelve, woke up sporting his usual grouchy look.

On his way to buy some soap at a sundry store in the alley, he had dropped a 50 *sen* silver coin on the earthen floor. He couldn't find it, no matter how hard he looked. He even got down on the ground to search, but in the process, he woke up from the dream and was overcome with regret. The fact that the loss wasn't real did little to allay his anxiety or discontent. (1: 301)

"Hyakkien's New Look" ("Hyakkien shinsō"), another in the series, is also one of his signature "poverty tales." Here, the professor reflects on the value of money, of which he is ever short.

Professor Hyakkien pondered the following: money is not a thing of substance but a phenomenon. It has no true shape. It is a form that comes into our subjective view. The more he thought about it, he realized that money is merely an idea. It is certainly not something that actually exists. Hence, the possibility of possessing it is a dream, an error in conceptual thinking.

Realistically speaking, no one ever truly owns money, least of all him. Money is an idea that is formed right before the cash comes into your hands or right after you have spent it. In the case of the former, you don't have any until you've acquired it, but the desire exists. As for the latter, once you spend it, you no longer possess it, and are left only with regret. Regret always follows desire. This is analogous to our understanding of time. The past connects directly to the future, and that which we call the present does not exist. Directly preceding any second in time is the past, and right after it is the future. Time has no duration, just the flow of past into future. We can imagine the present as a geometric line with no width. Time is money. Money is the present state of time. Such a thing does not exist in this world. Nobody possesses it. Nor is it possible to do so. (1: 257–58)

Hyakken was infamous for his surliness and lack of money, and he was constantly borrowing from friends and business associates to make ends meet. Both of the above examples showcase the light humor that, along with the autobiographical elements, is a hallmark of Hyakken's brand of *zuihitsu*.

Similar literary operations are at work in "The Continued Memoirs of Professor Hyakkien" ("Hyakkien sensei genkō-yoroku"), in which the protagonist is an exact match for Hyakken in age, marital status, occupation, and physical appearance.[21] This was published under the pen name Aochi Toyojirō, which also happens to be the name of a character in the works described below. The *zuihitsu* "Documentary Proof of the Existence of Half-Wits" ("Manuke no jitsuzai ni kansuru bunken") is a humorous portrayal of two bumblers, Aochi and Segawa, supposedly modeled on Hyakken and fellow author and Sōseki disciple Morita Sōhei. The novella "The Bowler Hat" ("Yamataka bōshi") is about two professors at the Military Academy, both of whom are verging on insanity.[22] As Aochi's condition improves, his companion Noguchi's grows worse, and the story builds toward Noguchi's suicide. Critics read this story as a tribute to Akutagawa Ryūnosuke, who worked with Hyakken at the Naval Engineers Academy and who also committed suicide in 1927. Hyakken, however, resisted this interpretation, arguing: "It's a novel. Akutagawa's name never even appears once."[23] Aochi also figures as the main character in Hyakken's *zuihitsu* "Gate of Hell" ("Jigoku no mon"), about a university professor who has to borrow money from a loan shark in order to pay his bills.

"Gate of Hell" holds further interest because it is one of the many *zuihitsu* that Hyakken critic Sakai Hideyuki claims is heavily based on episodes in Hyakken's diary, titled *Hyakkien's Diary* (*Hyakkien nikki chō*, 1935).[24] Hyakken acknowledges having recycled a 20-year-old diary entry—one in which he incidentally mentions a criticism of the national heroes, the Forty-Seven Rōnin—for use in *Hyakkien's Miscellany*.

I used parts of my old diary in *Hyakkien's Miscellany* for the scene with the condolence call, and the part about the Forty-Seven Rōnin also got included. Letters poured into the publisher: I could never read a book by an author capable of even thinking such disgraceful things. The complaints even came directly to me demanding an explanation.

The other day I was organizing my drafts for the soon to appear *Hyakkien's Diary*. The scene with the Forty-Seven Rōnin came up again. I realized I could run into problems if I use the original as is, because the criticism is far more stringent than in *Hyakkien's Miscellany*. Although it's a bother, I think I'll have to edit the diary. (2: 185)[25]

We can begin to see the opening of an "autobiographical space" located in the nexus of Hyakken's real life, his publishing history, his diaries, his *zuihitsu*, and his fictional writings.[26] We can also add in *Realm of the Dead*, another collection critics link to the diaries and subject to an autobiographical reading. By blurring the line between diary and fiction, creating characters that resemble him in name and physical description, and using character names as pen names, Hyakken encourages the reader to insert all his writing into this space.[27]

Although Hyakken encourages his reader to use his real life as a subtext for understanding his *zuihitsu*, to identify him with the characters Hyakkien and Aochi, and to accept *zuihitsu* as nonfictional, he also works at the same time to undermine these assumptions, or to pull us out of the "autobiographical space," and question the existence of the singular authorial voice. A month after "The Continued Memoirs of Professor Hyakkien," he published a *zuihitsu* called "The Dragonfly Marble" ("Tonbodama"),[28] which opens with the following line: "The word I here refers to the I of the story, not to the author himself" (1: 288). This line is isolated from the rest of the text, which begins "Now then, a lot of things bother me," and proceeds to describe the narrator's aversion to round objects.[29]

Critic Kōno Kensuke quotes this passage in order to examine Hyakken's relation to the printed word, and the textual level of *Realm of the Dead*, a level on which Hyakken's characters are trapped;[30] our present discussion, however, raises different questions. As readers, we have to wonder who exactly is speaking in this opening comment? It may be the author, or Hyakken may be warning the reader that the author is not present in the story and that the character is staking claim to his own identity.[31] This comment breaks the link between author and protagonist and undermines any comfortable autobiographical reading of Hyakken's work, especially if this one story is viewed as part of the collection, *Hyakkien's Miscellany*, as an integrated whole. This comment also highlights the tendency of the prewar reader to equate the "I" with the author, and brings the whole issue to the fore. By adding to the layers of interpretation, through embedded comments, confusing pen names, and the incorporation of biographical material, Hyakken problematizes the author-subject identification process and makes it difficult for his work to be read as pure autobiography, *zuihitsu*, or fiction. The range of *zuihitsu* writing in the prewar era easily encompassed all three of the above-mentioned genres, and the conventions of the *zuihitsu* allowed for Hyakken to create this "autobiographical space." An examination of the literary field of the 1930s reveals the repercussions of Hyakken's strategy to undermine this identification process, and to question the existence of an auratic voice.

## Blurring Generic Boundaries: *Zuihitsu* Meets I-novel

In an essay honoring the memory of fellow Sōseki disciple Terada Torahiko, Hyakken made the following puzzling statement:

> I can't define the word *zuihitsu*, nor do I have a clear grasp of the limitations of the term. . . . Recently I titled my collection *Hyakkien zuihitsu* and have since read a number of reviews comparing myself and Terada on the basis of our *zuihitsu*. I can't agree with such a comparison, and I think Terada would also be somewhat put off. I randomly hit upon my title because I liked the look and sound of the words. There was nothing deliberate in my use of the term *zuihitsu*. I never once thought in exclusionary terms about what was and wasn't a *zuihitsu*. (2: 323)[32]

By 1936, Hyakken would have been no stranger to the term *zuihitsu*, nor would he have been at a loss for examples of *zuihitsu* writing. A certain degree of skepticism is in order when gauging the validity of Hyakken's self-proclaimed ignorance of *zuihitsu* parameters. Hyakken's own work had been published in *zuihitsu* columns and the essay itself is dedicated to one of the great *zuihitsu* writers of the day. His reluctance to admit to having used a guiding literary principle when writing his work, or to accept the limits of such a term when applied to his writing, is curious given the very open-endedness of the genre. On the other hand, Hyakken may have been purposely articulating the ambiguity surrounding the *zuihitsu*. He used this ambiguity to his advantage as he played with narrative conventions and reader expectations in order to produce a confounding yet compelling hybrid text.

Judging from the comments of other contemporary writers and critics, Hyakken was not alone in his confusion about the *zuihitsu*—provided, that is, that we can take him at his word. There was little agreement in the 1920s and 1930s about the exact definition of *zuihitsu*. Additionally, Hyakken's constant crossing of generic boundaries and exploitation of reader expectations makes his writing difficult to analyze under any single literary rubric. However, since the works under consideration in this chapter were marked and marketed as *zuihitsu*, a closer look at commonly held assumptions about the genre provides the context for a better appreciation of Hyakken's experiments with the form, specifically his ventures into autobiography.

The title of *Hyakkien's Miscellany* would have both indicated the genre of the writing and resonated with other *zuihitsu* collections popular at the time.[33] Most major writers had a volume of *zuihitsu* in their oeuvre, such as Chikamatsu Shūkō's *Shūkō zuihitsu*.[34] Within this context, a reader in the 1930s would be inclined to believe the *zuihitsu* in *Hyakkien zuihitsu* were written by a person named Hyakkien. However, the name of the author, Uchida Hyakken, on the cover indicates otherwise. Hence from the beginning of the reading experience, readers are left to wonder who or what is this Hyakkien (literally translated as the "hundred ghosts garden"). Hyakken takes advantage of the prevalence of texts with similar titles and the mismatch in paratextual information to complicate the author-subject identification process.[35]

Although Hyakken did use the moniker Hyakkien in his real life, he breaks one of the cardinal rules of the genre in the title of this collection: that *zuihitsu* must "contain no fiction."[36] The question of fictionality is one of the central issues at stake in *zuihitsu*, and a point on which critics are willing to give very little. One of the most commonly held assumptions about premodern *zuihitsu* is that the label "is meant to signify the natural or unmediated writer, released from convention and presented without fiction."[37] In the Hyakken criticism discussed below, it is clear that these assumptions apply to modern *zuihitsu* as well. Critic Yoshida Seiichi admits that although miscellany are not completely devoid of fiction, the author's presence is much more direct, or raw, (unmediated) than in other genres, therefore eliminating the need for any conscious authorial pose.[38] This conclusion further strengthens the contention that the value of the work is inextricably tied to the reader's assessment of the author as a person.[39] This assessment complicates the case of *Hyakkien's Miscellany* because we are never sure if we are reading about the author Uchida Hyakken or about a fictional character closely resembling him.

Critical evaluation of *Hyakkien's Miscellany* and of *zuihitsu* in general supports the use of a biographical subtext. Murō Saisei praised the self-revelation in *Hyakkien's Miscellany* as lending a "human warmth" to the text.[40] Part of the appeal for Murō was the connection he could make between the author's name on the cover and the voice speaking out of the text. This is a standard feature of autobiographical texts, but one that is complicated in the case of *Hyakkien's Miscellany*.[41] The desire to read in an autobiographical fashion is not in and of itself that remarkable, given its prevalence in Japanese literature, but the degree of intimacy expected of the *zuihitsu* is extreme. It is not simply that we can hear the author speaking, but that we can see and smell him in all his glory and ugliness.

Critic Yoshida Seiichi explains that for the *zuihitsu*, "more than any other genre, the smell of the writer's bare skin and his way of thinking appear raw and unprocessed."[42] Hasegawa Izumi uses similar language when he refers to the "author's naked body," and to the subject matter that is "reflected in a raw state."[43] The emphasis on nakedness and rawness, specifically the term *nama,* is also found in descriptions of modern *zuihitsu*. Chiba Kameo states, "the author reveals himself with overwhelming closeness," or more literally, "the author is naked, which leads to an overwhelming intimacy."[44] Chiba also talks about "stripping oneself bare," and Yoshida comments on the "flesh and blood of the self" in Akutagawa's "Words of a Petty Man" ("Shuju no kotoba," 1923–25).[45] These physical metaphors are also used to describe the effects the *zuihitsu* has upon its readers. Chiba compares the *zuihitsu* to "the chill of icy water," imagery that resurfaces in Nakaya Ukichirō's recollections on the experience of reading Terada Torahiko, which he described as akin to drinking cold water on a day when dust sticks to sweaty, hot skin.[46]

These metaphors used to describe the *zuihitsu* imply a level of intimacy that verges on the inappropriate and even the sexual. The extreme closeness of the author binds the reader to the text. This emphasis on intimacy and unmediated self-revelation, although expected to an extreme degree in the *zuihitsu,* is not unique to *zuihitsu*. In fact, the locus classicus for this discourse in the late Taishō–early Shōwa period is the I-novel, the autobiographical stronghold of elite fiction, where writers bared their souls through the guise of thinly fictionalized characters. When examining the systems of expectation relevant to the modern *zuihitsu,* the semi-confessional, semi-autobiographical narratives of the I-novel provide insight on contemporary forces shaping the construction and consumption of the *zuihitsu*. It is not uncommon for genres to share textual and narrative features, and we can envision the *zuihitsu* and I-novel in a state of mutual adjustment.

The I-novel emerged as a form in the 1920s and debates about its authenticity and role in elite writing were revived in the mid-1930s. Hyakken was not only aware of these debates, but purposely employed the conventions of the I-novel when writing his *zuihitsu*. The *zuihitsu* was in competition with the I-novel for readers, publication venues, manuscript fees, and literary distinction. This happened at a time in the 1930s when calls rang out to rescue literature from its languishing state. Writers such as the modernist Yokomitsu Riichi were appealing to their compatriots to revitalize literature through the adoption of the themes and techniques of popular novels. While others turned to popular fiction to revive the flagging state of literature, Hyakken mined the shared territory with the I-novel, adhering to or ignoring its dictates as fit his needs. Just as the I-novel reading strategy of identifying author with subject was applied to the *zuihitsu, zuihitsu* writers such as Hyakken purposely mimicked the I-novel style to achieve certain literary effects. The shifting boundaries of literature allowed for such experimentation, and the public readily consumed these products.

In examining Hyakken's *zuihitsu* as an intrusion into I-novel territory, it is necessary to sketch out the narrative parameters and expectations for the I-novel, one of the most important being the rhetoric of truth. Adherents of the I-novel valued the artful recounting of personal experience, which they saw as the only viable means through which to express truth. The ability of the reader to place his trust in the story lay in the immediacy and verifiability of the author's experience. In 1924, at the height of the I-novel debates, Nakamura Murao commented on authorial presence in the *shinkyō shōsetsu* or "state-of-mind novel," a type of I-novel: "The author appears directly in the state-of-mind novel. The author speaks directly in the work, or rather, the novel appears to present the author's direct speech. . . . The main focus is not on what is written but rather on the person who wrote it."[47] Kume Masao, an outspoken proponent of the I-novel, stated unequivocally in 1925 "that the basis of all art lies in the self [*watakushi*]. It follows that the form that expresses this 'self' directly and frankly, without pretense and disguise, that is to say, the I-novel, should become the main path, the basis and essence of the art of prose."[48] Similar expectations were applied to the *zuihitsu* as it encroached on the I-novel in the 1930s.

In addition to the expression of authorial presence, similarities in content facilitated the *zuihitsu*'s adoption of the I-novel's conventions. Since interest in the author often took precedence over the narrated events, I-novels easily degenerated into plotless chronicles of daily life, records of the quotidian events of the everyday. I-novelist Chikamatsu Shūkō, in defending his choice of subject and his mode of writing, explains this link between content and form, a link we can also see in the *zuihitsu*.

> My writings—at least those collected in this volume—contain no plot or staging. Critics frequently declare this lack to be the great defect of my work. But plot has its drawbacks: it forces the author to embellish the facts of his own life. True, an author cannot but be satisfied

> when his imaginative technique has succeeded in pleasing his audience, but I am of the school that frowns on letting plot or fabrication needlessly violate the truth of lived experience. . . . I have swallowed my shame and presented before the public eye these frivolous incidents in my life out of a respect for historical truth.[49]

The emphasis Shūkō places on truth, or as he states "historical truth," is not echoed in *zuihitsu* criticism. But the historical truth of an I-novel readily equates to the "personal, individual, intimate truth of the author."[50] Such a "truth," based in personal experience, can only be subjective, and would be better labeled autobiographical truth. This truth of a subjective lived experience found in the I-novel is not far from *zuihitsu* territory.

The I-novel used the presence of the author as a type of plot or staging. This was a natural place to turn, given the I-novel's limited narrative perspective and emphasis on the self. Similarly, the author can be used as a means to bring order to the scattered *zuihitsu* text. Scholars and critics such as Itō Sei and Hirano Ken remarked on the resemblance of the two genres, with Itō describing the I-novel as "semi-autobiographical, containing characteristics similar to miscellanies (*zuihitsu*)."[51] But Donald Keene stated it most openly when he said:

> An essay in a book of *zuihitsu* may be no more than an intriguing sentence or two, or it may extend over several pages. In the end, after reading a series of seemingly unrelated anecdotes or impressions, we may nevertheless feel a great sense of intimacy with the writer, much as if we had read his diary or perhaps an 'I-novel' in which he laid bare the joys and sorrows of his life.[52]

My point in noting the similarities between the I-novel and the *zuihitsu* is to highlight the fact that genres are not discrete units. The premodern *zuihitsu*, which Linda Chance aptly describes as "outside the customary boundaries of narrativity, persona, fictivity, meter, and countless other limiting constructs," was in the modern period limited or bound by the surrounding discourse of the I-novel.[53] The expectations and reading strategies of the I-novel were applied to the *zuihitsu*, the rise of which was linked to the popularity of the I-novel.[54] As Tosaka Jun warned in 1936, pure literature was in a situation where it had to take on the characteristics of popular fiction, or risk having its essence stolen by a purer, more personal, I-novel-like *zuihitsu*.[55] Just as the *zuihitsu* could be bound by the interpretative strategies of the I-novel, the *zuihitsu* author could also use this association to exploit reader expectations and undermine the tendencies toward author-subject identification.

Hyakken creates a "self-conscious I-novel" in which the "author presupposes these autobiographical assumptions on the part of the reader."[56] He then employs the "autobiographical pact" to encourage the reader to see him in the text. But who exactly are we seeing—Uchida Hyakken, Fujita Hyakkien, or (in a later work) Ujita Hyakugen?[57] What is their relationship to Hyakken and what level of trust are we to place in these (mis)representations? Hyakken purposely makes it difficult for the reader to place his trust in a stable author-subject identification. He uses his "autobiographical space," to mock the serious I-novel and critique its basis, namely the representation of the self "directly and frankly, without pretense and disguise." He takes advantage of the unique features of the *zuihitsu* in order to take aim at this cornerstone of elite fiction. These features are characteristic of Hyakken's work in the genre, and they drive a wedge between the author and subject, differentiating his *zuihitsu* from the I-novel, and allowing the reader to see his critique.

Humor is a characteristic distinguishing Hyakken's *zuihitsu,* and *zuihitsu* in general, from the I-novel. In his 1948 essay "The Loss of Laughter" ("Warai no sōshitsu"), Nakamura Mitsuo points out that "a lack of distance between authors and their fictional egos, which was integral to the [I-novel], was hardly conducive to ironic distancing or a comic view of the self."[58] Certainly not all I-novels are humorless, but the genre's requirements for seriousness rarely permit the "comic view of the self" that we see in the character of Professor Hyakkien.

I-novelists often revealed their dark, unseemly side in their novels, and Professor Hyakkien is also cast in a negative light. But unlike the I-novelist's shocking confessions, these descriptions of the professor as lazy, insensitive, and self-serving mock him and provide a basis for humor. Far from the intellectual brooding we would expect from an I-novelist, the professor engages in discussions so inane as to send the hotel maid into fits of uncontrollable laughter. He is easily fooled and foiled, and is mocked by a variety of characters in the story, including the supposedly neutral third-person narrator, as seen in "The Memoirs of Professor Hyakkien." This comic distance keeps the author from expressing himself, as Kume Masao felt I-novelists should. It also impedes the reading of a work such as "The Memoirs of Professor Hyakkien" as an unmediated, nonfictional personal account—unless we are willing to believe Hyakken a liar or a fool.

In addition to the distancing effect of humor, Hyakken takes advantage of the loose author-subject linkage in the *zuihitsu* in order to critique this crucial function in the I-novel. The *zuihitsu* may have given readers a glimpse into the mind of the writer, but this was an inadvertent side effect of a casual, chatty, unstructured text. Unlike the I-novel, *zuihitsu* were not meant to be structured, aestheticized confessions. In fact, the *zuihitsu* offered writers a genre relatively free of the narrative constraints associated with the novel. Readers expected light, easy reading from the *zuihitsu*, not ponderous self-revelation. I-novelists, on the other hand, were not in the business of easy reading. In a time when capitalist production was replacing the unique experience with a plurality of copies, the I-novelists clung to the authentic, individual, yet highly crafted voice of their personal experience. Hyakken also reacted against this loss of aura at various stages of his career, as seen in *Realm of the Dead*. However, in *Hyakkien's Miscellany* he capitalizes on these features of the *zuihitsu* genre for the express purpose of creating multiple voices and personae (Fujita Hyakkien, Ujita Hyakugen, Aochi Toyojirō), the very plurality of copies the I-novelists feared.

The chatty, unstructured, loose narrative features of the *zuihitsu* allowed Hyakken to simultaneously encourage and discourage author-subject identification, highlighting the problematic nature of this association that forms the basic grounding for the I-novel. His success hinged on the tendency toward self-representation and autobiography on the part of both the literary producers and consumers of the 1920s and 1930s, and on the precariousness of authorial voice in the prewar era. Hyakken creates literary alter egos in *Hyakken's Miscellany* that he then proceeds to mock and undermine. In doing so, he mocks the seriousness of the I-novel depictions and throws a monkey wrench into the interpretative process of author-subject identification. He transgresses literary boundaries and plays with reader expectations, showing not only his awareness of literary trends, but of the fluctuations in narrative definitions. The *zuihitsu* and I-novel were in a state of mutual adjustment in the prewar era, and Hyakken crafted a *zuihitsu,* which in its similarities to the I-novel could function as a critique of this elite form. The successful *Hyakkien's Miscellany* showcases his hybrid text—a mix of fiction, nonfiction, narrative, and editorial—and in the process raises questions regarding the generic boundaries of the modern *zuihitsu*, and by extension, of the I-novel.

These boundaries were in flux in the late 1920s and 1930s as literature was being redefined by an emerging print market. In the following section, we will explore the disagreements over the definition and value of the *zuihitsu* among critics of that time. More important than the genre's definition is its function with relation to other literary modes, and the value—or risk—of writing *zuihitsu*. In the end, we will seek to answer the question: what did it mean for Hyakken to steal ground from the I-novel and write his particular brand of *zuihitsu*? Specifically, what did this mean within the writing community in the 1930s? Hyakken created an autobiographical space as a means to critique elite fiction, but he chose to conduct this critique through the *zuihitsu*, a genre that was under attack, despite its popularity, or perhaps because of it.

## The Genre Quandary: Writing *Zuihitsu* in the 1930s

Hyakken's *zuihitsu* functioned as a critique of the I-novel, but the question remains whether the ambiguous status of *zuihitsu* made it a viable means for critique. An evaluation of Hyakken's *zuihitsu* must take into consideration the state of publishing in the 1930s, the lack of a clear consensus on what constituted a *zuihitsu*, and the low status of the genre. Tosaka Jun proclaimed Hyakken the leading *zuihitsu* writer in 1936; however, as little as three years prior, his position was far from secure. Both the difficulty Hyakken encountered in finding a publisher for his first volume of *zuihitsu* and his eventual success with the medium were functions of the prewar literary field.

Hyakken's initial reputation as a *zuihitsu* writer was made in literary magazines, *the* active site for *zuihitsu* production in the prewar era.[59] His *zuihitsu* had originally appeared in such prestigious journals as *Chūō kōron* and *Bungei shunjū*, and so his difficulty getting his work published in book form is surprising. *Hyakkien's Miscellany*, although popular with readers, was initially a hard sell with publishers. Takeuchi Michinosuke, founder of the Mikasa Shobō publishing house, describes the reluctance of publishers to take on the financial risk of printing this collection of Hyakken's *zuihitsu*. Takeuchi convinced his brother-in-law to print the text, and to save on costs, Takeuchi set the type himself.[60]

The resistance Hyakken encountered is further puzzling, given the surge in the genre's popularity in the prewar era, first in the mid-1920s and then again in the mid-1930s. The earlier boom was strongly linked to the development of print culture, but this print expansion was slowing down in the 1930s, as one-yen book sales began to slump in the early part of the decade. These conditions, however, did not stop the *zuihitsu* from making a strong comeback. Articles in the Tokyo-based daily *Jiji shinpō* comment on the prevalence of this style of writing in 1934, with titles such as "The Flood of *Zuihitsu* and *Zuihitsu*-like Novels" ("Zuihitsu hanran to zuihitsuteki shōsetsu") and "The Deluge of *Zuihitsu* Books" ("Zuihitsusho no kōzui"). The term *zuihitsu hanran* was a catchphrase in the media of the day. The latter article dates the *zuihitsu* trend to 1933, and indicates that it climaxed in 1934. These articles discuss and review the merits of the *zuihitsu* books that shocked Tosaka in their vast quantity. Hyakken published his first collection of *zuihitsu* in the autumn of 1933, the first year of this *zuihitsu* resurgence, and he is mentioned alongside well-known and up-and-coming authors Satō Haruo, Satomi Ton, and Ibuse Masuji, among others.

The publishing difficulty Hyakken encountered was at least partly due to the negative effects of the one-yen book boom, which had raised the bar for publishing. "Reduced profit margins made the publication of books expected to sell only 500 to 1,000 copies . . . all but impossible."[61] *Hyakkien's Miscellany* was one such small printing with a first run of 1,000 copies, and two subsequent 500 copy runs made two and four months later. Takeuchi specifically states that his brother-in-law was very concerned about the financial repercussions of taking on Hyakken's text. This is understandable since the printing house where he worked would be burdening the costs in support of Takeuchi's fledgling enterprise. The head of the print shop was certain the book would not sell, and he suggested that the best thing to do would be to return the manuscript to Hyakken along with twenty yen for his troubles. Takeuchi's brother-in-law was not alone in his worries. The standards set by the one-yen book proved difficult for the small publisher to maintain. Even established houses such as Shun'yōdō almost went bankrupt after the success of *Complete Works of Meiji and Taishō Literature* (*Meiji Taishō bungaku zenshū*) eliminated the demand for more expensive volumes in their catalog.[62] By the time Hyakken's book came out in 1933, one-yen book sales had slumped, with volumes selling for as low as ten to twenty *sen*, one-tenth to one-twentieth of the original price.[63] Books had finally become affordable to everyone, but at a cost to the industry.

In Hyakken's case, the reluctance of other publishers proved to be unfounded, and Takeuchi's gamble paid off. Less than a month after it appeared in print, Murō Saisei praised *Hyakkien's Miscellany* in the prominent daily *Tōkyō Asahi Shinbun* (November 24, 1933). The success of *Hyakkien's Miscellany* secured the financial future of the then-small Mikasa publishing house; Hyakken's book was only their second publication. *Hyakkien's*

*Miscellany* originally came out in October 1933, and by February 1935 was already in its twelfth printing.[64] The favorable reception of the work certainly helped guarantee Hyakken a contract for his next book, *Triumphant March into Port Arthur,* with the young yet established publishing venture Iwanami Shoten.[65]

As mentioned above, Hyakken earned praise for his *zuihitsu,* even if the critics were not always sure which of his works actually fell under this category. This confusion indicates not only the lack of consensus in the prewar years over how to define *zuihitsu,* but also the tremendous flexibility of the genre. One noteworthy example is the inclusion of two short story collections in a six-volume series titled *Complete Hyakken Zuihitsu Collection* (*Zenshū Hyakken zuihitsu,* 1936–37). Volume six contains the entire contents of Hyakken's short story collections *Realm of the Dead* and *Triumphant March into Port Arthur,* originally published as separate volumes in 1922 and 1934, respectively. The confusion resulting from this loose categorization is apparent in the opening line of an essay by Hagiwara Sakutarō that was included in the series: "I'd heard of Uchida Hyakken before, but *Triumphant March into Port Arthur* is the first *zuihitsu* collection of his that I've read."[66] *Triumphant March into Port Arthur* may have been included in this *zenshū,* but the fictionality and novelistic structuring of these stories would seem to exempt them from a strict *zuihitsu* designation. Both collections were also marketed as *sōsakushū* or creative writing (fiction). But the comments of a sensitive reader such as Hagiwara further indicate the ease with which Hyakken's work was cross-categorized. In this essay, Hagiwara himself readily crosses genre boundaries by comparing Hyakken's text to premodern *zuihitsu,* to the Chinese-inspired ghost stories in Ueda Akinari's *Tales of Rain and Moon* (*Ugetsu monogatari,* 1776), and even to Poe. This example demonstrates the very flexible nature of literary genres, but more so the effectiveness of *zuihitsu* as a marketing tool in the mid- to late 1930s. For Hyakken, the *Complete Hyakken Zuihitsu Collection* not only increased his market value but also opened doors for him in other media forms: this *zenshū* formed the basis of the film discussed later in this chapter.

In addition to the marketing decision behind this *zenshū*, another reason for the cross-categorization—and, arguably, miscategorization—of Hyakken's work is the very mixed nature of the writing itself. Murō Saisei addresses this in an essay on Hyakken's *zuihitsu* collection *The Crane* (*Tsuru*, 1935). Murō argues that the reason Hyakken is well known and his *zuihitsu* are so interesting is because they are a hybrid of the *zuihitsu* and the *shōsetsu*; Hyakken is unique in his ability to blend the two forms. Murō considers Hyakken's use of language and expression to be less characteristic of the *zuihitsu* and more along the lines of a novel, or more specifically, novelistic structure (*shōsetsuteki kōzu*).[67] Murō finds this mixture appealing, but he regrets that Hyakken's tremendous skills as a novelist are being wasted on the *zuihitsu*.

Murō's comments raise important questions about the literary categorization of Hyakken's work. Indeed, many of his *zuihitsu* are emplotted stories that would easily fit into the *sōsaku* columns of the day. Hyakken acknowledged this in the abovementioned essay on Terada Torahiko: "The book [*Hyakkien's Miscellany*] is primarily narrative writing, but there are also some lyrical passages, and some *shōsetsu* that appeared in the creative writing columns of monthly journals. The volumes I've produced since have all been the same."[68] The seeming confusion over genre designation is not limited to Hyakken and can also be seen in critical discussions from the prewar. Even though Murō argues Hyakken is unique in his ability to blend the two genres, terms such as "novelistic *zuihitsu*" (*shōsetsuteki zuihitsu*), "*zuihitsu*-like literature" (*zuihitsuteki bungaku*), and "*zuihitsu*-novel" (*zuihitsu shōsetsu*) can be found in literary debates and critical reviews in newspapers and magazines from the prewar era.[69] Hence it is possible to see Hyakken's *zuihitsu* as part of a larger trend toward hybridization, a blurring of the generic boundaries. Despite this blurring, Murō not only tries to disentangle the two genres, but to legitimize Hyakken by disassociating him from the lesser-regarded *zuihitsu* and applying this label of *shōsetsu*.[70] As discussed below, in the prewar period, the term *shōsetsu* was a mark of distinction that elite writers sought to retain in the face of intense commercialization and the rise of popular literature.[71] What did Murō—and, by extension, Hyakken—have to gain from such a move?

In order to understand Murō's motivation, we must look at how the *zuihitsu* was regarded at the time, especially in relation to elite fiction. Despite Tosaka's praise, others saw far less potential in the *zuihitsu*: their remarks can be categorized as disdain for the form itself. In the late 1920s, both Murō Saisei and Hagiwara Sakutarō had openly spoken out against the poor quality of the *zuihitsu* and its deleterious effects on serious literature. Hagiwara lamented, "The *zuihitsu* favored by the Japanese literary elite is neither the Western essay nor the prose poems *Essays in Idleness* and *The Pillow Book*. What is commonly regarded in Japan as the *zuihitsu* is literary mishmash. By no means should this be considered real literature."[72] Murō, in reviewing *Hyakkien's Miscellany*, recalled that Akutagawa often spoke of the high quality of Hyakken's work, but despite the endorsement of this literary giant, Murō was surprised by Hyakken's artistry. Murō commends Mikasa Shobō for printing Hyakken's book, and remarks, "I dare say Hyakken has no equal in the *zuihitsu*. Unlike popular fiction where you are lucky to remember one page in a hundred, Uchida Hyakken stays with you right through page ninety-nine. I have much to learn from him."[73] Murō compliments Hyakken by way of contrasting his writing to popular fiction (*taishū shōsetsu*); there is no comparison between Hyakken's quality prose and the pulp aimed at the masses.

Murō's use of the term "popular fiction," alternately translated as "mass novel," is loaded. In the 1920s and 1930s the literary elite rushed to defend literature, or as they termed it, "pure literature" (*junbungaku*), against the rise of popular forms and publishing venues aimed at a much wider audience. The purity of literature was threatened in the 1920s by the rise of the mass market and by the strength of the new socially conscious proletarian fiction. However, by the mid-1930s, politicized fiction had effectively been stamped out by censorship and the government's campaigns against the left wing. Yet pure literature still assumed a defensive posture against popular fiction. With the withering of the proletarian movement, calls rang out for a literary revival. Mass writers were monopolizing the newspaper novels in the mid-1930s, and the elite rallied to try and take back these serialized publications.[74] The divide between the pure and the popular was shifting as new models for literature were being proposed through the one-yen book and other commercial means.

Murō is trying to maintain distinctions that are being eroded by the realities of the market, and he exhibits a high modernist insistence on the "inherent hostility between high and low."[75] Similarly, in a number of important literary debates in the 1920s and 1930s, writers and critics attempted to define and locate both the pure and popular modes in literary history and create a literary hierarchy. The placement of the *zuihitsu* within this hierarchy was clearly below that of the novel. But that did not keep pure literature authors from writing and profiting from the *zuihitsu*, which paid higher manuscript fees and was published in a wider range of venues.[76] Even so-called pure literature underwent a popularization as writers reaped significant profit for their contributions to the one-yen book boom; elite writers in the late 1920s and early 1930s gladly accepted royalties from publishing houses. The *zuihitsu*, like political and popular writing, was giving pure fiction a run for its money.[77]

The ability of a critic such as Murō to unequivocally term a work pure or popular gives the impression that there was a clear line between these two forms, with authors and works falling cleanly and uncontroversially on either side. But the designation of a work as pure or popular was not necessarily based on literary criteria.[78] The term "pure literature" was a literary fixture, but it remained undefined and ambiguous. Although the literary community was hard pressed to agree upon the exact qualities that made a work "pure," they retained the right to bestow this label upon works they recognized and deemed worthy as such. In some sense, the elite retained their hold on literary and cultural capital through the official dispensation of the label "pure." The seemingly fixed pure/popular divide helped the elite maintain the myth that literature could exist outside of the market, and that their pure creations of "art for art's sake" were qualitatively different than those produced as literary commodities. Despite the prestige of many of its writers, the *zuihitsu* was one such commodity. It was not granted this mark of distinction, and it remained more openly tied to the market. This connection is clear from its origins in the pages of *Bungei shunjū*, where Kikuchi Kan's advertising copy sold the *zuihitsu* as coffee and dessert, a side course to the regular fare found in other magazines.[79]

The pure/popular paradigm masks a complex relationship between literature and the market and further complicates the issue of how to evaluate Hyakken's work. Confining his writing to either side of this dichotomy overlooks the broad appeal of his work and the role the genre played in the prewar literary market. One means of investigating and escaping this conundrum is to look at publishing venue, a concrete factor that did affect such designations. Certain venues were considered legitimate sites for pure literature, while others were not. However, as in Hyakken's case, writers published in a wide range of venues, including the popular newspapers and women's magazines, the middlebrow general interest magazines, and the elite specialist journals, further highlighting the difference between theoretical debates and the reality of publishing.

In the 1920s, *Chūō kōron* stood at the top of the publishing hierarchy, and publication in its pages symbolized entry into the *bundan* (literary establishment) itself. Hyakken published not only in *Chūō kōron*, but in the other standard-bearers of the general interest magazine industry, *Bungei shunjū* and *Kaizō*, as well as in the highly regarded literary journal *Shinchō*. These prestigious general interest magazines were followed in descending order by the literary magazines and finally the coterie journals. Hyakken's appearance in these forums points to his successful bid for entry into the elite literary world. In many respects, he followed the code of the aspiring writer of the 1920s by publishing in important general interest and literary magazines, which were seen by many as the only legitimate sites for serious literature. However, Hyakken did not limit himself to these venues. He published in more popular journals and in two sites that had lost or were losing legitimacy with the *bundan*: women's magazines and newspapers. Both media reached wider audiences and paid higher manuscript fees, but in the eyes of the literary establishment, neither could grant the cultural authority elite writers desired, or professed to desire.

However, this did not deter writers such as Hyakken from publishing in the full range of venues. This demonstrates the mixed nature of the market, and the reality that Hyakken, as a representative author, did not, and probably financially could not, restrict himself to the general interest magazine.[80] An examination of the venues in which he published sheds light on both his readership and the financial and literary decisions made by authors at this time. It also shows the wide range of places that published *zuihitsu*.

The *zuihitsu* described earlier in this chapter provide a sample of Hyakken's publishing choices. Over a third of the works in *Hyakkien's Miscellany* originally appeared in newspaper dailies and weeklies.[81] "Frock Coat" was published in the *Ōsaka Asahi* and "The Farewell" and "Gate of Hell" in *Shūkan Asahi*, the weekly created by the *Asahi shinbun* in 1922.[82] Aimed at a middle-class audience, these weeklies popularized culture in the Taishō period. They featured commentary on current events, editorials, sports, novels, gravure pages, and matters of concern to women, children, and families. They also provided a welcoming forum for *zuihitsu*.

Other venues of interest were the specialty magazines aimed at an emerging middle class of aspiring intellectuals and professionals hoping to separate themselves from the lower class. "Amber" and "The Magic Carpet" appeared in *Kezai ōrai*, a *zuihitsu* economics journal started in 1926. The magazine may seem an unlikely place for Hyakken's literature, but *Keizai ōrai* had an editorial style similar to *Bungei shunjū*. The combination of *zuihitsu* selections, fiction, and economics articles appealed to the salaried worker who read a variety of specialty books and journals. *Keizai ōrai* broadened its scope around 1932 to include more literary interests, both pure and popular, and joined the ranks of the general interest magazine. Hyakken published in this magazine alongside many writers who commonly appeared in the pages of the more prestigious journals.[83]

If *Keizai ōrai* was marketed to salaried employees, *Josei*, the journal in which "Tale of Owl Woods" was originally published, also appealed to modern, urban, cultured readers, specifically women.[84] *Josei* is often said to be symbolic of Taishō modernism (*modanizumu*), and was packaged as a guide to modern urban living.[85] During the 1920s, *Josei* regularly featured the top writers of the era and was the most prestigious of the women's journals. The magazine featured both well-known and new writers during its short six-year life span (1922–28). In addition to fiction, it also regularly ran *zuihitsu* and criticism. Women's magazines reached a wider audience and paid significantly more than their literary counterparts, but by the end of the Taishō period these magazines came to be regarded as inappropriate sites for the publication of serious fiction.[86]

The "Professor Hyakkien" works appeared in *Chūō kōron* and *Bungei shunjū*, but also in places like the modernist and experimental *Shinseinen*.[87] *Shinseinen* started in 1920 and functioned primarily as a venue for detective stories, a subcategory of popular or mass fiction.[88] In addition to a few pages of *manga* or comics, the magazine showcased *zuihitsu*, original stories by Japanese writers, and translations of Western detective fiction, such as P. G. Wodehouse and Arthur Conan Doyle. In 1931, *Shinseinen* was dubbed one of the four "must-read" magazines for the modern person along with *Kingu*, *Modan Nihon*, and the cinema journal *Kinema junpō*.[89] Those seeking the modern lifestyle would have appropriated the cultural capital of *Shinseinen*, even though it may not have bestowed literary capital. *Shinseinen* could complement the more weighty offerings of the general interest magazine, and do so with an international flair. One sign of its success with the middle-class reader, specifically the salaried worker, is that sales at the Tokyo Station bookstore equalled those of *Bungei shunjū*.[90]

*Shinseinen,* like *Josei* and *Keizai ōrai,* appealed to an interesting blend of audiences crossing the pure/popular divide. It is important to recognize the existence and power of this literary hierarchy, but equally important to realize that neither readers nor writers were always so easily categorized. Writers ranged in their openness and opposition to the more popular venues; many of the elite authors regularly graced the pages of women's magazines or journals with a more popular slant. Neither did readers confine themselves to a small segment of this hierarchy, often subscribing to a selection of magazines and newspapers that ranged from general interest literary material to women's and popular magazines, technical journals, and newspapers.[91] In the case of the newspapers, they had such a large and wide-ranging audience that they are not readily placed in this readership hierarchy. There were, of course, more intellectual dailies, such as the *Asahi shinbun*, and popular or sensational ones, such as the *Yomiuri*, but the papers cut across class boundaries in a way that select magazines did not.[92]

Obvious differences, such as a phonetic gloss, separate the elite journals from the rest, but in terms of content, the *zuihitsu* Hyakken published in these magazines and newspapers differ little from those featured in so-called highbrow or pure literature journals such as *Chūō kōron*. The inability to differentiate Hyakken's writing by publication venue argues against the pure/popular paradigm as an analytical tool. Despite this, and other realities of the publishing market, critics such as Murō, Hagiwara, and Tosaka attempt to place Hyakken's *zuihitsu* on some higher level of the literary hierarchy, effectively engaging this debate. Murō laments that Hyakken is wasting skills that would be better spent writing novels. Hagiwara compares Hyakken's *zuihitsu* to classics of the past, describing them as "gems on a par with the classical *Account of My Hut* [*Hōjōki*, 1212] and *The Pillow Book*, both in terms of their poetic beauty and consummate literary form."[93] Hagiwara returns to legendary *zuihitsu* from the classical and medieval eras to strengthen his praise for Hyakken, and to combat the shifting definition of literature in a time of intense commercialization. Tosaka also praised Hyakken's *zuihitsu*, proclaiming that they are by no means a random scribbling of the brush. Rather, Tosaka was attempting to show that there are some *zuihitsu* worthy of being called literature, because he is trying to use the *zuihitsu* as a starting point for criticism.[94]

These critics seek distinctions between pure and popular literature, or stated otherwise, material they consider to be real literature and the pulp being produced for the masses, and we can see these debates play out over Hyakken's *zuihitsu*. Yet there is no indication that Hyakken was attempting to write novels, or was calling for a return to classical forms as a means to rescue the languishing state of literature in the 1930s. Neither is it clear that Hyakken's chatty and often solipsistic writing could serve as an example of the type of critical thinking Tosaka sought. The prewar *zuihitsu* was not a reprise of traditional literary models or a vehicle for critical thought.[95] Rather, it was marketed as light reading to relieve the pressures of modern life.

In the hands of a writer such as Hyakken, however, the *zuihitsu* did prove to be a ready site for literary experimentation and critique. But its lowly status and lightweight reputation made it difficult for critics to acknowledge it as a valid form. Critics felt the need to elevate Hyakken's writing further up the literary hierarchy in order to give it serious consideration. Hence, when Hyakken ventured into I-novel territory and critiqued elite fiction from the "autobiographical space" of the *zuihitsu*, his writing became subject to the standards of the very work he was mocking. Certainly many of Hyakken's *zuihitsu* are worthy of the level of literary analysis reserved for short stories or novels. However, these critiques miss the crucial point Hyakken was trying to make about the I-novel. Disassociating Hyakken's writing from the *zuihitsu* label removes it from the generic positioning that allowed him the freedom from narrative constraints necessary to mock the seriousness of the I-novel and its requirement for structure, authenticity, and truthful self-representation (authorial voice). It is only from within the literary confines of the *zuihitsu* that Hyakken's critique is effective. The work of critics such as Murō, although intended to provide a basis for praise, in effect and perhaps inadvertently also sought to nullify his critique.

The *zuihitsu* enjoyed overwhelming success within the commercial realities of the prewar publishing market. However, in the end, the established literary hierarchy did not recognize the *zuihitsu*'s contribution. Pure literature was propped up by institutions such as the Akutagawa Prize, but as militarism and nationalism gained traction in Japanese society during the 1930s, literature and literary journalism were grinding to a halt. The government succeeded in shutting down the major liberal magazines *Chūō kōron* and *Kaizō*, and although literature continued to be written, it was increasingly subject to censorship. In this climate, many writers sought cover in the chatty, unstructured *zuihitsu*. Hyakken continued to refine his critical expression of the realities of modern life through this genre, and this language would come into play when he attacked the war propaganda in his fiction. As Hyakken continued to write *zuihitsu* in the late 1930s, his work was adapted for cinematic and theatrical productions, and he crossed further boundaries into these entertainment media. Issues of literary hierarchy, distinction, and the authenticity of authorial voice reemerge in the following discussion of film adaptation, as does Hyakken's conservative stance seen in *Realm of the Dead*.

## From Page to Screen: *Zuihitsu* as Film

Riding the success of his *zuihitsu* in the 1930s, Hyakken's hybrid tales of the bumbling, financially pressed Professor Hyakkien were rewritten for the stage and the silver screen. The film script was based on the *Complete Hyakken Zuihitsu Collection* and Hyakken's personal life, further strengthening the link between author and subject in the *zuihitsu*.[96] Hyakken was notorious for his financial troubles, and readers familiar with Hyakken's *zuihitsu* and the literary establishment would readily recognize

Fig. 2 Hyakken on the set of the Furukawa Roppa film, *The Pale Faced Professor*. From *Uchida Hyakken*, vol. 42 of *Shinchō Nihon bungaku arubamu*. Courtesy of the Okayama Culture Foundation (Zaidan hōjin Okayama-ken kyōdo bunka zaidan).

the characters and storylines. The star power of the famous vaudevillian actor Furukawa Roppa was used to market the film, *Roppa's The Pale Faced Professor* (*Roppa no Hoojiro sensei*, March 1939; see Figure 2). Roppa also played the title role in the play *Professor Hyakkien* (*Hyakkien sensei*), which ran during the entire month of April 1939 at the Yūrakuza theater in Tokyo. This connection with film and popular theater demonstrates the active intermingling of literature and entertainment for the mass audience, one of the many such hybrid creations in the prewar period. Not only did *The Pale Faced Professor* mix media by combining literature and film, but the movie itself, by nature of Roppa's inclusion, also crossed genre boundaries within cinema, namely, between art films and popular movies. Despite the enticement of this new medium, the adaptation process proved to be difficult for Hyakken. His flexibility and playful attitude in the *zuihitsu* disappeared once his work was transferred to the screen and he lost control over his words. As early as 1922, Hyakken had recognized that authorial voice and literary distinction meant little in the modern market, but this brush with film, a media aimed at the masses, left him longing for that which he could no longer have.

*The Pale Faced Professor* moves between humor and melodrama as it recounts the tale of a university professor with financial and familial problems.[97] The screenplay centers around the character Professor Aoji Hōjirō as he attempts to borrow and repay money to loan sharks and to his colleagues, and to keep up relations with his three daughters, although he moved out of the family house close to ten years prior.[98] Roppa played two roles, Aoji Hōjirō and Fujita Hyakuan, professors at Kokumin Daigaku (The People's College). The names for both characters are variations of those used by Hyakken in his *zuihitsu* and fiction. The film capitalized on the comedic value of Roppa appearing in both of these roles, and the screenplay suggests that other than clothing and hairstyles, the two were indistinguishable.[99] Cinematic technology would have allowed for both characters to appear onscreen at the same time, adding to the appeal and humor. It is also implied in the script that Fujita is Aoji's alter ego. In one scene in the film, Aoji visits a moneylender and is surprised to discover that he claims to know Professor Fujita.[100]

Other literary references include a young musical prodigy on the Japanese *koto* named Kawabata Ryūsuke, a reference to Hyakken's *koto* playing, and to the well-known writers Kawabata Yasunari and Akutagawa Ryūnosuke. For international flavor, the screenwriter threw in a French professor named Lupin, played by a foreign actor. Added to this is the fact that Roppa bore an uncanny resemblance to Hyakken, which was remarked upon numerous times and noted in Roppa's diary.[101] Roppa also shared Hyakken's love of word games and his peculiar eating habits.[102] Hyakken was famous for giving himself and others amusing nicknames and for his picky love of food, seen in his *Notebook of Feasting* (*Gochisōchō*, 1946).

Besides the humorous characters, a serious aspect of the film, which also draws directly from Hyakken's *zuihitsu*, is the depiction of poverty. Hyakken employed a light touch in his *zui-*

*hitsu* when discussing poverty, a topic painfully close to home for many readers of the time. "Hyakkien's New Look," the first of Hyakken's signature "poverty stories," describes the Professor's humorous attempts to replace his threadbare coat and old hat without spending any money. He convinces a friend who is hospitalized to give him his hat, since he will not be needing one in the hospital, and later proudly returns home with a hand-me-down coat. The Professor sports this oversized, red plaid jacket, while his wife tries not to tell him how ridiculous he looks in something better suited to the racetrack than the classroom. In a scene translated earlier in this chapter, the text turns quasi-philosophical as the Professor engages in a discussion on the conceptual and hence unattainable nature of money. When he compares it to such other abstract concepts as time and arrives at the Western saying "time is money,"[103] he feels justified spending that which he does not have (1: 258).

This lighthearted portrait of a financially strapped couple would have struck a chord with the reader of depression-era Japan. Between the aftereffects of the depression and the increasing economic burdens of the imperial campaigns, poverty became a part of prewar daily life. "Hyakkien's New Look" is datable by the newspaper mentions of Manchuria and Korea, and hits closer to home when the wife complains that even though the paper mentions rents are going down, she cannot get the landlord to fix the leaky roof. The title of the last work in the Professor Hyakkien series, "Bankrupt Serenity" ("Mukō saisha mukō shin"), is a parody of the *Mencius*: "If the people have not a certain livelihood, they have not a fixed heart,"[104] which Hyakken reworked to read: "If they have not steady debt, they have not a fixed heart." The main character dreads payday because it only reminds him of his increasing debt. Not only is there something reassuring in the constancy of his debt, but he decides his personality is better suited to borrowing money than to working for it.

Two other *zuihitsu*, "Gate of Hell" and "The Cruel Collector" ("Saiki"), deal directly with moneylenders and were most likely also used as a basis for the screenplay. The *zuihitsu* describe visits to loan sharks by professors, soldiers, and troubled wives. At one point in the film, the following newspaper advertisement is shown on the screen, implying that Professor Aoji Hōjirō is not the only one in financial trouble: "Government workers, teachers, businessmen—confidential, emergency funds with no guarantor required—Contact Mr. Washino."[105] There are similar advertisements in "Gate of Hell," a story about a Professor Aochi's meetings with the moneylender Mr. Tajima. Aochi is a professor at a public institution but has to borrow money to pay his bills. After borrowing from a number of lenders, Aochi comes to appreciate Tajima's professionalism and kindness. Tajima dies and the story turns poignant as his wife tries to hide his death in order to keep the business going.

The depictions of moneylenders range from humorous to frightening. There are a number of comic scenes in the film between Aoji and Oda, a moneylender who is in a particularly difficult economic situation. Aoji uses overly polite speech towards Oda, and offers moral support for this down-and-out loan shark. The tables are turned as the lender relies on Aoji to help him make ends meet. In an expression of gratitude, the loan shark even gives Aoji a gift.

A second and more frightening moneylender is Washino Takeshi from the advertisement mentioned above. His name roughly translates to the "Fierce One of Eagle Field," a joke about his hawk-like nature. When Aoji asks Washino about his prosthetic arm, the lender tells him that he lost it in the February 26 Incident (the attempted military coup of 1936). He was injured in the line of duty and jokes, mockingly calling it an admirable story about giving your life for the cause. He took his generous retirement settlement and started up as a moneylender. Since neither job—soldier nor moneylender—is very popular, he has no qualms about his current profession. Hyakken shows the human side of these lenders and their struggle for survival in the economically depressed Japanese metropolis. His *zuihitsu* also reveal an interesting interaction between the middle-class intellectual and the lower class, underground figures that kept these precarious middle-class lives afloat.

The film ends with a shot of Aoji's *koto* teacher and Kawabata sitting inside the teacher's darkened, empty house. His electricity has been cut off and his belongings either repossessed or sold to pay overdue fees. Other than a well-to-do lawyer, almost everyone is afflicted by poverty in the film, even the loan sharks who are hard pressed to pay their medical bills, and are fearful of others cutting in on their business. Aoji has to quit his job to pay off his debts with his retirement funds, and jokes with the loan shark that maybe he should go into business as a moneylender too. But he has already decided to try making a living as a writer. He expresses his decision to write in crass commercial terms, telling the loan shark that he will live by selling his words (*bunsho demo utte kurashimashō*).[106] This is no art-for-art's-sake, highbrow conception of literature; rather, it is a comment on the reality of life in late 1930s wartime Japan.

The film also details Aoji's family situation. His wife is having trouble making ends meet and their daughter has taken on a job. He has been living separately from his wife and daughters for almost ten years and although a cousin tries to get the couple to reconcile their differences, the marriage is beyond repair. Aoji's wife is portrayed as cold hearted and hysterical, and even her daughters make fun of her. But there is a painful scene in which she explains to the daughters why she cannot take her husband back. When he moved out he said terrible things to her, calling her cold hearted and inflexible, and after ten years she has become that curmudgeonly woman.[107] He will never take her back now. There are a number of touching scenes between Aoji and his daughters, especially the youngest played by Takamine Hideko, a hugely popular actress. Takamine's role in the film further testifies to its star power.

Given the very personal nature of these scenes and the resemblance of the film to the actual details of Hyakken's life, it is understandable that Hyakken's family would feel their privacy had been invaded.[108] But Hyakken himself often purposely blurred the line between himself and his characters through the creation of a literary "autobiographical space" in his *zuihitsu*. The film also demonstrates this very public side of a writer's private life. Hyakken must have been aware that the screenplay would draw from his personal life; he agreed to have his work adapted for film and stage, and even visited the play the day before it opened, as noted in Roppa's diary entry for March 31, 1939.[109] These cinematic and dramatic adaptations may have intruded on Hyakken's privacy, but they also raised his stock as a writer and a public figure. We can imagine the middlebrow urbanite readers of *Bungei shunjū*, *Shinseinen*, *Kinema junpō*, and Hyakken's *zuihitsu* purchasing tickets for *The Pale Faced Professor*. The film opened on March 20, and Roppa remarks in his diary on the 23rd that reviews were positive. His friend, Kawaguchi Matsutarō, the first Naoki prize winner, whose story was adapted for a Roppa play, concurred.[110]

Critic Satō Tadao describes *The Pale Faced Professor* as one of Roppa's representative films.[111] If anything, the movie is a cross between an art film (*bungei eiga*) and the comedies on which Roppa's fame was based. Roppa's presence would have captured the popular audience familiar with his Asakusa work, as well as the middle-class viewer attracted to his cultured background. He was the comedian for the new age. The inclusion of Roppa is just one of the many noteworthy aspects of this hybrid film. In order to contextualize *The Pale Faced Professor* within the 1930s market, it is necessary to take a brief look at the production of the film itself and at the state of prewar cinema.

Roppa's high birth, elite education, and literary talents made him an unusual choice for the vaudevillian stage.[112] Roppa came from an illustrious line: his grandfather was the highly respected philosopher and educational statesman, Katō Hiroyuki, and his father a baron and a medical doctor in the service of the Taishō emperor. His brothers went on to become viscounts and presidents of prestigious schools in Tokyo. All but the eldest son were sent into adopted families, and Roppa's surname, Furukawa, comes from his adopted father, an employee of the South Manchuria Railway (Mantetsu) and a member of upper class society. Roppa is a pen name from his grammar school days. His cultured upbringing led him to enter Waseda University's English literature program, only to drop out for a career as a film critic. Literary entrepreneur and founder of *Bungei shunjū* Kikuchi Kan gave Roppa editorship of the magazine *Eiga jidai* in 1924, and Roppa eventually took full control in 1930, only to see the publication fail. He continued to contribute essays to *Kinema junpō*, the *Tōkyō Nichinichi shinbun*, the *Sandē Mainichi*, and *Ōru yomimono*.

Through his career as a critic, he became acquainted with directors and other figures in the film and theater industries, and got his start on the stage in 1932. Kikuchi suggested that Roppa meet Kobayashi Ichizō, real estate magnate, entertainment promoter, and creator of the all-girl Takarazuka troupe. Between 1932 and 1934, Kobayashi organized the troupe as an official theater company and acquired and built theaters, including the Hibiya Theater, Yūrakuza, and the Tokyo Takarazuka Theater in downtown Tokyo. Kobayashi secured his empire by forming the Tōhō Motion Picture Distribution Corporation to distribute films produced by the P. C. L production company and the J. O. Studio, precursors to the giant Tōhō Motion Picture Company created in 1937.[113] By 1933, Roppa was billed as a top star in the Asakusa revues. He appeared in plays in Kobayashi's theaters and in films such as *The Pale Faced Professor*, produced by Tōhō.

Film studios used vaudevillian stars Roppa, his rival Enomoto Ken'ichi (better known as Enoken), and others to boost sales in the 1930s. With the introduction of the talkies, the film industry in Japan underwent radical changes and turned into a large scale business enterprise. Films had long been based on dramatic adaptations of popular fiction, and often used stage actors. In this same vein, studios enlisted Asakusa stars for musical comedies with vaudeville songs and nonsense gags.[114] However, in the mid-1930s, after the talkies were firmly established in Japan, many directors began searching for more substantial material to raise the artistic level of their films above the typical melodramas. The resulting art films drew on works of pure literature such as Kawabata Yasunari's "The Izu Dancer" ("Izu no odoriko," 1926), which was made into a film of the same title in 1933, and Tanizaki's "A Portrait of Shunkin" ("Shunkin shō," 1933), which became *Okoto and Sasuke* (*Shunkin shō: Okoto to Sasuke*) in 1935.[115] Other authors whose works were adapted for the silver screen include Yamamoto Yūzō, Kishida Kunio, Mori Ōgai, and Hayashi Fumiko. A director who distinguished himself both artistically and commercially in the literary film was Toyoda Shirō, starting with his hit *Young People* (*Wakai hito*) in 1937 for the small independent company Tōkyō Hassei.[116] The director and screenwriter of *The Pale Faced Professor*, Abe Yutaka and Hatta Naoyuki, also produced films for Tōkyō Hassei.[117]

Abe Yutaka directed *The Pale Faced Professor* for Tōhō in 1939. He was long known to the film industry from his days in Hollywood as "Jackie" Abe. He acted and wrote scripts in Hollywood, trained as a director, and was influenced by the style of Cecil B. DeMille and Ernst Lubitsch.[118] Abe returned to Japan in 1925 and earned a reputation for bringing modern, American-style films known as *modan mono* to Japan.[119] Directing with a megaphone—shouting in English, "Camera! Action!"—Abe brought his international flair to films such as *The Girl Who Touched His Legs* (*Ashi ni sawatta onna,* 1926), which won the highly respected *Kinema junpō* "Best One" Award.[120] Hyakken's *zuihitsu* readers would have been drawn to *The Pale Faced Professor* by the appeal of the modern director Abe Yutaka and their interest in the intellectual lifestyle portrayed in the film.

Tōhō distinguished itself with major directors, screenwriters, and actors, many of whom were lured away from rival studios. The company's connections with smaller independent studios, such as Tōkyō Hassei, provided them with high-quality movies and innovative filmmaking techniques attractive to others in the industry. In the latter half of the 1930s, Tōhō rose to prominence and emerged as the "virtual ruler of the Japanese film industry."[121] *The Pale Faced Professor* could boast the backing of a major studio, an international director, famous stars, and a well-known author.

Despite the commercial success, or perhaps because of it, Hyakken was disappointed with the film as an adaptation of his literature. In the introduction to a subsequently published volume titled *Professor Pale Face and Professor Hyakkien* (*Hoojiro sensei to Hyakkien sensei*, 1939), Hyakken takes a roundabout way of criticizing the film industry in general. He is concerned that the screenwriters failed to capture the essence of his writing. He pledges to work his hardest to achieve a level of pure expression (*junsui bunshō*), ensuring that the only way his work could be captured would be through the act of reading. For Hyakken, film and theater adaptations left only the dregs.[122] His writing was cheapened by the transfer into these popular media. Hyakken experienced the loss of aura and distinction inherent in the massification process. Unable to control his literary productions in this new market, he seeks refuge in the illusory realm of pure language.

Hyakken's comments reveal the tension inherent in the "Great Divide" separating high art and mass culture.[123] Many writers were engaged with the cinema as a means to find a voice in this new medium that was stealing ground from literature.[124] Although Hyakken may initially have been enthusiastic about these adaptations, the resulting products were disappointments. Hyakken wants to retain the artistry and quality of his prose after an ill fit with a medium aimed at the masses. Hyakken was unwilling to accept the compromises literature made to film. This was the only film adaptation made during his lifetime.

Hyakken's reaction to *The Pale Faced Professor* is ironic given his openness to more popular forums. Like other writers of his generation, Hyakken regularly crossed the pure/popular divide by publishing in venues aimed at an audience ranging from elite to mass readers. His discontent with the film industry lay not in its popular nature, but in the loss of control over his artistic craft. He could publish a *zuihitsu* in the newspaper or a popular women's journal, but still retain power over the word itself. Although Hyakken was making a living off of his writing, the words were his; the craft remained in his hands. However, once transferred to film, screenwriters changed his words, adapting his stories to fit the needs of this openly commercial venture.

In his writing, Hyakken was willing to play with identity and risk losing the authorial voice and literary distinction. He created alter egos and mocked the seriousness of literature. However, once his control over the written word was lost to the medium of film, Hyakken's playfulness disappeared. Like the I-novelists he readily critiqued, in the end, Hyakken was also unwilling to relinquish his unique authorial voice. The plurality of copies, so integral to film and his version of the *zuihitsu*, proved troubling to Hyakken. In the end, Hyakken attempted to reclaim the very thing he so successfully undermined in *Hyakkien's Miscellany*: the individual, auratic voice. In his reluctance to yield to this form of muteness, Hyakken resists the mechanisms of modernity. He also begins to trace a path toward the possibility of critique, emphasizing the value of the individual in the militarist climate of the 1930s.

# THREE

# *Reliving War, Rewriting History: Film, Architecture, Memory*

> I couldn't understand why I was so moved by the bluish images of the mountains surrounding Port Arthur, but it was like seeing my own memories up on the screen. What a terribly somber mountain it was. A dim glow emanated from behind the hills, but the sky blanketing the peaks was devoid of light. I knew that the port lay under the darkest spot in the sky.
>
> —Uchida Hyakken, "Triumphant March into Port Arthur"

Everyday life in the 1930s was increasingly dominated by the presence of the military and the imperialist campaigns in Asia. Japan was expanding its holdings overseas, while back home the nation was shaken by mass arrests, political assassinations, and no fewer than three attempted military coups between March 1931 and April 1932, signaling the end of party government.[1] It was impossible to ignore the shifting tides as the media was filled with images of the war. Hyakken published his second fictional collection, *Triumphant March into Port Arthur* (*Ryojun nyūjōshiki*) in 1934, three years after the first attack in a series of military campaigns that came to be collectively known as the Manchurian Incident (September 18–19, 1931). These offensives launched between 1931 and 1933 brought Manchuria fully under Japanese control. This incident signaled the shift from "the era christened 'Taishō demokurashii' to what Japanese called the 'national emergency' (*hijōji*) of early Shōwa."[2] The invasion of Manchuria was woven into the national remembering of the Russo-Japanese War (1904–05), a costly battle from the past that also took place on Manchurian soil. The losses of the past were transformed into justification for the new war on the continent.

As the war progressed in Asia, it became increasingly difficult for writers to express themselves without the threat of censorship or imprisonment. Armed with the Peace Preservation Law of 1925, the government began suppressing leftist movements in the later half of the decade and into the 1930s. The death of proletarian writer Kobayashi Takiji at the hands of the police in February 1933 set off a wave of political renunciations (*tenkō*) by imprisoned leaders of the Japanese Communist Party and proletarian writers, decimating the left wing in Japan by 1937.[3] As the war progressed, even writers without political affiliations felt the pressure to conform. Hyakken responded to this new crisis of representation and language by drawing again on the symbols of cultural modernism. Since he did not use the vocabulary of the politicized left, his work was not seen as a form of resistance. But the idiom of cultural modernism afforded Hyakken the means to escape censorship and to protect the literariness of his writing from the dictates of ideology. In his emphasis on the fleeting nature of the present and the ruptures of history, Hyakken found a means to critique the production of memory and the discourse of immutability vital to the propaganda of war.

This chapter examines two of Hyakken's short stories from this collection that recreate the experience of an overseas war for a nation of readers back home: "Triumphant March into Port Arthur" (1925) and "The War Museum" ("Yūshūkan," 1929).[4] Hyakken never set foot onto these foreign battlefields, and both stories were originally published before the events that precipitated the Manchurian Incident. Hyakken's titles would have reverberated with 1920s readers, bringing back memories of the Russo-Japanese War and drawing their attention to the Yasukuni Shrine in Tokyo, specifically to its war memorial museum, which was undergoing reconstruction after the Great Kantō Earthquake of 1923. However, the memories and feelings these images stirred up in readers during the 1920s cannot compare to the potency the titles and their referents held in the 1930s. With the onset of the Manchurian Incident, the government recycled the discourse of an old war to justify a new one. As soldiers began dying at the start of Japan's Fifteen Years War (Jūgonen sensō) in Asia, the Yasukuni Shrine, the central site for enshrining Japan's war dead, became increasingly prominent in everyday life.

In order to fully flesh out the implications of publishing a book in 1934 titled *Triumphant March into Port Arthur*, we must analyze Hyakken's stories within the context of the militarism of the 1930s. To consider the stories only as products of the 1920s would be to overlook the intersection of Hyakken's literature and the prominent national discourse surrounding the war. Hyakken was not blind to the significance of using an old Russo-Japanese War slogan as a title when the book was printed in 1934. Indeed, it shows his consciousness of the power of language. To be sure, the public, now inundated with images and talk of Manchuria and the "boom of Russo-Japanese War theme products," would little realize or care that Hyakken's stories were written in the 1920s, and would read them within this new context.[5] Manchuria became a product of national discourse and popular consumer culture in the 1930s, at a time when Hyakken's stories received their broadest possible exposure through the publication of his book.

This conflation—of present and past, Russo-Japanese War and Manchurian Incident, personal and public memory, fiction and history—is a pattern that we can not only observe in Hyakken and prewar culture, but also perpetuate in our analysis of his stories. The act of reading his works through reprints is a critical move, a mimicking and highlighting of the patterns of conflation and of memory found in the works themselves. We should not approach Hyakken's stories by viewing them solely through a literary lens, but rather by locating his work within the cultural setting that emerges in it and around it.

Conflation is a crucial trope in these short stories, since war is not represented as part of a glorious national history, but as an unreliable memory, as an uninvited intrusion of the past, in the form of phantom soldiers and shrines. "Triumphant March into Port Arthur" takes up the decisive battle of the Russo-Japanese War through the viewing of an old actuality film.[6] The protagonist identifies and merges with the soldiers on the screen as memories of the war, cinematic ones, come to life. The viewer is transformed into an imperial subject, but one who is able to make a subjective interpretation of the images he sees. In "The War Museum," Hyakken superimposes the Yasukuni Shrine's old war museum (Yūshūkan), a site redolent of Western modernization, onto the empty space of reconstruction. This space is the future site of a new museum, a pan-Asian-style building that was completed shortly after the Manchurian Incident. Hyakken's protagonist is haunted by a menacing soldier whose eerie yellow-toned skin resembles the mannequins in the museum. Just as the context of the Russo-Japanese War and the intervening decades of Western modernity were erased in national discourse on the Manchurian Incident, the history of the Yūshūkan was also lost as a new architectural structure overcame the modernity of the earlier building.

Hyakken's protagonists—and by extension his readers—experience the horrors of war, psychologically reliving the battle. But in these stories, this is always one step removed. The past is accessible only through film, dreams, or distant memories, and the experience itself is transitory. Not only is it removed in terms of medium and time, but the vision of the past is an obstructed vision. Employing the language of silent film, Hyakken represents the war as a series of blurry, indistinct images spliced together in random order. As readers we are not sure if we, or the characters in the story, are seeing the real war or fabricated celluloid images of it. Similarly, in "The War Museum," Hyakken's protagonist is never sure if his meeting with the phantom soldier actually happened or is part of his dreams. There is always a gap between what is seen and what is represented, and no guarantee that the representation is real. Hyakken employs these potent war images to comment on the shifting meaning of national symbols, telling us that as citizens of modernity we have lost the ability to perceive the real, but that this gap indicates an erasure of history inherent in the rhetoric of propaganda.

Hyakken contests the suturing of historical gaps, the substituting of the Russo-Japanese War for the Manchurian Incident, through the language and tropes of modernism, specifically the idea of history as fleeting and ephemeral. He returns the reader to a time when our means for interacting with the world still held the possibility for transformation, and when these images of the war, now a part of everyday consumer culture, still held a visual power. Hyakken finds aura in the outmoded—an old actuality film and a building from the era of "civilization and enlightenment"—and deploys this in order to defamiliarize the commonplace image of war, and to enter the realm of the extraordinary. Hyakken accomplishes this by severing these images from their referents and reinscribing them with a subjectivity and indeterminacy. He counters the seamless narrative of propaganda with a fragmentary aesthetic, showing how the past is open to interpretation and that history exists outside of the homogenizing discourse of nationalism.

Before examining Hyakken's stories, we should consider some background on the reproduction and circulation of war imagery in the early twentieth century, shedding light on their significance in Hyakken's work.

## War Reportage and Repackaged Propaganda

The Russo-Japanese War was the culmination of a series of events that placed Japan on a par with Western nations and resolutely took the nation into the modern era. Japan's victory represented a watershed in the nation's attempts to enter the international stage, as the Japanese gained respect for defeating a European power. Japan now claimed the Russian rights and interests in southern Manchuria, but the rest of Manchuria remained under Chinese control. Japan could not advance its interests without engaging in intricate and difficult diplomacy with China.

Such diplomatic efforts came to a halt in the early 1930s, when the Kwantung Army, Japan's field army in Manchuria, took matters into its own hands under the guise of protecting Japanese colonists and properties, mainly the South Manchuria Railway Company (Mantetsu). Mid-echelon staff officers decided on a violent means of separating southern Manchuria from China without military or civilian authorization. The army attacked the Chinese garrison at Mukden as retribution for a "supposed Chinese attempt to destroy the tracks of the South Manchuria Railway just north of the city, an act that had in fact been secretly perpetrated by Kwantung Army staff officers."[7] This act heightened tensions with China and the Soviet Union and propelled Japan along its course of military expansion.

The Manchurian Incident was soon recast as a second chance to redeem the losses of the earlier battles. The old slogan "payment of 100,000 lives and a billion yen in blood and treasure for Manchuria" was revived to equate the Russo-Japanese War with Manchuria, making Manchuria the "sole compensation for this past sacrifice."[8] The original aim of the Russo-Japanese War was control of Korea. But by 1931, Korea had long been under Japanese rule, having been annexed in 1910, and Japan's goals were shifted to the new Manchurian front. The imperialist government of the 1930s skillfully capitalized on lingering resentment in presenting this new war as an opportunity to right the wrongs of an old peace treaty that the Japanese populace perceived as denying the nation full compensation for its suffering in the Russo-Japanese War. The events of the Russo-Japanese War had entered the discourse of everyday culture and had featured in the rhetoric of the anti-peace demonstrations that roiled the nation after the peace treaty of 1905.[9] Over a quarter of a century later, at the time of the Manchurian

Incident, the government took advantage of the central place of the Russo-Japanese War in national memory.

The state was aided in its efforts as national memory was converted into a profitable commercial memory. The modern mass media system saw a lucrative opportunity in the marketing of Manchuria. Stage productions, films, popular music (such as the 1932 hit song "Manchuria March"), and even consumables (such as "three human bullets" candy and *sake*) told the tales of the empire, as the war flooded mass consumer culture in the 1930s.[10] Many films were shot on location in Manchuria solely as a means of selling the movie.[11] Over five hundred books came out on Manchuria in 1932 alone, as publishers catered to both adults and children. Journals such as *Bungei shunjū* and *Kingu*, aimed at the middle- and lower-class reader, also ran special sections and even whole issues on the war.[12]

Newspaper companies capitalized on the Manchurian Incident by showing newsreels of the key events of the war.[13] Within days of the events, *Tōkyō Nichinichi*, *Tōkyō Asahi*, and *Ōsaka Asahi* sponsored films were traveling to the major cities, playing in parks, department stores, and elementary schools. These raw newsreels were subsequently edited into documentary films (*kiroku eiga*) with titles such as *Protect Manchuria and Mongolia* (*Mamore Man-Mō*) and *The Radiant Imperial Army* (*Kagayaku kōgun*).[14] Such films played at movie theatres in the early months of 1932, and shows regularly sold out across the country. In conjunction with the films, the newspapers organized exhibits of photographs and military paraphernalia, such as the one at the Nagoya Matsuzakaya department store, and lecture series featuring reports from the front by war correspondents. These also welcomed over-capacity crowds.

These cultural products and productions were not limited to the immediate aftermath of the Incident. A half-page advertisement for a Manchurian revue in the September 12, 1933 *Tōkyō Asahi* newspaper shows the lingering nostalgia for Manchuria, or as it came to be known after 1932, the Japanese puppet state of Manchukuo.

The Manchukuo Entertainment Delegation Is Coming!
Remember September 18th!

As we approach the two-year anniversary of the Manchurian Incident, the Empire is once again moving forward in this time of national emergency. Our friends in the Manchukuo Entertainment Delegation are coming!

Come gather for this great event! This friendly union between the Japanese and Manchurian peoples shines with hope for the world! Let's sing these Manchurian songs together.

The show included songs and performances by Manchurian entertainers, and a film titled "Manchukuo, the Whole Story" ("Manshūkoku no zenbō"). Sponsored by the cosmetics company Utena, the revue played in the Hibiya area of Tokyo and Yokohama. The promotional language describing the "friendly union between the Japanese and Manchurian peoples" echoes government propaganda and incorporates Manchurian cultural tradition into Japanese national memory and popular culture, hiding the fact that Manchuria was violently colonized by the Japanese.

In their move from fact to fiction, these "infotainment" materials transformed history into an entertaining public spectacle, becoming pseudohistory in the process.[15] The difference between these two wars, as well as the intervening years of Western-inspired modernity, were glossed over as these public spectacles served the interests of the military state in rallying support for their imperialist incursions. Remakes from the early 1930s participated in this cross-over from fact to fiction, or fact to propaganda.[16] One of the more popular topics for such films in the 1930s was General Nogi Maresuke, who also appears in Hyakken's "fictional" film. Nogi is one example of the way in which the government and the media engaged in the production of memory.

Despite tremendous losses and bungled leadership, General Nogi was recognized for his heroism in the Russo-Japanese War. He became the consummate military man, righteous and virtuous. He shocked the nation by committing ritual suicide (*junshi*) following the death of his lord, the Meiji emperor, in

1912.[17] Nogi remained true to his beliefs in the old samurai code of *bushidō*, the Way of the Warrior, but not everyone in the country felt that he should have sacrificed his individual self for the spirit of the late emperor and the traditional codes of the past.[18] Despite the ambiguity surrounding his death, the legacy of his heroism lived on, partly, if not wholly, due to the efforts of the state. A shrine was posthumously dedicated to Nogi in Tokyo in 1923, and films, such as those described below, were made about him in the 1930s.

Nogi came into vogue in the form of films, plays, children's books, and minstrel songs, such as *Remember General Nogi*, which opened on the stage and screen in early 1932.[19] Documentary filmmaker Tsuchimoto Noriaki focuses on these so called "Nogi mono" by looking at two films that employ original actuality footage from the Russo-Japanese War: *Immortal Nogi* (*Fumetsu Nogi*), a 45-minute talkie, and *March Tenth* (*Sangatsu tōka*, 1933), an unusual film that mixes actuality footage and animation.[20] Both express loyalty to the Emperor and are militaristic tools. The former has the feel of a school ethics text, while the latter is more of a propaganda film capitalizing on the current anti-Soviet climate.

*Immortal Nogi* is basically an introduction to Nogi's life, and more than anything, a nostalgic look at the Meiji era.[21] The second film, however, is far more vitriolic in its message. It was clearly made to justify the establishment of a Manchurian state and Japan's policy of manifest destiny in Asia. The title, *March Tenth*, is a reference to the Japanese victory in the famous battle at Mukden, which in reality cost far greater human loss than Port Arthur. The film explains that 30 years have passed since Nogi taught the Russians a lesson, but the Red Army has once again set its sights on Manchuria, and preparations should be made to replay Nogi's battle.[22] The narrative of the film effectively weaves Nogi's heroism into the current Soviet threat the Japanese perceived in Manchuria, and uses it as a means to promote the new war.

*March Tenth* uses animation to supply the historical background to both the Sino- and Russo-Japanese wars. This is especially prevalent in the scenes of Nogi, where an attempt to rewrite history is clear. Those gains for which Japan had fought so hard in the Russo-Japanese War were again being threatened by the Soviet army. The highlight of the film is a map with a star marking the Japanese occupied areas. The film builds to its climax as the area around the star expands out from Port Arthur to encompass the former Manchuria, then China, and the whole of Asia.[23]

Hyakken's story would have been read against the context of these 1930s remakes. However, the film in "Triumphant March into Port Arthur" is not one of these films, but an actuality of the Russo-Japanese War from the time of the battle. Hyakken returns the reader to the early twentieth century with his use of these silent, rough-edited films, which were one of the many media used in the early 1900s to bring war into everyday life in Japan, along with newspapers, woodblock prints, postcards, personal accounts, and government campaigns.[24] Peter High remarks in "The Dawn of Cinema in Japan" that "documentary war footage" was the vehicle through which film infiltrated "the mainstream of public life and entertainment."[25] Unlike the sophisticated, crafted narratives of the 1930s, these actualities were often no more than scenes of soldiers advancing and firing cannons, but they had a tremendous impact on the viewers of the time. Film critic Satō Tadao mentions Hyakken's story, "Triumphant March into Port Arthur," as an example of one such actuality, or as they were known in Japan, *jissha*.[26]

## Cinematic Phantoms of Manchuria, Past and Present

The story "Triumphant March into Port Arthur" first appeared in print in the July 1925 issue of the popular women's journal *Josei*, alongside the last installment of Tanizaki Jun'ichirō's *Naomi* (*Chijin no ai*, 1924–25), a story about the main character Jōji's slavish love for the "modern girl" Naomi. The date, venue, and proximity to *Naomi* firmly set Hyakken's story in the era of modern life (*modan raifu*), the cultural production of social modernism depicted in Tanizaki's novel. This physical proximity to the modernist culture of the 1920s is countered by the temporal proximity to the Peace Preservation Law enacted two months before the story appeared in *Josei*. This law, which turned out to be a crucial tool in government suppression of political dissent, provided legal powers that became increasingly necessary in the militarist climate of the 1930s. In this short story, Hyakken calls on the language of modernism to reread the images of war.

Of the 29 stories in Hyakken's collection, "Triumphant March into Port Arthur" was chosen for the title of the book published in 1934. Regardless of whether the decision was Hyakken's or that of a representative at the Iwanami publishing house, the significance of the title could not have escaped Hyakken's notice given the societal context of the time. It was not possible in the 1930s to mention Port Arthur, one of the most famous battles of the Russo-Japanese War, a public rallying cry, and the current headquarters of the Imperial Japanese Army's field command in Manchuria, without calling up these more recent militarist associations. Nor would the book have escaped the public's notice. In the 1930s, "the process of empire building in Manchuria touched the lives of most Japanese."[27] The book was also published by one of the major companies of the era.[28] The analysis in the following pages reads Hyakken's story against the cultural context of the 1930s, purposely switching back and forth between the Russo-Japanese War, the 1920s, and the 1930s, as well as between his fiction and the discursive and material reality of Japan after the Manchurian Incident.

"Triumphant March into Port Arthur" is set in Tokyo before the earthquake, opening with a film screening on May 10, 1921, the silver wedding anniversary of the Taishō emperor. The prominent mention of the emperor at the beginning of the story clearly indicates a connection between this film and the imperial seat of power. Another intentional aspect of the story is the location of the screening at a university, the site of the intelligentsia. There were many movie theatres in the metropolis by this time, but Hyakken sets his story in a darkened lecture hall at Hōsei University.[29] The cinema is often seen as an object of the masses, but here Hyakken shifts the focus to his own social strata, the middle-class literary elite, as he recreates the viewing conditions of early actuality films, which were often shown in locations other than theaters.

> I went to a film festival of old moving pictures at Hōsei University on Sunday May 10, the day of the Imperial Silver Wedding Anniversary Celebration.
>
> The windows in the lecture hall were covered with black cloth, throwing the room into darkness. Thin shafts of afternoon light snuck in with an eerie blue glow.
>
> Random, confusing landscapes and faces flashed before me. The smoke-screen shootouts from the Ministry of War advanced with an exciting and relentless pace. Thick smoke enveloped the picture, obscuring my view. I thought I could see the screen growing brighter through the dissipating smoke, but the images disappeared, and the lecture hall suddenly lit up. (1:137)

Hyakken recreates the experience of viewing early silent films. The quick pace of these often blurry, roughly edited newsreels and actualities from the early twentieth century is reflected in Hyakken's narrative style. Images, literally "photographic images" (*shashin*), appear and disappear (*utsuru, kieru*), and murky figures and unfocused landscapes flash before his protagonist's eyes as the room darkens and lightens with the disconnected action on the screen. These early actuality films lacked the coherence and narrative purpose associated with documentaries and with the propaganda films of the 1930s.[30] Hyakken's film easily fits with descriptions of early silent films as the "cinema of attraction," a cinema not dominated by narrative, but based on "its ability to *show* something."[31] In this cinema, the attraction "aggressively subjected the spectator to 'sensual or psychological impact.'"[32] This impact is readily seen in "Triumphant March into Port Arthur," as these images, not the narrative, drive the film and shock the protagonist / viewer.

Hyakken uses images and vocabulary of early film, such as a newsreel aesthetic of realism that wins out over the cohesive requirements of fiction. The aesthetics of the *jissha*, this shock experience of early cinema, is a formal principle of film and a characteristic of modern, urban life itself.[33] Hyakken's fragmentary narrative draws on both the experience of the modern everyday and on the artistic response of modernism, making the actuality an apt tool for commenting on the crisis of representation and language seen in the rhetoric of immutability. Through this "fictional" film, Hyakken cuts between seemingly disconnected scenes of war and comments on the recycling of history as he critiques the unified narrative of government propaganda in the 1930s. In the process, Hyakken is also able to question the intersection of the individual and the nation, the visual and the imaginary, and the inherent ambiguity in these quintessentially modern relationships. The internally generated memories of a lost childhood in "Realm of the Dead" are replaced in "Triumphant March into Port Arthur" by mechanically created and commercially marketed national memories of an overseas war.

The thick smoke that obscures the picture in the above quotation was, in fact, such a problem with filmmaking that many "made-up" documentaries were produced in an effort to overcome the difficulties of filming on the front lines.[34] But in Hyakken's retelling, the smoke seems to fill the lecture hall itself, as the images on the screen and the viewer start to merge. Throughout the story, the protagonist crosses over and enters the film, or conversely, the film fills the hall. Neither side is confined to their space as they merge and pull back. This effect provides the power behind Hyakken's story and brings twenty-year-old images to life for an audience who, like the protagonist, relives distant memories.

After a few American comedies and more actualities, an officer from the Ministry of War introduces the main feature, a film of the Japanese capture of Port Arthur: "This film was originally shot by a German military observer and only recently came into the hands of the Japanese Ministry. There are scenes not only of the famous meeting at the naval base of Generals Nogi and Stessel, but also of the bombing of the fort at Niryuzan. Quite the cinematic treasure, the officer explained"

(1: 137). This scene with Japanese General Nogi Maresuke and Russian General Anatolii Mikhailovich Stessel is none other than Stessel's controversial surrender of Port Arthur to Nogi, an event immortalized in black-and-white photographs and filmic images at the time (Figure 3). Such images were regular fare in films depicting the Russo-Japanese War.

Back in Hyakken's lecture hall, the Ministry officer concludes his comments, the lights dim, and he sinks into the blackness of the room. But before this khaki-colored, uniformed image fades from the protagonist's retina, another is projected onto it—a soldier leading a parade of men headed for the front. Just as in "Realm of the Dead," the eye serves as screen, placing the protagonist in the unusual position of both observer and part of the viewing mechanism. The overlap of these two men—one from the present and one from the past, one in the flesh and one on the screen—collapses the temporal gap and triggers an auditory memory of an old military tune, the kind of war songs (*gunka*) that became so nostalgic in the early 1930s. The new vogue for Russo-Japanese War songs recalled painful memories of the human cost of the war, and skillfully transferred that loss to the soil of current-day Manchuria.[35] Although these old elegies feature in the background of Hyakken's stories, his nostalgic use of them is tinged with a dangerous ambivalence.

The next scene shifts from the farewell parade in Yokohama to the mountains surrounding Port Arthur itself. Space collapses as the bluish image of these mountain peaks connects directly with the protagonist's memory banks, throwing them open and producing a strange sense of pathos. But what exactly is he remembering, the actual war or old newsreel footage he saw during the war? In Hyakken's story, this is purposely unclear. We cannot know if his memories, his existing images of the war, are from first-hand experience or were also products of this new technology. Additionally, the fact that so-called actuality films of the war were regularly faked raises issues about the authenticity of the protagonist's memories

Fig. 3 "Russo-Japanese War: Meeting of Generals Nogi and Stessel at the Surrender of Port Arthur," January 8, 1905. Reproduced by permission of Mainichi Shinbunsha.

of the war and about the current film he views in the story. Hyakken suggests that the very memories of the war that the government was mining for nationalist pride exist only as celluloid phantoms, and possibly fakes.

In the dark, blurry images that follow, a group of panting soldiers drags a cannon up a hillside. Watching the movements of this undifferentiated mass, our protagonist sympathizes out loud with their plight—"Poor bastards"—and an unnamed voice from this side of the screen, the crowd of viewers, speaks out in agreement. When one of the soldiers unexpectedly lifts his head to the sky, the protagonist enters the scene in the film, crossing from spectator to participant: "Cutting through the dark sky like a dog with its head hung low, a towering peak jutted up before *us* as *we* climbed" (1: 138).[36] The protagonist sees his own face in this anonymous soldier and that recognition allows for the fusion of viewed object and viewing subject. The protagonist's strong identification with this soldier and the war would seem to be in line with the military government's desire to foster support for their troops and the battle itself. However, this identification is only temporary and the protagonist's position soon shifts back to the lecture hall when he asks aloud the name of the mountain he had previously ascended. He continues to move between the present and the past, between the darkened lecture hall and the ominous mountains surrounding Port Arthur, as he crosses back and forth from one side of the screen to the other. Despite the power of these images, Hyakken emphasizes the fleeting nature of the reactions and associations that are formed.

The protagonist's tension level rises as the artillery campaigns increase, and time slows down as the bombs rain endlessly day and night. Hyakken captures the mental wear of the constant bombardment during which soldiers "remained for days continuously under fire," a tactic not known in military engagements prior to the Russo-Japanese War.[37] This is said to have contributed to the Russian soldiers' failure of nerve, but must certainly have affected the demoralized Japanese troops as well. Again, the protagonist identifies with the plight of the men on the screen, these soldiers from an old war. The bombings wear down the protagonist as he grows anxious watching a group of soldiers return cannon fire: "Those soldiers in the hollow reacted out of fear. I got nervous when smoke cleared from the cannon. If they'd only just fire again quickly, who cares where it lands!" (1: 138). The battle is so relentless and damaging that it transforms the very landscape of Port Arthur. As the sound of the bombs is "sucked into the belly of the dark mountain," the protagonist feels sure that "the echo must certainly have died there as well" (1: 138).

The protagonist comments that the two sides let out "a frightening barrage of sound" (1: 138), which is curious because these early actualities were undoubtedly silent films. Such actualities were, in fact, viewed with the accompanying narration, dialogue, and commentary of the *benshi,* and possibly also by live music, all used to "whip the crowd into a patriotic frenzy."[38] But any such external interpretative means are absent in Hyakken's story, despite the fact that *benshi* were actively being used up until the talkies took over in the early 1930s.[39] It is possible to consider the Ministry officer as a type of *benshi*, but as soon as the film starts, he fades into the blackness and is not heard from again until the end of the film. And Hyakken's protagonist does not mention any musical accompaniment. The viewing is stripped of these heuristic frameworks of popular culture, which Hyakken purposely removes from his fictional viewing, reducing the experience to viewer and silent image. But this is not to say that the images are completely "raw." At a minimum they were framed and composed by the cameraman, and the possibility exists that they were staged.

All sound and analysis are represented as internal, taking place in the protagonist's mind. Hyakken spoke about this process in an essay titled "Film and Imagination" ("Eiga to sōzōryoku") in *Eiga Asahi* in 1938.[40] He enjoyed the silent films *The Cabinet of Dr. Caligari* (*Das Kabinett des Doktor Caligari*, 1920) and *Dr. Jekyll and Mr. Hyde*.[41] However, he dislikes the talkies; not only are they an insult to his imagination, but when their sounds are different than the way he imagined, he gets annoyed. Even though the films he saw were silent, he claims to have heard the guns in the war movies and the rushing water at Niagara Falls. Similarly, the protagonist in "Triumphant March into Port Arthur" hears the bombs, feels the reverberations of cannon fire, and literally struggles to see through the smoke. In his film essay, Hyakken talks about the interaction of personal memory and screen images, admitting that he cried during a scene from Charlie Chaplin's *Modern Times* (1936). Hyakken asserts this was not a result of the images on the screen, but of what was in his mind, namely his own sense of loss and nostalgia for the past.

In "Triumphant March into Port Arthur," the visual image interacts with the subjective vision of the observer. Just as fake newsreels sought to "re-create . . . the drama of the cameraman's presence, i.e. the photographic subjectivity through which the event was captured on film," Hyakken's story recreates the drama of the observer's presence, the photographic subjectivity of the act of viewing the film.[42] This emphasis on the subjective nature of viewing runs counter to the goals of propaganda, which does not allow for the indeterminate meaning associated with an individual viewing.

This connection between image and mind is important for Hyakken's literature, but we cannot ignore Hyakken's reaction to these films (and his character's reaction to the war actuality) as speaking to the power of the visual, specifically the visual medium of the cinema. As in the story "Realm of the Dead," we are in a nostalgic era—only the magic lanterns have been replaced by the flickering images of the early silver screen. Hyakken returns to the early 1900s, to a time when film still retained an aura. Viewers of these early actualities were transfixed by the alienness of seeing their own troops amidst such foreign landscapes and shed tears regularly over scenes of battlefields strewn with war dead.

Audiences, however, soon adapted to this medium. Peter High argues that by 1904, a mere seven years after film had been imported to Japan, "attentive watchers of the screen" had already emerged.[43] More important for Hyakken is the fact that by the time he wrote his story in the mid-1920s, film had become a part of mass consumer culture. "Triumphant March into Port Arthur" is set in a post-photography era where visuality is now part of the cultural economy of consumption and circulation. By the mid-1930s when his collection was published, "Triumphant March into Port Arthur" was readily integrated into the economy of images of the Russo-Japanese War, the endless production and reproduction of scenes and events from these watershed battles. The process of replication is present in the word Hyakken uses to describe the way in which his images are projected onto the screen. The Sino-Japanese character used to represent the verb *utsuru* is not the same character used in "Realm of the Dead." In this later story, Hyakken employs a character that means "to photograph, copy, duplicate."[44] Hyakken makes it clear we are viewing copies.

The earlier story focused on the play of light and darkness, and the world of reflections. But in "Triumphant March into

Port Arthur," Hyakken's images are purposely replicated, both on the fictional screen in his story and on the pages of his book being marketed to modern consumers. These images also reverberate with those being used by the media and the government to support the war. The very reproducibility of these images, the doubling mechanism of modern capitalist culture, deprives them of an originality and of an aura. Not only can we question the authenticity of these images, but also the value of the visual experience, observed and consumed. However, at the same time, the constant reproduction of the images severs them from their specific historical referent, the Russo-Japanese War. Once floating freely, the images are released from the requirements for authenticity and hence can be reused and reinterpreted in any number of contexts. These images are open to interpretation and to the reinscription of new meaning. By returning to the anti-narrative of the cinema of attraction, Hyakken restores the power of aura to these images, removing them from the level of mundane, everyday consumer culture. He creates the possibility of critique by further severing them from the inscribed narrative of propaganda and leaving them open to a subjective interpretation.

Hyakken does so by carefully selecting the images he invests with the power of visuality. But these are not always what we might expect. Historically important images that should create powerful responses in the viewer are reduced to passing scenery, while preference is given to anonymous, frightened soldiers and Russian prisoners of war. An example of this is found in the following scenes of Nogi and Stessel. The two generals met at a small stone cottage and formal arrangements were made for turning over the fortress to the Japanese. A famous black-and-white photograph from 1905 shows the men and their officers seated in front of the cottage wall (Figure 3). Images of this meeting circulated at the time of the Russo-Japanese War in photographs, on film, and in the popular song "Meeting at the Base" ("Suishiei no kaiken"), which describes this famous encounter, a proud moment in Japanese history.[45]

This moment is an excellent example of how history was reconfigured to meet the needs of the state. Stessel, the Russian commander of the garrison at Port Arthur, surrendered the strategic port to Nogi on January 1, 1905, but not without great cost to both sides. Nogi was only successful in breaking through to the port on his fourth attempt, when he finally gained control of 203 Meter Hill on December 6, 1904, but at the cost of 15,000 Japanese lives in the first attempt alone.[46] The tremendous losses of this critical battle had, in fact, resulted in public outrage in Japan at the "Port Arthur massacre." Nogi became a national villain: citizens threw stones at his Tokyo house, accosted his wife, and penned insulting letters.[47] His stubborn reliance on outdated ideas of samurai honor led more than one-third of his soldiers to senseless deaths in the first of three unsuccessful frontal attacks on the port.

The horrors of the battle for this hill were described in the Western press and in Japanese fiction of the era.[48] Novelist Natsume Sōseki captured the tragic meaninglessness of these suicide attacks in his story "The Heredity of Taste" ("Shumi no iden"), which he published in January 1906. The story opens with a homecoming for Russo-Japanese War veterans. The protagonist is unable to join the crowd in their celebratory cheers of "*Banzai*!" since he is forced to painfully remember that his friend, Ko-*san*, will not be returning. Ko-*san* died in the attack on Port Arthur. In imagining his friend's death, the protagonist compares a swarm of Japanese soldiers to ants scattering in disorder, a "wriggling stream," a "black writhing thing."[49] As the mass advances, the protagonist searches the landscape in vain for Ko-*san*. When the soldiers fail to climb out of a ditch, the protagonist realizes that his friend Ko-*san* "lies at the bottom of that ditch . . . just as dead and just as cold as any other soldier." The narration switches abruptly from this scene to the end of the war: "Stessel surrendered. Peace was signed. Our general came back home in triumph."[50]

The ending to this scene in Sōseki's story is indicative of how the horrors of the war were quickly displaced by victory celebrations, and Nogi was turned into a folk hero, a valiant warrior who ended the battle and gained public sympathy for losing his sons to the war in Manchuria. The pivotal battle at Port Arthur came to signal a key victory for the Japanese. The rehabilitation of Nogi's image was important for the project of nation-building in the 1910s and again in the 1930s. "The Meiji regime as well as subsequent Japanese governments transformed Nogi Maresuke into a formidable instrument of militaristic and national propaganda."[51] Writing twenty years after these events, Hyakken echoes the sentiments of his mentor, Sōseki. He comments on this scene, and the battle as a whole, in a way that makes it impossible to take the title of his story, "Triumphant March into Port Arthur," as genuine.

> Next came the long-awaited encounter at the naval base. Amidst the bleak scenery I could barely make out the faint image of a cottage with stone walls. From off in the distance indistinguishable figures on horseback grew in size as they approached, but the blurry image never came into focus, it just faded away.
>
> A formation of Russians on horseback rode unsteadily past a row of storehouses. The ceremony at the base was over. Nogi and Stessel's expressionless faces passed quickly before my eyes like a bank of fog. (1: 138)

This scene of would-be triumph is reduced to somber, pale images of vanquished Russian soldiers. The celebrated mien of Nogi passes before the protagonist's eyes "like a bank of fog," an unclear, ambivalent image, hardly the impression-making, legendary moment it was reputed to be. This was an important historical event and a well-circulated image symbolizing Nogi's heroism, but it lacks the expected weightiness. The protagonist is far more moved by the frantic soldiers, the ominous mountains, and the prisoners of war—in other words, those images not invested with national importance.

Hyakken's story may be a representation of just such a film, and this may account for the naval base encounter's failure to make an impression on his protagonist.[52] According to critics, Hyakken did in fact see a Russo-Japanese War film at Hōsei University in 1921. But we must remember that Hyakken's is a fictional story, a representation, a copy of an actuality film.

Hyakken is using this story as a means to comment on the recycling of war images. It was not a random choice on his part to have this most important of scenes, the meeting at the naval base, pass before the protagonist's eyes like a bank of fog, rendering it insignificant and meaningless. This interpretation would have contradicted the heroic images of Nogi that were circulating in the 1930s. Hyakken reminds the reader that there is more than one way to view this image of Nogi, and that Nogi's heroism is more a construction of the state than a reflection of the reality of the war. Nogi himself is reduced to a celluloid phantom as Hyakken's protagonist "misinterprets" this national icon.

The movie in Hyakken's story closes with another parade, only these men carry no arms or knapsacks, and their empty faces and lifeless marching bring the protagonist to wonder if he is not witnessing dead soldiers risen from their graves on the war-torn mountainside. The image undoubtedly portrays Russian prisoners of war. The movie ends and the crowd breaks out in applause. But the images from the screen continue to be projected onto the protagonist's mind. As the audience files out of the lecture hall, the protagonist continues to "see" these dead soldiers, but his vision is clouded with tears, and he loses his way.

The film ends much as it began, with a set of superimposed images: the marching soldiers (POWs) and the crowd filing out of the lecture hall. The collapsing of these images is intentional given the similarity in language Hyakken uses to describe the two groups.

"The Triumphant March into Port Arthur!" boomed the voice of the officer on the stage.

The audience, crammed into that dark room, broke out in loud applause.

Tears streamed down my face. The row of soldiers marched on and on. My eyes clouded with tears, obscuring the people in front of me. I lost my bearings and was set adrift in an unfamiliar place.

"Quit crying" said a man walking next to me.

Someone behind us was weeping.

> The crowd kept clapping. My cheeks wet from crying, I fell into formation and was led out into the quiet of the city streets, out into nowhere. (166–67)

Tears obscure the protagonist's vision, turning it into the blurry landscapes of the actuality film. He is unable to see where he is going, but at this point in the story, we imagine he has not yet started filing out of the lecture hall. The protagonist envisions himself as part of the parade on the screen. Hyakken uses the word *retsu* (列) to describe the "row of soldiers" in his mind, and also the formation his protagonist joined. At the point when his protagonist says he "fell into formation," or more literally, joined "that row" (*sono retsu*), he is referring to the prisoners and to the crowd filing out of the lecture hall. The protagonist cannot see the person in front of him and the surroundings grow unfamiliar, as though he has lost his way in a strange landscape. He follows the crowd but does not share in their enthusiasm for the film. In fact, the patriotic applause of the audience causes the defamiliarization of the landscape, as he is drawn into the crowd much like the unwilling soldiers sent to battle. The disconnect between the crowd's reaction and the image of the POWs disorients the protagonist. But an important point is that Hyakken identifies first with the defeated Russian enemy, and only by extension with his fellow citizens.[53] The story ends as the viewers file out into the streets of the imperial capital on the anniversary of the Taishō Emperor's wedding. The crowd has been transformed into a group of imperial subjects.

By having the film end with an image of prisoners of war, Hyakken is making a clear unpatriotic statement in identifying the crowd with the vanquished enemy soldiers. Even if the soldiers were Japanese, they are not marching victorious, but walk like the living dead, defeated and unarmed. The protagonist comments: "There was something eerie about these lifeless men. Weren't they in fact the war dead risen from their graves on the shadowy mountain for one final march?" (166). POW or Japanese war dead, the effect is equally subversive. Unlike the earlier scene in which the protagonist identifies with the soldier, this later association is clearly not what the government intended. These men on the screen are not portrayed as having died bravely in battle nor are they reliving their glory. The viewers in the lecture hall become captives, or worse, casualties, of war. On a large scale, the Japanese public was a casualty of the Russo-Japanese War, a conflict touted for elevating Japan's status as an international power, but which in reality caused its people to suffer a tremendous loss. Hyakken's story would have been powerful in 1925, but it had even stronger—and more dangerous—connotations of neutrality and indeterminacy in 1934, as war again raged in the Far East. Despite the government's rhetoric glorifying the earlier battle, the Japanese public once again became victim, this time in a new era of imperialism.

Hyakken reconstructs a personal and commercial memory of this decisive national battle in the context of a remilitarizing, imperially expanding Japanese empire. The images and narratives of the Russo-Japanese War were reconfigured in the national memory of the 1930s as a means of justifying Japan's incursions into Asia. The nation underwent "a very successful public forgetting" of the "great human and financial costs of the [Russo-Japanese] war, and the inconclusiveness of its ending."[54] Along with this forgetting, "the human and financial costs were remembered only in a positive light, as irrefutable evidence of Japan's right to control Manchuria."[55] Although Manchuria initially occupied a "peripheral position" in the growing Japanese empire, it became the "jewel in the crown" of the new kind of Japanese empire after 1931.[56]

The officer from the Ministry of War who introduced the film can be seen as the voice of the state recrafting a prior war to serve new imperialist purposes in the 1930s. The cheering crowd is the willing partner to this "public forgetting." In a time of strict censorship and the patrolling vigilance of the Special Higher Police Section (Tokubetsu Kōtō Keisatsu, or the "Thought Police"), Hyakken manages to present these memories in an ambiguous and even frightening manner, all the while evading the nationalistic fervor of the official retellings of past wars. Whereas the state's intent was to support the new imperialist campaigns by reliving the glory and sacrifice of the earlier battle, Hyakken presents the Russo-Japanese War as a frightening, depressing, disorienting, and ultimately ambiguous experience. Hyakken's protagonist is not the only person crying when the film ends. There are others disturbed by these images. Citizens were being arrested for antiwar comments in 1937, in a battle of personal memory versus national, official discourse.[57] During the time of the Manchurian Incident, Japanese children were told tales of bravery about soldiers in the Russo-Japanese War,[58] but Hyakken's protagonist sees the soldiers as they really were, not as the propaganda they were made out to be. They are driven by fear, not bravery or love of country. The soldiers are animals, shouting out orders "like the howl[ing] of a beast" (1: 137), as they march off to war with somber faces.

Read from the perspective of Japanese nationalism after the Manchurian Incident, Hyakken's story successfully recreates the patterns of conflation used by the state and the media to marshal the memory of the Russo-Japanese War in support of new conflicts on the continent. Hyakken fuses these two time periods, creating a temporal discombobulation. A reader from the 1930s would little realize that Hyakken's story had been written six years before the Manchurian Incident. Hyakken also collapses the distance between viewer and viewed, protagonist and narrated, allowing for a dangerous identification, albeit temporary, with suffering Japanese and Russian soldiers. Hyakken allows for his reader to relive the sorrow and losses of battle, hardly the triumphant images necessary to fuel the new war of the 1930s.

## Ghosts of Yasukuni

Hyakken recreated the war experience a second time in his story "The War Museum" ("Yūshūkan"). In place of the actuality, Hyakken uses an architectural symbol of the modern nation. He returns to a building from yesteryear, to a phantom structure, to raise the grim specter of war. In this story, he switches back and forth between reality and dreams without any clear line separating the two; the illusory is real and the real illusory. The story was originally published in October 1929 in *Shisō*, an academic monthly with a narrow, intellectual readership.[59] The initial audience for this story was limited by the venue, but it received a much wider circulation when reprinted in the *Triumphant March into Port Arthur* collection in 1934. Like "Triumphant March into Port Arthur," "The War Museum" would have been read against the cultural context of militarism in the 1930s. In this case, the reference point is not a particular battle, but a museum on the grounds of the Yasukuni Shrine, the national site for commemorating the nation's wars and war dead.

One of the most structurally complex of Hyakken's tales, "The War Museum" is a multilayered nine-part sequence, in which the protagonist shifts back and forth between what we assume to be dreams and reality, although the transitions are not always clear. The fragmentary nature of the narrative is akin to the aesthetic of the *jissha*; the story jumps around without a clear narrative or temporal line. The protagonist visits the Yūshūkan war museum at the Yasukuni Shrine, and in turn is visited by a ghostly soldier. The Yūshūkan in Hyakken's story is neither a sacred space nor the site of national militaristic pride. The building and the Kudan district in which it is located, as well as the lieutenant who appears in the first scene, are sources of great trepidation for Hyakken's protagonist.

The story opens with a description of the weather: "The rain that had been falling since afternoon suddenly stopped. But the sky darkened, and oppressive clouds descended onto the eaves" (127). As in other Hyakken stories, the sudden change in the weather signals the onset of the surreal, the alternate space that opens up from within the fabric of the mundane. Hyakken reveals that which is hidden by the homogenizing discourse of propaganda and nationalism; in "The War Museum," this is the true face of war and the history of the museum, not as a symbol of war, but as an icon of Western civilization and enlightenment.

The protagonist, Professor Noda, hears a voice in the entryway of his house, which turns out to be an unexpected visit from an imposing artillery lieutenant. Noda's attention is drawn to the eerie yellow tone of the lieutenant's skin and the bluish hue around the edge of his face. The lieutenant, who remains nameless, claims to know the protagonist, but Noda has no memory of him. The soldier explains that he has recently been posted to Tokyo, and so he stopped by to see the Professor. He also claims to have seen the protagonist at Kudanzaka the previous day, but Noda was at home all day. The mention of this hill leading to the Yasukuni Shrine gives the protagonist the chills.[60] For the avid Hyakken reader, the word *kudan* also brings up memories of the cow-man in *Realm of the Dead,* a reminder of an eerie tranformation from the past where the protagonist himself was turned into a mythical beast. The association with the *kudan* portends ill for Professor Noda.

The protagonist hears someone in the distance singing or perhaps crying, and the lieutenant's expression changes. His narrow forehead grows pale and the luster on his cheeks disappears. Noda grows frightened and, like his counterparts in *Realm of the Dead,* is rendered speechless. He is unable to make sense of the visual and aural stimuli. He is shaken out of this stupor by the sound of heavy rain, and notices he is alone. But the surroundings indicate that someone had been there with him, and the afterimage of the lieutenant ready to storm out of the room flickers across Noda's eye. Hyakken once again employs the language of the visual, just as he did in "Triumphant March into Port Arthur," when the image of the officer remains on the protagonist's retina. Only here Hyakken presents an image even more elusive and ephemeral than the cinematic ones in the earlier story. The lieutenant's mysterious disappearance with the sound of the rain makes the reader think he may be a ghost. While visiting with Noda, the lieutenant had remarked on how much Tokyo had changed. Perhaps this is because he lost his life in the Russo-Japanese War and has been dead for over twenty years. The city the lieutenant remembers has long since disappeared in the wake of modernization.[61]

Section two opens as the protagonist ventures out into a wind storm to visit the Yūshūkan. Again, the unsettled weather indicates that Noda's experience will be out of the ordinary. As he enters this realm of the extraordinary, the true history of the war museum is revealed. In place of the clean, managed space of a national monument, the area outside the museum resembles a battle scene. To get to the entrance, the protagonist must walk over artillery shells and horse legs, which give way beneath his feet in an uncomfortable, pliant sensation. The gatekeepers are earless, and inside, in place of armor and swords, Noda sees dead soldiers irreverently piled high in large glass cases. The stench is overwhelming and he runs for the door.

These scenes both outside and inside the museum are reminiscent of eyewitness accounts of battles in the Russo-Japanese War. The following description is from an English attaché who fell prisoner to the Japanese in the battle of Mukden: "Many corpses were lying about, the wounded were neglected, and the fields were strewn for a dozen miles with provisions, rifles, cartridges, and dead horses."[62] At the time the story was written, this would have been the most recent major battle to have been added to the museum's display. It is as though the battle has been transported from the continent over to the site of this museum commemorating the war dead. In place of exhibits, the protagonist experiences the destruction of the front lines. As he is leaving the shrine, he sees a giant cannon, as long as ten telephone poles and as wide as the Kudan slope. It is facing west and smoke is coming out of the mouth as though it had just been fired. The direction here is not meant to signal the West, but the area to the west of Japan, in this case, China, Korea, Manchuria, and by extension, Russia. The battle has come home in all of its chaos, ugliness, and death. There is no sign here of the glory of war. The description of the Yūshūkan as a battle scene combines with the lieutenant's mention of Kudanzaka to strengthen the association with fallen soldiers from the Russo-Japanese War.

The action in the subsequent sections moves between a small restaurant in the Kudan district, the protagonist's home, Tokyo Station, the Yūshūkan, and finally the Tokyo suburbs. Transitions between sections are rough, often nonexistent, and the timeline is nonlinear. Hyakken again uses the aesthetic of the fragment to undermine the national narrative of war memory. For example, in the first section the lieutenant claims to have seen the protagonist at Kudanzaka the previous day, but the protagonist does not visit this neighborhood until the next section. The mere mention of the Kudan slope generates Noda's experience the following day. As in *Realm of the Dead,* Hyakken evokes the modernist power of language: a single word has the power to shift the protagonist into the everyday as Other, especially when the characters are confined to the textual level. It is possible we are not in the realm of reality, but in the shifting landscape of the protagonist's mind. However, the Yūshūkan is real, as are its connections with the war. Unlike those in *Realm of the Dead,* this story is anchored to a historical reality: the building, and by extension, the war.

The third section is set in a restaurant hidden in the back streets of the Kudan district, the area around the Yasukuni Shrine. Although the protagonist seems familiar with the shrine and its surrounding neighborhood, this area is completely new to him, almost as though it did not previously exist. He is led to this eatery by his friend Kimura, and the introduction of this heretofore unknown space bodes ill for their evening together. This back street is infused with the mysterious spatial qualities of *Realm of the Dead,* as phantom spaces open up in the modern city.

While celebrating Kimura's new teaching assignment in the country, the two men proceed to get drunk, and the lieutenant with the yellow skin unexpectedly enters the room. After sharing a drink, he convinces them to go for a drive. Vague shapes and shadows appear outside the windows as they speed through the dimly lit town. Suddenly the scene shifts to the bright entryway of a building. The men are served dinner and drinks, and the lieutenant starts singing. The protagonist is on the verge of remembering something, and he looks around him, but the edges of the room are shrouded in blackness, a representation of the reaches of his own mind and of the limits of the text's history. The lieutenant's song reminds Noda of something he heard on a stormy day in the past. This is an obvious reference to the opening segment of the story when Noda hears a song in the distance and then heavy rain starts to fall. This may also be a reference to old war tunes that came back into vogue. This is not just nostalgia, but an active recycling of history.

The lieutenant abruptly stops singing and reaches his yellow hands for the protagonist's neck. A geisha manages to calm the soldier, but the protagonist is thrown out of the restaurant and put into a car, which he tells us "sped off on a pitch-black river, the dark water catching the light and flickering back at me" (131). The section ends as the protagonist is spirited home across a surreal landscape, having left his friend Kimura behind. The next section opens with the protagonist in bed. He has been transported from the restaurant directly to a sleeping-dreaming state. This segue takes on significance as he relates a dream in the following section. He dozes and wakes to the sound of the wind battering the house as though somebody were rapping on his windows, perhaps another unexpected, unwanted visitor, like the past itself arriving uninvited. He is startled from sleep by an animal-like cry emanating from his wife, a cry that reminds the reader of the howling soldiers in "Triumphant March into Port Arthur." He wakes her and she relates a nightmare about sleeping next to a large corpse. This body started moving and grabbing for her, but she was awakened by her own screams. Noda touches his wife's shoulder just as the corpse did, scaring himself.

The protagonist listens to his wife apprehensively, and in the following section has a dream of his own. The wind dies down and the silence makes him feel as though he is sinking underwater, another common image used as a slippage point in Hyakken's texts to enter the realm of the extraordinary. Noda thinks about his wife's dream while he is asleep.

First the lieutenant and now this corpse. They couldn't have been real. The dead body was in my wife's dream so the lieutenant must have been in mine.

But what about Kimura?

I left him with the lieutenant and that geisha. What happened back in that restaurant with the dark garden?

I realized the soldier must have killed him.

Or maybe that happened in somebody else's dream.

It was even possible that I had already been killed in some stranger's dream.

But to die like that . . . It just couldn't be.

But my wife hadn't mentioned the smell. (132)

It is not necessarily clear if this analysis of his and his wife's dreams occurs while he is awake, or is part of yet another dream sequence. The wife's dream seems to be the connection point for the various sections of the story. The body in the wife's dream resembles the bodies the protagonist saw at the Yūshūkan, hence his surprise that his wife did not mention the smell, presumably of dead bodies. But this is not Noda's last encounter with these yellow-toned corpses.

From Noda's dream, the story segues into a scene at Tokyo Station. Kimura is scheduled to leave for his job in the country and Noda goes to see him off. Pigeons fly around the famous clock tower at the station, another building emblematic of Western modernity. There is no sign of Kimura, and the protagonist searches the crowd in vain for a familiar face. The train departs, yet his friend is nowhere to be found. Despondent, Noda leaves and enters a Chinese restaurant staffed by menacing employees. He worries about Kimura, only to have one of the Chinese staff tell him that his friend is dead. The sequencing of these scenes after Noda's dream leaves the reader wondering if this is still part of his reverie. Hyakken offers some clarification in the following section.

Noda returns to the Yūshūkan, only this time the weather conditions are the exact opposite of his earlier visit. In the previous episode the wind was blowing so strongly that the protagonist could hardly tell where he was, but in this scene, the sky is a clear, beautiful blue, the cherry trees glisten in the sun, and the stone pavement is cleanly swept. This description leads us to believe that the museum will be returned to a state of normalcy. There is something odd about the military policeman standing outside the museum, but the protagonist is sure that once he enters, he will feel better. He comments that he knows that such frightening things cannot really exist, but he hesitates all the same. In saying this, Noda references his prior experience at the museum, and by extension, the story as a whole. He speaks on a metalevel, stepping briefly outside of the text to comment on the past and to throw its existence into question.

The museum is smaller and brighter than he expected, and the requisite flags and armaments are all in place, but the anxiety he felt before entering is not readily dissipated, rather it intensifies. Running past the exhibits on his way toward the exit, he glimpses something disturbing: "Hidden in the shadows was another, larger display case. Behind the glass were five or six mannequins in uniform. They looked almost real to me. Then I saw their faces and hands—that eerie yellow skin—I retched" (1: 114).

The mannequins have the same yellow skin as the lieutenant and the dead bodies Noda saw piled up behind the glass cases on his previous visit. Hyakken explicitly draws the protagonist's experience into the dream world, only to later contradict it. When in the dream world, neither protagonist nor reader is able to tell the real from the illusory. Also like the cinema, images can seem more real than reality, but they can also be complete fabrications. Hyakken takes advantage of the blurry line between reality and representation to comment on the national retelling of the Russo-Japanese War as a purposeful mixing of the two. But Hyakken does not leave the reader guessing. By having his protagonist return to the Yūshūkan on a clear day, Hyakken signals that we have returned to the realm of reality. The war is real and it is within this realm that the protagonist confronts its horrors. The sight of the eerie yellow skin causes Noda to retch. Hyakken affirms the reality of war, in all its stomach-turning wretchedness. Unlike his counterpart in "Triumphant March into Port Arthur," Noda does not sympathize with the plight of Japanese soldiers. The military is clearly represented as menacing.

It is important to recognize that Hyakken's story would have been read in the context of Japan after the Manchurian Incident, but the real key to understanding the power behind Hyakken's story lies in the original publication date. In 1929, the original Yūshūkan no longer existed, having been destroyed in the 1923 earthquake. Like the lieutenant, the museum itself is merely a phantom, a reminder of something that used to be—in this case, a forgotten past. Hyakken returns to this original building from the late nineteenth century, a symbol of Western modernity, to show how the government later attempted to overcome that very modernity in its recreation of a national past. To appreciate fully the repercussions of Hyakken's use of this structure, we need to review the history of the museum.

The title of Hyakken's story is a reference to the annex of the Shōkonsha, the central shrine to the war dead in Tokyo, better known as the Yasukuni Shrine (Shrine for the Repose of the Nation). The shrine was originally built in 1869 as the Kudan Shōkonsha, a shrine in the Kudan district for inviting the return of the spirits of the dead. The shrine was renamed Yasukuni in 1879, and established primarily for honoring those who died in disturbances surrounding the restoration of the Emperor in the transition to the Meiji period. The annex opened its doors on February 25, 1882 as a war memorial museum housing exhibits of weaponry and other military paraphernalia from the battles that led to the Meiji Restoration.[63]

The Yūshūkan described in Hyakken's story was a Western-style building designed by Italian architect Giovanni Vincenzo Cappelletti in the style of an ancient European castle (Figure 4). "Stylish and enlightened," it sat atop the steep Kudanzaka, one of the highest spots in Tokyo in the late nineteenth century. The building stood out in the city's landscape as a symbol of Western modernism, in the style of the Rokumeikan (Deer Cry Pavilion), a famous building used for entertaining foreign guests at lavish ballroom dances.[64] At the Yūshūkan, the locals roamed the gardens and the first floor exhibits, which were open only on Sundays. Japanese military elite used the large room on the second floor to entertain Western guests of honor.[65] In 1908, two years before Hyakken moved up to Tokyo, the annex was remodeled to include items from the recent Sino- and Russo-Japanese Wars.

The Yūshūkan's early associations with Rokumeikan-era modernization were soon forgotten—or erased—as the Yasukuni Shrine took on nationalistic and militaristic overtones in the early part of the twentieth century. The Western look was abandoned when the museum was rebuilt after being destroyed in the Great Kantō Earthquake of 1923.[66] At the time of the Shōwa Emperor's coronation in February 1928, interest was growing in restoring the museum. Committees were formed, an architect chosen, and plans drawn up. In a move telling of the times, the army appointed a lieutenant general to be head of the architectural committee.[67] Preliminary construction began in July and August 1929, and the official groundbreaking ceremony was held on March 3, 1930.[68] The museum reopened with a visit from the Shōwa Emperor on April 26, 1932.[69] Hyakken's story was reprinted two years later.

The original Western style was replaced with a "modern Oriental" style (*kindai tōyōshiki*), specifically an Imperial (Diadem) or Japanese gable-roof style (*teikan yōshiki*), a return to tradition and a nod to pan-Asianism (Figure 5). This new building stood in stark contrast to the modernist architecture of other neighborhoods in Tokyo, specifically Ginza.[70] Modern buildings had dotted the landscape since the Meiji period, but whole neighborhoods took on a Western feel with the comprehensive urban planning of the 1910s and 1920s. Tokyo was remade into a modern city. This return to an "Oriental" look—a rejection of Western modernism and the building's own history—is not coincidental given the backdrop of growing militarism and impending war. Conservative ideology also had its expression in architecture in the 1930s: "the question of how to express Japanism in design became frequently discussed among Japanese designers."[71]

Fig. 4 The original War Museum (Yūshūkan), 1882. Courtesy of the Yasukuni Shrine.

Fig. 5 The new War Museum (Yūshūkan), rebuilt in 1932. Courtesy of the Yasukuni Shrine.

Hyakken chose to write about a building symbolic of war and of death, but also of a Western-inspired modernity, a modernity that was being redefined at the time he was writing. The museum commemorated soldiers from a war that brought Japan into the modern, Western world. Originally constructed at a time of nation-building, it was rebuilt during a second phase in the building of the nation, namely the creation of an empire. The Yūshūkan would become a site of memory for native casualties in the empire's wars. This symbol of Western-style modernity, enlightenment, and civilization came to stand for an alternate modernity, one wrought through military might as Japan imposed its will on Asia.

Yoshida Tsukasa argues that the story of Yasukuni as a symbol of modernization came to an end around 1906 with the large-scale military parade celebrating Japan's victory in the Russo-Japanese War.[72] But a different type of modernization had begun. The Russo-Japanese War had put Japan on the international stage by defeating a Western power. The Fifteen Years War established Japan's empire within Asia. Japan was no longer interested in joining the ranks of the Western powers, but in overcoming them and their Western modernity by "liberating" Asia. This potent site of war memory also overcame its own modernity to better serve the ideology of the state.[73]

The Yūshūkan was a part of Hyakken's daily landscape: he worked, literally, in its shadow at Hōsei University. He would have known of the plans for reconstructing the museum as he was writing his story. He was also well aware of the potency of images of Yasukuni and the museum in the daily lives of his fellow citizens. The museum, and Yasukuni Shrine in general, had stood as symbols of national mourning throughout their history.[74] The association of the War Museum and dead soldiers from the Sino- and Russo-Japanese Wars remained strong in the public imagination during the early Shōwa period.[75] Yasukuni itself became prominent in everyday life of the 1930s through venues such as NHK's live broadcast of three prayer ceremonies at Yasukuni in 1932, part of the new radio coverage of military ceremonies.[76]

Like Hyakken's protagonist, the nation as a whole was haunted by the Russo-Japanese War, but Hyakken points out the unreliable, ephemeral, elusive, and constructed nature of that memory. In writing about the old Yūshūkan, a structure whose history precedes the militarization of early Shōwa, Hyakken takes the nonexistent building, the phantom space of the destroyed Yūshūkan, and makes it part of the new narratives on the war in Manchuria. The ghost of the original museum, the symbol of modern, Western enlightenment, is superimposed on the empty space of reconstruction and on the new pan-Asian museum that surfaced little more than half a year after the Manchurian Incident. Hyakken conjures up the aura inherent in this early site of modernity and recreates the powerful experience of the Russo-Japanese War. But the building is merely an echo of the past and of a modernity now overcome by the rhetoric and actions of imperialism.

Amidst the crisis of representation in the 1930s, Hyakken turns to the surreal and the fragmentary to counter the national narratives on war memory. Hyakken returns to a time when our means for interacting with the world retained an aura and the possibility of transformation. He employs the language and narrative techniques of modernism to make his war critique. His fragmentary aesthetic, seen in the actuality film and in the disjunctive narrative in "The War Museum," allows Hyakken to "misinterpret" war images and to undermine the seamless narratives of propaganda. By returning to a time of aura and defamiliarizing the imagery of the Russo-Japanese War common at the time, Hyakken can reinscribe a transformative power into the actuality film and release its images from the crafted remakes of propaganda.

Hyakken was fully cognizant that the war was more than illusion, a trick of light and screen. The Japanese empire of the 1930s was not an abstract concept, but a reality for the soldiers who were cycled through it on duty, and for the colonists, many of whom worked for the South Manchuria Railway. By 1930, there were already a quarter million civilian Japanese living in Manchuria.[77] For those living in the homeland, images of the empire, past and future, were transmitted to the average citizen through the media, and became a part of everyday life. Hyakken drew on this everyday imagination in his stories that recall the past through potent sites of memory and trauma. The building in "The War Museum" functions like the silent film in "Triumphant March into Port Arthur"; the original was part of a different era and of a different war, yet it comes to symbolize the government's new military desires in Asia. Once again the old war is relived in a new context. But Hyakken teaches us that these images from the everyday are part of the lived moment, not an unchanging past. Amidst the conflation is a clear sense that history is discontinuous and is populated by phantoms.

# FOUR

# *Return to the City: Excavating Memory in "Tokyo Diary"*

> The wind picked up, lifting dust from the crevices of the pavement, and ran along the dark street corners like a living thing.
>
> A shift in the breeze carried the dust from the back streets and filled the plaza with a thick smoke, turning the distant city lights reddish brown.
>
> Shivering in the cold air, I stamped my feet atop the streetcar platform. As I turned around, I saw a pack of wolves emerge from behind Commander Hirose, his bronze statue now buried in the recesses of the city. Running in the border between pedestrian and car space, the wolves headed silently for the Kudan district.
>
> —Uchida Hyakken, "Tokyo Diary"

Wolves run down city streets, giant eels rise out of the moat surrounding the Imperial Palace, and landmark buildings disappear in Hyakken's 1938 "Tokyo Diary" ("Tōkyō nikki").[1] The story features 23 vignettes set in neighborhoods around the Imperial Palace, mostly in the middle-class, "high city" known as the Yamanote.[2] Hyakken's protagonist wanders about Tokyo, as "the order of the city is negated in favor of a drift that allows the disordered forces of the city to be revealed."[3] This wandering does not take place in the traditional, plebian flatlands of the low city, nor at the poetic locales famous from classical travel diaries, but in and about important sites of modernity: Tokyo Station, the Marunouchi Building, Ginza, and the Imperial Palace. Situated within these symbolic locations of modernity, capitalism, and imperialism, Hyakken performs a literary archeology. The strata of the past rupture the present. Through "Tokyo Diary," Hyakken critiques the homogenizing effects of the capitalist standardization of the 1920s, and in the process uncovers the uneven, discontinuous, hidden times, spaces, and narratives of the urban everyday experience.

Writing "Tokyo Diary" in 1938, Hyakken looked back to Taishō, the age of the city and "city stories" (*toshi shōsetsu*) and evoked the changing metropolis of the 1910s and 1920s, the era of urban planning. Hyakken firmly locates himself within Tokyo, this monument to modernity, but he is also engaged in the production of memory. By the time "Tokyo Diary" was written, literary tides had shifted away from the city to the war. Modernist and proletarian writers had abandoned the metropolis as a literary setting and a physical home, many seeking refuge in the countryside. Those who continued to write on the city, such as Nagai Kafū, looked back through the lens of nostalgia. Unlike other modern writers, Hyakken was not seeking to erase, abandon, escape, or eulogize Tokyo.[4] The importance of these sites of modernity had been supplanted in national discourse by the war, but Hyakken purposely returns to the outmoded cityscape and language of cultural modernism to access the forgotten in order to construct his critique.

Hyakken's evocation and critique of the city, and his return to the past, must be read against the backdrop of the war and the conservative voices of the late 1930s, specifically within the Return to Japan movement. Their discontent with modernity and the decadent, contemporary Japanese culture led the writers and thinkers of this movement to wander homeless. They decried the cultural invasion of Americanization represented in the metropolis and the subsequent loss of traditional ways, yet they found themselves unable to go back to their countryside homes (*furusato*). The combination of cultural particularism, nationalism, and revolt against the West that informed the movement also led it to seek an identity and a home in the return to an immutable, ahistorical Japanese past. This combination and the rhetoric it produced proved to be dangerous in the climate of the 1930s, when the war came to be portrayed as a struggle against modernity itself.[5]

The discourses of capitalism, modernism, and nationalism converge in this movement and on the symbol of the city. Writing one year after Japan plunged into full-scale war with China, Hyakken returns to the city to make his critique of both modernity and militarism. But unlike these conservative voices, Hyakken was not rejecting modernity or embracing an idealized, "Japanese" past. If there is a return in "Tokyo Diary," it is a literary one, a return to his first short story collection, *Realm of the Dead*, but even this is contingent and ultimately unsuccessful. This failure serves to counter and undermine the homogenizing forces of modernization and the manufactured nostalgia of the war machine in the late 1930s.

## Figuring the Urban Landscape

The modern city truly emerged as a literary topic in the late 1920s and early 1930s. Writers in previous eras had written about cities, such as the foreign capitals of Berlin and London in the works of Mori Ōgai and Natsume Sōseki, or the Naturalist reconfiguration of Tokyo by writers from the countryside.[6] However, the "city story" came into its own in the 1920s, a time when Japanese writers discovered and celebrated the modern urban landscape.[7] Well-known landmarks, neighborhoods, and prominent features of Tokyo's new urban reality commonly appeared in literature, as the city became an oft-used setting.

Taisho was the age of the city and the era of urban planning that wrought the largest changes on the local landscape. In fact, the Japanese translation of the term urban planning, *toshi keikaku*, was created and popularized in the 1910s.[8] The 1910s and 1920s witnessed a transformation of everyday urban spaces: avenues, street corners, parks, and plazas. The Meiji Era was known for its modern, Western buildings, such as the Rokumeikan, the First National Bank, the Yomiuri Shinbun Building, and the Kankōba Exhibition Hall, but they were often isolated from the surrounding street architecture. In Taishō, the city underwent fundamental changes that shaped it into a prototype of the present day metropolis, integrating monuments, buildings, and plazas into the city design.

Tokyo as a city "was remade along modern lines," not just in terms of physical construction, but in the conceptualization of the metropolis.[9] Tokyo was expanding, with unchecked development of suburbia outside the city limits, and hence the need arose for a conceptualization of the city as a unit. A number of committees were set up for the comprehensive planning of the city, and in 1919 the City Planning Act and Urban Building Act were passed. The destruction of the earthquake in 1923 opened the land for reconstruction along planned lines, and drastically changed the face of certain neighborhoods, especially the old low city. The urban structure of later Tokyo was further determined by influential zoning laws in the mid-1920s.[10]

Asakusa was one locale that often featured in the new city literature. The neighborhood had long been a site of tradition and the old ways of premodern Japan. This imaginative cultural home for Japanese identity was also a physical home for the many rural, working poor who entered the city and found refuge there. But in the 1920s, Asakusa was also a *sakariba,* a modern entertainment district replete with films, follies, panoramas, and other amusements. Many modern writers focused on this site of popular culture in the low city of the urban masses. It was a place where one went to become lost in the crowd. Asakusa was another world, an escape from modern life, a place to go and forget about the trials of daily life in Tokyo.[11]

Modernists of the Newly Arisen Artistic School, such as Yoshiyuki Eisuke and Ryūtanji Yū, celebrated the experience of living in the city in works such as "The Apartment, the Women, and Me" ("Apāto to onnatachi to boku," 1928) and "Pavement Snap" ("Pēvumento sunappu," 1930).[12] Writers from the New Sensationalist movement, Kawabata Yasunari and Yokomitsu

Riichi, penned the "cartographic" *Scarlet Gang of Asakusa* (*Asakusa kurenaidan*, 1929–30) and *Shanghai* (1928–32), which are "organized around the mapping of a specific urban topography," a downtown neighborhood in Tokyo and a city in the new Japanese empire.[13] Marxist critic Hirabayashi Hatsunosuke observed the relationship between the technological material change in the city and the new attitudes and social problems such as the liberation of women and the break-up of the family.[14]

By the 1930s, post-quake reconstruction was complete and interest in the city, as an object of cultural and political concern, had faded. As the military agenda took over, the city largely disappeared as an idea in Japan.[15] As a result of this shift, the urban narratives never reached full expression, and the 1920s disappeared from the work of proletarians, modernists, and other city writers. In the early 1930s, Hori Tatsuo underwent a private, self-motivated turn away from the city. Hori's *Beautiful Village* (*Utsukushii mura*, 1933), set in the unnamed K village, refers to the protagonist's and Hori's retreat to Karuizawa, a high-class resort town. Writers such as Hori fled the excesses of the city, as it took on menacing overtones. The urban lifestyle, once the site of modernist revelry, gave rise to sickness, a physical and mental deterioration. In its place, writers sought refuge and recuperation in the countryside.

Unlike the self-motivated retreat of the modernists, proletarian writers, many of whom were arrested, imprisoned, or otherwise silenced, forcibly underwent a public renunciation (*tenkō*) of their beliefs.[16] Their literature, filled with factories and urban workers, would now be abandoned—a shift that occurs in Nakano Shigeharu's writing after his apostasy in 1933. "House in the Village" ("Mura no ie," 1935) recounts in semi-autobiographical fashion the homecoming of a young man who has renounced his Communist beliefs. In an oft-cited passage, the protagonist realizes that he cannot follow his father's advice to throw away his pen in order to save his literary legacy. Like his fictional character, Nakano kept writing, but felt the loss of the 1920s.[17] The "city story" itself disappeared from literary history as authors denounced their productions from the 1920s, some even deleting these stories from their collected works.[18]

One notable case of an author who wrote about the city in the late 1930s is Nagai Kafū. In 1937, the year before "Tokyo Diary," Kafū published *A Strange Tale from East of the River* (*Bokutō kitan*). The protagonist, a collector of old magazines, kimono, and other antiques, wanders into the unlicensed prostitute district of Tamanoi and meets up with an old geisha. She is an antique herself, her beauty reminiscent of Edo-era aesthetics. He returns often to the battered houses of this derelict quarter as he develops a relationship with the geisha and gathers material for his novel. The work was popular, serialized in both the *Tōkyō* and *Ōsaka Asahi* newspapers from mid-April to mid-June, and was praised as one of Kafū's finest. Kafū had long been known for eulogizing the old downtown neighborhood of Asakusa; his was a nostalgic view of an older Tokyo that was disappearing.

While some writers found comfort in their retreat to the country or the nostalgic warrens of the old downtown, others, such as poet Hagiwara Sakutarō, completely rejected the idea of a home. He escaped his hometown of Maebashi to move into the liberating metropolis of Tokyo. Once relocated, he struggled financially and found himself looking for consolation from modern city life; however, the comforts of the new consumer lifestyle only served to intensify his sense of loss. Hagiwara felt the "disillusionment and loneliness of a new generation of Japanese who were now as ill at ease in the modern city as they had been earlier in the countryside."[19]

Hagiwara was unable to accept city or country, and identified himself, and the Japanese, as wanderers (*hyōhakusha*).[20] This homelessness led him to search for a true home within his identity as a Japanese. In 1936, he joined the Japan Romantic School (Nihon Roman-ha), a group of writers who advocated a return to an "authentic literary tradition" and native aesthetics free of the influence of the West.[21] This came at a time when questions of national identity became increasingly politicized. As intellectuals searched for their identity in an ethnic, national past, the modern Western city became symbolic of their loss of culture and their alienation from their own history. Some perceived a "threat of cultural hegemony" in the crass materialism associated with the Americanization of both city life and everyday Japanese culture in the 1920s.[22] By the mid-1930s, modern, Western values, ideals, and innovations had permeated the lives of the average urban dweller and had transformed the Japanese landscape. The romantics sought the "restoration of 'timeless' cultural values" to counter these trends.[23]

The retreat from the city took place in the climate of growing conservatism and nationalism in the 1930s. Modernization had fundamentally changed Japan, and those changes were especially evident in the metropolitan centers. Intellectuals such as those in the Return to Japan movement rejected the cosmopolitanism of the previous decade in favor of culturalism.[24] They sought to remedy the problems of modernity by rejecting Western thought and embracing a timeless Japanese tradition. This broad-based intellectual movement "became a rallying cry for a broad spectrum of Japanese society including romantics, fascists, government officials, and traditionalists."[25] This sentiment found its expression in literature, philosophy, and political activism ranging from nostalgia to extreme nationalism. Despite the lure of this movement, the path back to tradition was fraught with difficulty. Hagiwara encapsulated the problematic in his famous literary essay aptly titled "Return to Japan" ("Nihon e no kaiki," 1938): "But we had been traveling abroad for much too long a time. And now, having returned home, we saw to our surprise that everything was lost: no trace remained of the days of old, the eaves on the houses were all broken, the gardens overrun; not a single memento of what is Japanese was left."[26]

Hagiwara knew that a pure Japanese cultural identity was gone forever, if it had ever existed; the Japanese were homeless and could only make the return through irony. The leader of the movement, Yasuda Yojūrō, also realized that the "conditions for modernity necessitated eliminating those elements and forms from the past that he and his associates sought to preserve."[27] But other romantics, such as Kamei Katsuichirō and Hayashi Fusao, believed a "return" was possible.[28] The Japan Romantic School may have realized the artificial nature of culture, but it still struggled "to produce a memory that belonged irretrievably to an earlier generation."[29] They never found an answer or a way to return. The critical possibilities of their project were muted by the totality of the culture they created and embraced. The adherents of the Return to Japan movement rejected modernity only to find they had nothing with which to replace it, except a dangerous complicity with the rhetoric justifying the war.

Hyakken's "Tokyo Diary" must be considered against this background of rising nationalism and militarism. Writing in the same year as Hagiwara, Hyakken does not reject modernity, but he does "produce a memory" of a past. He locates this past not in native tradition, but in the "disjunct and defamiliarized urban spaces" of the metropolis, the very site of the modern everyday that intellectuals rejected as the site of loss.[30] Hyakken discovers these spaces through his wandering in "Tokyo Diary," but this is not the rootless wandering of Hagiwara. Hyakken engages in a form of *dérive,* a type of drifting about the city akin to that in which the Surrealists and the Situationists engaged. This wandering is a practice for understanding the transformational possibility within the urban everyday. It is through this "free association" that the hidden secrets, spaces, and temporalities of the city are revealed.[31] But unlike his Surrealist counterparts, Hyakken does not wander off the beaten path; the "temporally outmoded" is not found in the "spatially marginal," but within the physical centers of modernity, capitalism, and imperialism, such as the Marunouchi Building and the Imperial Palace.[32]

This wandering allows Hyakken to conduct a literary archeology, excavating the strata of memory buried in the urban. In addition to finding the history of modern city planning, he also uncovers oral myths and local superstition, histories outside of the crafted discourse of a national Japanese tradition. In these modern urban spaces, the past returns as a disruption of the present, momentarily revealing that which was lost in capitalist progress and nationalist discourse. This experience does not hold the promise of a "return," but these momentary and ambiguous disruptions allow Hyakken to offer an alternate view of the past, one that reveals the history of an urban modernization erased by the homogeneous narrative of modernity and militarism. Hyakken's placement of his protagonist in the high city is both an affirmation of the middle-class modern life and a rejection of the cultural home of the low city. The use of these material symbols of modernity demonstrates the ways in which the physical restructuring of the 1920s was also an imaginative reshaping of the local and national, the mythical and the real, the traditional and the modern, as a new Japanese identity was forged in the metropolis.

## Images of Empire Fabulous and Forgotten

Hyakken's protagonist finds a moment of historical disruption while waiting for the train at Kanda in Episode 17 of "Tokyo Diary," quoted in the epigraph of this chapter. On this quiet night, the recently widened street at Sudachō is transformed into a vast, open plain. The hour is late and the streets deserted. Wind blows dust into moving clouds, and when the protagonist turns around, he sees a pack of wolves emerge from behind a statue of Naval Commander Hirose Takeo and run toward the Kudan district. The mention of Hirose touches off a string of associations, linking the modern city with war and a history of recent imperialism. Hyakken's story unfolds in the nexus of geographical locations, sites of memory, and the language of modernization and empire.

The previous chapter examined the cultural setting of the early 1930s as the backdrop and context with which to interpret Hyakken's recreations of the war experience. "Tokyo Diary" was written after the China Incident of 1937, as Japan expanded its violent imperialism to encompass this Asian neighbor. Just as in the earlier stories, in "Tokyo Diary" Hyakken references the current conflict via the Russo-Japanese War. But this time he does not recreate the experience of the overseas battle. Rather, Hyakken conducts a type of literary archeology, uncovering layers of both Tokyo's and the nation's history. Through this image of the Hirose statue, Hyakken examines the historical shifts in meaning of such national symbols, tracing them from the Russo-Japanese War through the era of city planning and back into the war rhetoric of the 1930s. Chapter 3 of the present study examined the ways in which these images from the Russo-Japanese War were recycled in the national imagination through consumer and propaganda films and architectural sites in the early 1930s. Hyakken showed the erasure of the losses of the earlier battle necessary to feed the nationalist fervor for the new war. In "Tokyo Diary," the erasure of history is not that of the old battle, but the era of modern urban planning. By linking icons of the Russo-Japanese War to the metropolis, Hyakken is problematizing the claims of the various conservative voices who advocated the rejection of modernity (and by extension the city) in favor of a heroic, national past, which in a time of war would include heroes like Hirose. He demonstrates how the martial is intricately intertwined with the modern. If modernity is rejected, so too is the role of the war in its construction.

One of the icons of the Russo-Japanese War, Hirose Takeo died fighting in 1904 while trying to help seal off the Port Arthur harbor. He was killed while searching for one of his men and later revered as a war hero (*gunshin*).[33] Hirose was remembered for his great act of courage and compassion, qualities often associated with war heroes from the Russo-Japanese conflict. However, Hirose's image was not used solely to support the war. In the 1910s, he came to symbolize the modern city.

Eight years after his death, Hirose was memorialized with a statue erected at the Manseibashi Station plaza, the eastern terminus of the Kōbu Railway (predecessor of the present-day Chūō Line of the East Japan Railway Company). Adorned

Fig. 6 Manseibashi Station, 1912. Courtesy of the National Diet Library.

with an impressive brick station house, Manseibashi served as Tokyo's first genuine station and city plaza (Figure 6).[34] Construction of such station plazas formed an important component of the modernization of train lines and city space. Manseibashi's location along the Kanda River had been an important site for water and land traffic since the Edo period. With construction of the plaza, Manseibashi quickly became a new Tokyo landmark.[35] The site resembles the subsequently opened plaza of Tokyo Station, on which the same planners worked.[36]

Hyakken links Hirose to the construction of the modern city by showing how images from the war were recontextualized within modern architecture. Hirose was no longer simply a symbol of military power—he came to represent Western modernity. This is akin to the original Yūshūkan war museum; the building that housed artifacts of the nation's wars was designed after an Italian castle and was redolent of Western modernism. The nation that had emerged from the Russo-Japanese War was now defining itself in a nonmilitary context by building public spaces such as Manseibashi Station plaza. As memories of the war were displaced by other concerns over the 1910s and 1920s, Tokyo's inhabitants came to associate Hirose with the efficiency of the trains and the public spaces of the modern station plaza.

Pictures from the Taishō period show Hirose overlooking the busy intersection at Sudachō. The statue was centrally placed in the open plaza in front of a stately brick-faced train station. The streets in front of the station were clogged with the chaotic mix of rickshaws, automobiles, city trams, and pedestrians. Hyakken's story starts by mentioning the urban renovation of Sudachō, which resulted in the street being widened. He employs the new language of urban planning, the *kukaku seiri* or land readjustment of streets and lots that reassigned spaces in the modern cityscape. In the protagonist's opinion, the new street was too wide, creating the impression of crossing an open field. Such urban planning projects dramatically changed the feel and look of the city, removing the close-knit spaces of the old capital. These new traffic plazas created such vast, open spaces that local residents had difficulty developing a sense of familiarity with the site.[37] However, these plazas were important in creating new landscapes and new patterns of urban life.

By the time Hyakken was writing "Tokyo Diary" in 1938, however, the once centrally located Manseibashi plaza had become an out-of-the-way place, Hirose's "bronze statue now buried in the recesses of the city."[38] As Surrealist writer Louis Aragon once noted, these are "places that were incomprehensible yesterday and that tomorrow will never know."[39] As the architectural landscape of Tokyo changed, Manseibashi's history became physically and mentally buried. Hyakken crosses a 25-year gap to rediscover this lost space. He returns to a time when the Manseibashi plaza was bustling, and the busy streets turned into a desert as dust clouds filled the air in the dry months. This was a common occurrence on the unpaved streets of the city. Although the street in Hyakken's story is paved, he retains this memory of the dust storms and uses it as a slippage point to transform the landscape and enter the realm of the extraordinary.

Hyakken's decision to represent Manseibashi plaza in 1938 as a forgotten space is ironic, since Hirose Takeo and the Russo-Japanese War took on new importance in the 1930s. During the Manchurian Incident, Hirose was eulogized in children's stories and songs. One popular boys' magazine, *Shōnen kurabu*, included a play paper construction set of the Hirose statue with their illustrated article on his "final glorious hours."[40] The statue's geographic centrality may have been diminished, but its symbolic significance grew in the national imagination and discourse. Hyakken creates a strong link with the current war through his use of the wolves. The pack emerges from behind the Hirose statue and runs toward the Kudan district. This is not a casual mention of the Kudan neighborhood. Rather, it links Hirose with the Yasukuni Shrine, and by extension, with the new war on the continent. Hirose was enshrined at Yasukuni and his memory resurrected to support the war in the 1930s. Hirose's connection to the war was further strengthened after World War II when the statue was forcibly removed by order of the Allied Occupation. (A plaster cast of it now resides in the Yūshūkan.) The statue was removed from its original location and distanced from its role in the urban planning of the modern city. But Hyakken shows that even in the 1930s, Hirose was losing significance as a symbol of modernity.

Hyakken references various eras and events in this episode of "Tokyo Diary," creating a multilayered history. Chronologically speaking, Hyakken refers to the Russo-Japanese War of 1904–5, the Manseibashi era of urban planning starting in the 1910s, and the militarism of the late 1930s, during which the interest in the city and city planning became buried along with Hirose's statue. In this wartime context, Hirose reemerges as a symbol of the war, a national reaction against the westernization of the previous decades, and an overcoming of that earlier modernity. Hirose's history as a symbol of urban planning is erased by the rising nationalism.

On one level, Hyakken is saying that the era of urban planning and the liberal cosmopolitanism of the modern city are lost. But they are not completely lost, for the past is an uncontrollable disruption of the present. Michel de Certeau describes the modern city as haunted by its past, by "heterogeneous references [and] ancient scars." De Certeau envisions those parts of the city that survived the destruction of urban planning, the old buildings and closed factories, as wild objects and spirits of the past that haunt the city. There is a lurking uncanniness in the everyday urban life of the city, an uncanniness that is ever present in "Tokyo Diary."[41]

Hyakken not only reveals the city as an "accumulation of topoi replete with expressions of memory and meaning," but he accesses this hidden memory.[42] The trigger for this memory is found in the geographical location, in the weather conditions, in the appearance of strange beasts. These moments of rupture occur, as de Certeau says, like "slips of the tongue from an unknown, perhaps unconscious, language."[43] As in *Realm of the Dead*, Hyakken moves from the everyday as quotidian into the everyday as Other. Through these intrusions of the past, Hyakken temporarily escapes a historical narrative that has erased these other historical moments. Unlike *Realm of the Dead*, the past is not found within the traditional pastoral, but in the modern city itself. The act of remembering the old site of Manseibashi Station causes a disruption of the present and transfigures the landscape. In this encounter with the extraordinary, the wolves appear to Hyakken's protagonist, and he is allowed to return to the earlier era of modernization. But this return is also an acknowledgment of the new configuration of the war and its recycling and reformulation of that very history. Hyakken makes clear that it is not possible to erase the era of modernity symbolized in the city.

In "Tokyo Diary," Hyakken mixes the historical past of war and modernization with an ahistorical, fantastic past of mythical beasts. In the Hirose episode, Hyakken may also be commenting on the fantastic tales of the Edo period, stories that lie below the surface of the modern city.[44] Hyakken does draw on one such tale in the opening episode of "Tokyo Diary," a story about a giant eel residing in the moat of the Imperial Palace. But this folkloric history cannot exist outside the context of the metropolis. It cannot be assigned to a native folk past. Such beasts are produced, reproduced, and revealed by and in the new spaces of urban planning. Hyakken's protagonist in "Tokyo Diary" does not encounter the animals in the rural settings of *Realm of the Dead*, but within a city replete with trains, traffic lights, modern office buildings, and widened streets.

Like the Hirose story, Episode 1 of "Tokyo Diary" opens with a train:

> The train descended Miyakezaka and came to a stop at Hibiya crossing. The driver informed us the car was out of service, and asked everyone to get off.
>
> In the looming darkness, rain fell in large drops. The air was still, thick and warm.
>
> It didn't seem that late, but light seeped out from the windows of the surrounding buildings and glittered in the darkening sky. (3: 191)

Although it is raining hard, the drops seem to have no substance, and turn to mist on contact, creating a smoky effect. Mishima Yukio remarks that this description of the unusual weather conditions signals the reader that something out of the ordinary will happen. This line about the raindrops acts as "a bridge connecting the real and the surreal."[45] The Hyakken reader knows that we are about to enter the everyday as Other.

Although night is falling, the water in the Imperial Palace moat is strangely illuminated. Despite the size of the raindrops, there is barely a ripple in the water's surface. The noisy, unsettled crowd waiting on the platform watches the moat as the water moves back and forth, rising and falling so as to make the protagonist dizzy.[46] The water eventually overflows onto the street, carrying with it a giant eel, larger in size than a cow. The sky darkens and the colored lights of the traffic signals reflect off the eel's wet body as it slithers across the intersection toward Sukiyabashi. The protagonist cannot tell if the eel is headed toward the canal at Sukiyabashi or the shopping district of Ginza, but he does not stay long enough to find out. He tries unsuccessfully to flee by taxi, and ends up walking to Yūrakuchō, where countless, small, two to three-inch eels cover the buildings.

The giant eel can be traced back to Edo-period oral tales of a beast rumored to live in the Imperial moat.[47] Hyakken uncovers another layer of meaning underneath the modern city. The Imperial Palace is a perfect place for his literary archeology, since it is a visible reminder of an earlier age. The scholar Jinnai Hidenobu argues that the basic structure and layout of modern Tokyo is not far removed from the previous capital of Edo. Jinnai overlays maps from different eras in the Edo-Tokyo timeline to show how the new city can be read via these old maps. In a way, Hyakken is doing a similar thing. He reads into the hidden spaces of the city to find forgotten histories and spirits of the past, which lie outside the rational discourse of modernity and the official history of the nation's capital.

The eel is not the only mythical animal residing at the palace, which is guarded by other beasts, namely the lions and dragons on the bridges leading into the main grounds. These animals are much clearer symbols of power, the lion coming from the West and the dragon from China.[48] The lion and dragon reaffirm the seat of Imperial power, and their physical representations, in concrete statues and decorated metal bridges, adorn the entry points to the palace. The eel, however, exists only in the imagination and in the realm of spoken language. Hyakken can give life to this eel within the limits of his textual, linguistic space, evoking the modernist fascination with the power of language.

The location of the eel in the palace moat is a clear link both with the center of power and with an unnamed, alternate history. The eel is produced as a wild, indecipherable disruption of the premodern and the local into a modern, national, official history. However, this eel is observed not from the position of folklore, but from the train platform. The trolley is not only the catalyst for Hyakken's story, it also provides a new space from which to observe the events. The protagonist and his fellow passengers stand on the streetcar platform as they watch the eel emerge from the moat. The eel follows the train tracks toward Sukiyabashi, the streetlights reflecting off its wet body. This disruption of the past traverses the city using the same paths as the trains, an invention that not only revolutionized transportation but that also simultaneously expanded the boundaries of the metropolis while shortening those very distances.

The trolley Hyakken rides was a common feature in modern Japanese fiction. Well-known examples include Nagai Kafū's

"Fukagawa Song" ("Fukagawa no uta," 1908) and Natsume Sōseki's *Sanshirō* (1908). Sōseki uses the train as a means to introduce his young countryside student, Sanshirō, to the modern city. Kafū, on the other hand, laments modernity and the loss of old Edo. His travels into the low city are brought about by a power outage on the trolley line, which forces him to change destinations.[49] Such breakdowns on the train lines provided a useful literary device. But unlike Kafū, we do not know where Hyakken's protagonist is headed. His departure at Hibiya leaves him centrally located in the city. Hibiya was a major stop for the *shiden*, the city line installed in 1903. Close to the palace, Hibiya was also famous for the mass protests over the peace treaty that ended the Russo-Japanese War. The unruly crowd is present in "Tokyo Diary," only now they are waiting for the train. The war, which was currently raging in Asia, is strangely absent, and the crowd's attention is drawn instead to mythical history.

Hyakken's choice of the Imperial Palace as the opening location for "Tokyo Diary" cannot be overlooked. The palace is the center of the city, even if it has been characterized as the empty center.[50] In the late 1930s, the palace was clearly tied to the Emperor and the nationalistic discourse of war. In Hyakken's story, the palace is associated with a giant, mythical eel, a beast who is equally a part of the folkloric past and the technological present. Critic Marukawa Tetsushi compares Hyakken's eel to Godzilla, who destroys Tokyo, but never approaches the palace. Godzilla is banished from the city and ultimately killed. The eel is a longtime resident of the palace moat who is able to invade Tokyo, slithering down major intersections and covering walls and windows. The beast is an irrepressible part of unofficial memory that is woven into the fabric of the modern city. This past has the power to disrupt the homogeneous discourse of nationalism, which seeks to erase the history of modernity and of the local.

References to the current war of the 1930s, the Fifteen Years War, are strangely missing in "Tokyo Diary." But the conflict is present through its conspicuous absence. In these two episodes, Hyakken looks at the shifting meaning of national symbols. Both Hirose Takeo and the Imperial Palace were representative of the war in the 1930s, but Hyakken uncovers other layers of meaning associated with these two sites of memory. Just as Hirose stood guard over the modern space of the Manseibashi Station plaza, the palace belonged to a premodern, local history of myth, now transplanted into the urban. Hyakken realized the war itself was a manipulation of symbols, and in a countermove to the growing nationalism, he provides us with an alternate means of interpreting them and seeing the inherent discontinuity in the discourse of the return to Japan.

## Missing Buildings and the Empty Middle-Class Landscape

Episode 4 of "Tokyo Diary" is set at the Marunouchi Building, an urban landmark and a symbol of middle-class culture and American-style modernization.[51] It was the first of its kind, a boxlike modern office building with Western amenities such as flush toilets. Major publishing houses Chūō Kōron and Josei had offices in the building. The salaried workers who commuted to the Marunouchi Building regularly consumed one-yen books and *zuihitsu* magazines, as they pursued modern life. Construction on the building was completed in 1913, the second year of Taishō, and it became symbolic of the new Taishō look. Poet Kawahigashi Hekigotō described the building in a 1927 article:

> Nobody could overlook the large matchbox style of the Maru biru [the commonly used shorter version of "Marunouchi Building"] as an example of Taishō era architecture. This building is, without a doubt, a product of the strikingly new Taishō reality. Those worshippers of European civilization, who deplore the nouveau riche Yankee culture, frown upon this shameless American mockery. Could this building really be in Tokyo, or are we in the outskirts of Chicago? Regardless of such opinions, it is a permanent reminder of Taishō period tastes.[52]

Hekigotō testifies to the power of the Marunouchi Building, both as a positive and negative marker of the new Americanism. Writing in the late 1920s, Hekigotō cites the opposition of Europeanists, holdovers of an earlier decade of European-inspired modernization, who looked down on American culture and the Americanization of the 1920s. The building is so American looking that it makes Tokyoites wonder if they are in Japan at all. It was this very Americanization represented in the "modern girl" (*moga*) and the "erotic/grotesque" culture of early Shōwa that native traditionalists rejected in the 1930s as a form of "foreign cultural domination."[53] Hyakken opens this episode of "Tokyo Diary" at this commanding site of modernity.

Hyakken's protagonist gets off a train at Tokyo Station and notices that the crescent moon seems oddly out of place in the sky. Normally the moon would not be visible, because it would be blocked by the Marunouchi Building, but the building is no longer there. He walks over for a closer look and finds an empty lot with puddles of water and tufts of grass. Since the Marunouchi Building also had a basement, one would not expect the ground to be so flat and even, indicating that the building could not have been demolished. It simply disappeared.

The next day the protagonist returns to the site for an appointment at a law office in the Marunouchi Building. The building is still missing, but the area is now fenced off; however, the wire is rusted and the wood worn, as though the fence could not possibly have been constructed the day before. Light flickers off the puddles as water striders skip across the surface. Nobody else seems bothered by the fact that a major landmark has disappeared; the bus driver calls out the name of the stop "Maru biru" and another man looks confused when the protagonist asks what happened to the building, as if he had never heard of it before.

The protagonist visits a journalist friend and takes him to the site. He is equally shocked. The next day, however, when the protagonist returns, the building is back. His lawyer cannot confirm the building's disappearance, since he was not at work the day before. The protagonist is tempted to ask people on the street, but he decides against it: "On the way home I stepped outside and turned around for one last look at the Marunouchi Building, but there wasn't a thing out of place. I now knew that strange things do occasionally happen to large buildings like this. But I couldn't stop wondering—wasn't the grass being crushed and where had the water striders flown off to?" (3: 195).

Mishima remarked that this scene is so realistic that the open space becomes the real and the Marunouchi Building the phantom.[54] If the building is a phantom, so too is the modernity it symbolized. The Marunouchi Building was strongly associated with the business district after which it was named and with the capitalist Taishō culture. But the history of the neighborhood stretches back to the transferal of power from the shōgun to Emperor Meiji, and is not without its own ghosts. Hyakken evokes this past in his story.

In 1890, the Mitsubishi company bought 35 hectares of land in the Marunouchi area just in front of the palace on the eastern side. The land had formerly been warrior estates during the Edo period, and became a military parade ground after the Meiji Restoration. However, the military moved to other areas of the city and the Mitsubishi Meadow—or Gambler's Meadow as it was also known—turned into a "weed covered wasteland."[55] Mitsubishi started construction in 1894, and by the time Tokyo Station opened in 1914, there were over twenty Mitsubishi brick-clad office buildings, commonly known as "Little London" (*itchō Rondon*).[56] Tokyo Station established Marunouchi as the preeminent business district, replacing Ginza as the "doorway to Tokyo."[57] The Marunouchi Building was prominently located, facing the large station plaza.

Although the area soon came to symbolize the capitalist power of the modern city, memories of the old meadow were not far in the past. The haiku poet Takahama Kyoshi described the meadow circa 1910:

> It was a day when people spoke of the row-houses, four in number, on the Mitsubishi Meadow, otherwise the abode of foxes and badgers. Here and there were weed-grown hillocks from aristocratic gardens. The murder of O-tsuya was much talked about in those days. . . .

> Marunouchi was a place of darkness and silence, of loneliness and danger. If one had to pass the Meiji Life Insurance building, a black wilderness lay beyond, with only the stars to light it. Darkness lay over the land on which Tokyo Central Station now stands and on towards Kyōbashi, where a few lights were to be discerned.[58]

Hyakken's open field recalls the weeds and foxes of the old Mitsubishi Meadow, as he layers the modern and premodern, creating strata of memory and myth. For the reader of his works, the moon and fenced in area will recall the space of "Kudan," the short story from *Realm of the Dead* in which the protagonist is penned in by the masses who await his prophecy. But in "Tokyo Diary," the surrealistic space is transported to the middle of the city, replacing a major urban landmark. References to foxes and badgers, animals traditionally associated with folklore and bewitching, fit well with the mood of Hyakken's Taishō-era fiction. But they are only temporary occupants of this new space, which was completely transformed through the power of modernization. The open field is an integral part of that self-same process.

Hyakken's story could be a reference to the destruction of the Great Kantō Earthquake, but the landscape he paints is not one of chaos and destruction. Rather, Hyakken's field is disquietingly calm and empty, its only occupants puddles and water striders. The phantom field of the Marunouchi Building functions much like the plaza of Manseibashi or the intersection at Hibiya. These newly opened spaces created feelings of disorientation in the city dweller used to the warrens of the old town. It also functions like the Yūshūkan, the phantom space of emptiness is projected onto the discourse of modernity and militarism.

In the Hirose episode, Hyakken's protagonist compares the newly widened street at Sudachō to a vast, open field. He implies there is something disturbing about this space when he says that the street was too wide. This fear of open spaces was considered a side effect of modernization and is also featured in "The Bowler Hat," a story of two professors working at the Military Academy, another important site of modernity and war. The campus, replete with imposing Western architecture, stood on a hill in Ichigaya (Figure 7). The protagonist, Aochi Toyojirō, crosses a large courtyard on the campus in order to get to his office. He comments that the distance across the narrow end of the yard was so great that it was difficult to make out the faces of passersby on the far side. Aochi develops a debilitating fear of open spaces, as the courtyard is transformed into a frightening sea by a light snowfall: "The shallow snow gave way with a crunching sound, and when I'd gone about thirty feet, I was suddenly gripped with fear. My legs cramped up, and I froze in my tracks. I was floating amidst a vast ocean. The waves reflected the sky as they closed in above me, splashing my chin. I couldn't move forward, I couldn't move at all, I felt near collapse" (109).

A friendly colleague comforts Aochi, telling him that he never crosses the yard alone, especially on snowy days when the lack of markers makes the space seem even more vast. The colleague reassures that this panic attack of Aochi's is not uncommon, and nobody would think anything amiss had it been a case of vertigo instead. Aochi, however, starts to worry that perhaps he is losing his mind, and that this experience is symptomatic of something serious.

The defamiliarization of space was a common event in the changing city, such that mental illness was referred to as "American disease" (*Amerikabyō*), "modern disease" (*gendaibyō*), and "city disease" (*tokaibyō*).[59] These terms are linked in the disappearance of the Marunouchi Building, a symbol of the modern, urban, American aesthetic. This aesthetic was viewed by conservatives of the 1930s as the root of society's ills. Kamei Katsuichirō saw the modern as an "unyielding illness."[60] But, the Marunouchi Building was also representative of the business district, the capitalist center of modern Tokyo. In this episode of "Tokyo Diary," Hyakken offers us another explanation for the disappearance of the building, an explanation not dependent upon mental instability. Hyakken's story is a literal interpretation of Jonathan Crary's assertion: "Modernization

Fig. 7 The Military Academy (Rikugun Shikan Gakkō), 1903. Courtesy of the National Diet Library.

is a process by which capitalism uproots and makes mobile that which is grounded . . . and makes exchangeable what is singular."[61] The building itself is literally uprooted and made mobile, disappearing and reappearing at will. The open field that remains can be exchanged for other fields, be they from the history of the land, some mythical past, or the fictional creations of the author. If capitalist history can so readily disappear, then so too can the ethnic past promoted by the Return to Japan movement.

Not only are the buildings missing in Hyakken's stories, but so is the war and the nation's citizens. Absence is a marker in "Tokyo Diary," as seen in the opening to the Hirose episode: "I tried my best to catch the last train home, but as always I ran late. Buffeted by the wind that suddenly turned cold with nightfall, I stood on the platform headed toward Kudan, waiting for the city train, but the train didn't come. It had gotten late and there were no taxis about, and neither was there anyone on the street" (3: 210–11).

Hyakken's protagonist waits alone on the train platform, and in the emptiness of the evening landscape, wolves appear from behind Hirose's statue. Hyakken's protagonist can justify the empty landscape in this episode because it takes place late at night. But even in the daytime, normally crowded places are devoid of people. Episode 6 of "Tokyo Diary" is one such setting. The story opens as the protagonist's friend takes him to a restaurant specializing in *tonkatsu*, fried pork cutlets, in a back street in Ginza: "Because I hadn't been there yet, my friend took me to the *tonkatsu* place. It was on a narrow alley on the backside of Ginza, and the street in front was totally deserted. 'Pretty quiet, huh,' I remarked amiably as I followed my friend into the restaurant" (3: 197). The protagonist's friend voices his surprise at the emptiness, since the restaurant is normally crowded. The protagonist does not seem disturbed by the lack of crowds, as he and his friend settle into their seats. In fact, when the restaurant becomes crowded, he feels claustrophobic. The majority of the episode is dedicated to describing the different sounds inside and outside the eatery. The hiss of the frying oil drowns out the pounding rain. Lightening flashes outside, but the protagonist cannot hear the thunder. The restaurant is filled with the sound of customers and clinking glasses, and mixed amidst the others is a sound the protagonist is unable to identify.

The protagonist hears someone coughing or choking in a doglike whine. A blue flash of lightening illuminates the inside of the restaurant, followed by a loud clap of thunder. The protagonist leaps from his seat, and the customers turn to face him. In that instant, he sees they have the faces of dogs and foxes; they are beasts in Western clothing, and in their midst some lick their chops with long tongues. The crowds, who were at first missing, have been replaced by animals. The sounds of the oil and thunder allow the protagonist to see these customers for who they truly are. The extraordinary emerges from within the everyday.

This is reminiscent of the scene from "The War Museum" in which Kimura leads the protagonist "to a restaurant down an alley off a side street that [he] didn't even know existed at the base of Kudanzaka" (1: 109). At this restaurant they meet the lieutenant with the eerie yellow skin. Although we are rightfully led to believe something strange will happen in this backstreet of Ginza, we are no longer in the shadow of the Yasukuni Shrine, but are in the main upscale shopping district. Ginza was home to the nouveau riche and the pursuers of modern life, who engaged in *ginbura*, a practice of strolling about the Ginza that started around World War I.[62]

Ginza was a site of modernization from the 1870s on, but after the earthquake it became a national symbol of modernity. By 1930, the name Ginza became synonymous with Tokyo for citizens across the nation.[63] The word Ginza was used as a catch phrase in the names of suburban shops and as a means to describe the modern style of various consumer goods.[64] Modern life was being lived on the streets of Ginza; this was the place where people went not only to look at merchandise through the new glass display windows, but to be looked at, to parade themselves about the streets.

In these episodes, Hyakken focuses on sites of middle-class culture, namely the business and commercial districts of Tokyo. These are not the places of mass culture, or the crowds of anonymity, but sites of distinction. It is telling that Hyakken chooses the Marunouchi business district and the Ginza over a place such as Asakusa. Many authors wrote about the amusement centers of Asakusa, which continued to be popular gathering places up until the 1930s. However, Asakusa did not have the cachet of Ginza. It was cheap and easy compared to the high-class diversions of Ginza.[65] One went to Asakusa to forget about life in Tokyo, but went to Ginza to live it.[66] The modern girl (*moga*) and modern boy (*mobo*), two new subjectivities, strolled about Ginza, not for the purpose of blending in, but in order to be recognized. Similarly, in the business district, the salaried employees commuted to jobs in modern office buildings, and also sought distinction in their new professional status. Hyakken's choice of locale, sites populated by middle-class subjects who had the means to live the modern life, further reinforces his focus on the unmistakably modern aspects of the city.

It is in these spaces of power, commerce, and cultural capital that Hyakken finds emptiness and beasts. Both stories function as a critique of capitalist modernity. In the first example, the site of capitalist modernity is found to be ephemeral, disappearing and reappearing without notice or reason. The citizens are so used to the exchange of signs in the new consumer culture, that they do not even notice that the building is gone. They are blind to the reality that capitalism uproots the stable and is constantly producing the new. As victims of this disorienting landscape, they have lost all grounding, be it in tradition or cultural identity, and hence they are unable to see that which has been lost. In the second story, Hyakken portrays the nouveau riche and new professionals who shop in Ginza as frightening beasts in Western clothing, hungrily licking their chops. Here, too, we can read a critique of a modern consumer culture that emphasizes both the act of looking at exchangeable goods, and the act of making oneself into an exchangeable good to be looked at and consumed.

Such a critique echoes and supports arguments made by the Return to Japan conservatives, who lamented the ready adoption of Western material culture by the denizens of Tokyo. However, Hyakken's critique is not unequivocal. He may be critiquing the modern system and revealing its flaws, but this is not a rejection of modernity, as was seen in the discourse of the 1930s. Hyakken is not looking to return to the Japan of some "traditional" past. There is no promise, or even a desire, to return. The past is as incomprehensible as the present. Hyakken's protagonist is unable to make sense of the open field at the Marunouchi Building or of the bestial crowds in Ginza. If these ruptures do point to some past, it is a fantastic and fabulous one that offers no comfort or security. Hyakken's embrace of modern life is an uneasy one, but he is even more uneasy with the illusory embrace of Japan's traditional past.

## Tokyo Station and the Literary Past

Tokyo Station serves as the middle and end point for "Tokyo Diary." The station links a number of themes through its ties to

Fig. 8 Tokyo Station, 1918. Courtesy of the National Diet Library.

the era of urban planning, middle-class culture, the business district, and imperialism. But for Hyakken, it is also a site of memory used to evoke the dark nostalgia of and the possibility of return to *Realm of the Dead*.

Construction on Tokyo Station was completed in 1914, two years into the Taishō period. It was one of the great station plazas, with a French-style brick building that housed three towers and adjoining galleries (Figure 8). The orientation of the building, specifically its entrance, became an object of controversy: the station opened onto "Little London" and faced the Imperial Palace, benefiting the business district. By doing so, it was cut off from the low city on its back or eastern side, separated by tracks and a moat, cementing its association with the high city of Yamanote and modernity, and by extension rejecting tradition.[67] Not only was the orientation a problem, but the name of the station itself was an affront to other stations, such as Shinbashi, that had been important transportation centers in the city. However, the station did live up to its name in the years after the earthquake, when it became the central exchange for north-south train lines.[68]

In Episode 11 of "Tokyo Diary," the train station takes on new meaning within the context of the war in the Far East. The protagonist arrives at the station early and spends the free time before his departure having a beer at the Tokyo Station cafeteria. The seat next to him is open, and a student with a dark complexion asks if he can join the protagonist. There is something familiar about this student; he reminds the protagonist of somebody from the past, but the protagonist's teaching career ended over twenty years ago. He assures himself that this person could not be a former student because he is too young. Despite the obviousness of this observation, the protagonist must repeat it in order to convince himself.

There is something uncouth and rough about the young man's mannerisms. He offers the protagonist beer and cigarettes, and despite the protagonist's refusals, the student does not relent. This behavior is unsettling and makes the protagonist nervous. When the protagonist asks where the student is headed, he replies that he is Manchurian (*Manshūkoku no mono*). A friend of his is returning home to Mukden and he has come to see him off. Like the protagonist, he also had time to spare, and is passing it in the restaurant. He apologizes for his poor Japanese and hopes he has not offended the protagonist. His friend later joins them and the two students become loud and argumentative, frightening and embarrassing the protagonist.

For readers of "Tokyo Diary" in 1937, this reference to Manchuria would have clearly pointed to the war, specifically to Japan's colony Manchukuo. The location of these two Manchurians at Tokyo Station is not coincidental. Two of the most important buildings in the 1920s and 1930s were the National Diet Building and Tokyo Station.[69] The former, a physical representation of the government, and the latter, a central point for traversing the capital, both buildings represented the local (Tokyo) and the national (Japan), but also the empire (Japanese colonies in Asia). As the previous chapter argued, Manchuria became a part of daily life for the average Japanese, through mass media coverage and the production and consumption of Manchurian "theme products." Not only was it possible to read about and plan travel to the colonies through advertisements and articles in magazines, but "in the 1930s it was possible to go to Tokyo Station and obtain information about train timetables all over the empire."[70] Tokyo Station linked both local and foreign cities. The geographical reaches of the empire could be realized through the train timetables, which allowed Japanese citizens to conceptualize the empire as an imagined community, a tourist attraction, and a series of exotic place names with numerical representations of the distance between them. In this episode of "Tokyo Diary," Tokyo Station is linked with these menacing students from Manchuria and distant images of the empire. This episode affirms the strong connection between modernity and the war, a connection the Return to Japan members sought to dismiss along with the modernity project itself.

The final vignette, Episode 23, calls up the failed reunion of father and son in "Realm of the Dead." In place of the chophouse under the embankment, the protagonist is now at one of the restaurants outside the ticket entrance to Tokyo Station. This episode in particular abounds in references to *Realm of the Dead*, both the collection and the short story. The reader is undoubtedly meant to recall the earlier collection and wonder about its relationship to "Tokyo Diary." Hyakken leaves numerous clues for the avid reader, leading them back to this failed reunion. Hyakken adds the premodern, pastoral landscape of *Realm of the Dead* to the strata of memory buried in the station's past. He teases the reader with the possibility of a literary return, only to reject it.

The protagonist is staying at the Tokyo Station Hotel, and as a means of breaking up his routine, descends to a restaurant in the station at least once a day. The eatery is noisy and crowded, and at first this unsettles him, but after a few drinks the noise grows distant and he is no longer bothered by his surroundings. As he drinks, the images of the people flickering before his eyes no longer assault his vision. He describes these images as *hitokage*, a term that means the "human figure," but which literally translates as the "shadow or silhouette of a person."

There are a number of obvious references here to "Realm of the Dead." In the original story, images appeared to the protagonist like shadow pictures from a magic lantern, and he struggled unsuccessfully to see and hear clearly. But in the later story, he chooses not do so, purposely drinking so as to phase these shadows out of his visual field. The protagonist of "Tokyo Diary" has the ability to control his perception, and he chooses not to see. He has become the modern urban dweller, inured to the shocks and stimuli around him.

Somewhere in the cafeteria crowd, the protagonist hears a familiar voice, but cannot tell from where it is coming. Like in "Realm of the Dead," he cannot place the location of the sounds, nor can he judge the distance between himself and the voice. He tries coming to the restaurant at different times, but still hears this hoarse voice of an older man. It is as though the voice is waiting for him. Rather than being troubled by this, the protagonist finds it reassuring. Like the earlier story, he is unable to make out the meaning of the man's words. The voice of the man's conversation partner is also lost in the noise of the restaurant. This reminds us of the scene in "Realm of the Dead" in which his father appears like a shadow, but the other men are obscured in the darkness. In "Tokyo Diary" the other man or men are obscured in the din. The unidentified voice in "Tokyo Diary" is isolated from the crowd, but this isolation does not imply clarity of perception. Although the protagonist in the later story is unable to make out any of this man's words or hear the voice of this man's companion, he looks forward to his trips to the restaurant.

Once when the protagonist is particularly drunk, he hears the voice much clearer than before and can almost make out the conversation. A week or so later, the voice coughs and the protagonist is taken aback: "The sound of that cough was an exact match for that of my father, who died thirty years ago. I thought perhaps it was my father, but I realized that my father was younger than me when he died, and the voice I heard was definitely older. Unless you continue to age after death, my father's voice would most certainly sound younger" (3: 218). This aural realization is akin to the visual memories in "Realm of the Dead," the only thing that the protagonist is able to see clearly. But just as in the earlier story, the act of remembering is not productive. It does not lead him to a reunion.

Once the protagonist decides that this cannot be his father's voice, the coughing stops and the voice returns to its former talking state. It is only a familiar voice, no longer the voice of his father. Although there are similarities to "Realm of the Dead," this final recognition, that it is someone else's voice, returns the story to the realm of the mundane. For a moment, the protagonist in "Tokyo Diary" believes he is hearing a voice from beyond, and had it turned out to be true, we can imagine him searching the restaurant for his father, as did the character in the earlier story. If indeed this episode of "Tokyo Diary" is meant to reverberate with "Realm of the Dead," it is also in some ways a rejection of it. The earlier story adds force to this one, but our protagonist is now older and less inclined to have the encounters experienced by the dark riverbank.

Hyakken's protagonist rejects the homecoming, realizing that it is not possible for him to reunite with his father. He is not in search of the past. He does not return to the countryside in order to find his lost parent. It is chance that almost brings them together at Tokyo Station, the gateway to the modern city. When the reunion does not materialize, the protagonist does not forsake the city for failing to provide a memory. Rather, he realizes the potential for encountering passing memories and layers of meaning within the city. The protagonist is not traumatized, as was his counterpart in "Realm of the Dead." He is comfortable with this vague level of familiarity and with his ability to wander through the landscape as an observer of modernity.

Hyakken, speaking as an intellectual in the 1930s, rejects the concept of a national homecoming so prevalent in the conservative discourse of the time. He is not in search of Japanese tradition, but offers the reader glimpses of alternate pasts—myths, oral tales, urban legends, and the history of modernization—buried within the fabric of the modern city itself. These pasts have been erased by the narrative of homogeneous Japaneseness. Unlike conservative voices of the Return to Japan movement, Hyakken emphasizes that the nation's history lies within prewar modernity, and this modernity cannot be rejected in favor of an immutable, yet illusory, ideal of cultural identity. The story of war heroes such as Hirose Takeo are intertwined with the history of modern buildings and urban spaces. Hyakken warns that history can only be experienced as momentary disruptions, and he observes the shifting meaning of national symbols. The temporary nature of these ruptures leaves Hyakken unwilling to commit himself to any one interpretation or ideology of history.

Lastly, Hyakken as author signals the reader that he is not making a return to his literary past. He rejects the possibility of a return through language to an "authentic literary tradition" and a realm of native aesthetics. He samples the moods and gestures of *Realm of the Dead*, but he has evolved as a writer. His style in the late 1930s was a hybrid of the fictional and nonfictional, the short story and the *zuihitsu*, the narrative and the fragment. In "Tokyo Diary" he revisits themes from earlier stories, but his tone has changed. The prewar atmosphere would continue to figure as an element in Hyakken's writing, but never with the intensity of these years. "Tokyo Diary" completes the circle, bringing us back to *Realm of the Dead* in order to release us from its grip, and from the lure of the past.

# *Epilogue*

Less than a decade after Hyakken's death in 1971, a wide range of his writings—fiction, diaries, and even love letters to his wife—were reissued in a flurry of reprints.[1] News weeklies pondered the "Hyakken boom" and scholarly studies of the author were winning literary awards.[2] Critics looked to cult director Suzuki Seijun's *Zigeunerweisen* (*Tsigoineruwaizen*), the "must-see" film of 1980, which was based on Hyakken's prewar fiction, as a means of explaining this resurgence of interest. Hyakken's work made the silver screen again in 1993, as the world renowned director Kurosawa Akira paid tribute to his life in wartime and postwar Japan in *Madadayo*. This final section examines these late postwar films as artistic interpretations that rework issues prevalent in Hyakken's prewar fiction and *zuihitsu*, and comment on the meaning of Hyakken's work in late postwar Japan.

Suzuki's film closely echoes Hyakken's expressive methods, while Kurosawa nostalgically evokes the mentoring relationship Hyakken had with his students. Akin to the literary works from which they draw inspiration, both films are episodic, lacking a formal plot. However, unlike Hyakken's work, both exhibit an elision of history. Suzuki avoids the political in his recreation of prewar life, and Kurosawa moves the war and subsequent Allied Occupation off screen. The absence of history is not limited to these two directors, but is a symptom of the cultural amnesia common to late capitalist societies, including Japan. The question remains as to whether or not Hyakken's critique of militarism can be meaningful in a world that has witnessed "the undisputed waning of history and historical consciousness."[3]

## A Phonographic Voice from the Past

*Zigeunerweisen* is loosely structured around the lives of two academics and their intellectual and sexual endeavors in prewar Japan. The film takes it title and most memorable and haunting scenes from "The Sarasate Disc" ("Sarasāte no ban," 1948), one of Hyakken's best-known works.[4] Suzuki uses Hyakken in a variety of ways, drawing freely from his prewar writings. With the help of his script writer, Tanaka Yōzō, Suzuki fills *Zigeunerweisen* with images, dialogue, characters, settings, incidents, and atmosphere from Hyakken's fiction, in the process creating a pastiche that eschews plot. Despite the fact Suzuki and Tanaka lifted whole lines of dialogue from Hyakken's stories, the author is not credited in *Zigeunerweisen*. But for the avid Hyakken reader, the references are readily apparent, and the film crafts a new narrative from the gaps in Hyakken's writing. In this section we will analyze Hyakken's story alongside selected scenes from Suzuki's film that further themes found in Hyakken's prewar fiction: the use of autobiography, doubling, and the intrusion of the past.[5] In the subsequent discussion, the names of Hyakken's characters are followed by their film names in parentheses. For those characters who remain unnamed in Hyakken—the protagonist, his wife, and Nakasago's first wife—the names of the corresponding characters from *Zigeunerweisen* will be used.

"The Sarasate Disc" is a story about two friends and a 78-rpm recording of Pablo de Sarasate's famous 1904 violin composition "Zigeunerweisen," a song that was popular in Japan in the decades preceding World War II. Although Hyakken's story was written after 1945, it reflects his prewar style, especially the atmosphere and setting. The Sarasate disc of the title was an actual record; Hyakken was given the 78 by the Natsume family after his literary mentor Sōseki died in 1916. Sōseki's son Jun'ichi brought the family's old Victor to Hyakken with 20 or 30 records, among which was the Sarasate. Both Hyakken's daughter and Sōseki's son Shinroku have commented on the record's eerie quality and the strange, muttering voice of Sarasate audible through the music.[6]

Hyakken's story comprises eleven short sections that tell the story of his protagonist, a teacher (Aochi), and his late friend Nakasago. The friend's widow, Ofusa (Oine), pays repeated visits to the protagonist's home to retrieve her dead husband's books and records, including the Sarasate. The story moves back and forth in time as it chronicles Nakasago's first meeting with Ofusa, formerly a geisha in the Tōhoku region where Nakasago was teaching. After resigning his post, Nakasago moves back to Tokyo, marries an old sweetheart and they have a daughter. The wife dies shortly after, and Nakasago, in need of a wet nurse, comes upon Ofusa by coincidence. They live a strained existence, with Nakasago dying a few years later. Ofusa cares for the daughter, Kimiko (Toyoko), and they move to a smaller house, bringing the story up to the narrative present. The Sarasate record figures again in the end of the story, as Ofusa keeps returning for it. This is because Kimiko has a recurring dream in which she mentions Aochi's name and house. Ofusa thinks Kimiko is talking to her dead father in the dream, and takes the mention of Aochi as a sign that there is something of her late husband's at Aochi's that is meant for Kimiko. When the protagonist returns the record to Ofusa, she has a strange, emotional response to Sarasate's garbled voice.

Like many of Hyakken's works from the Taishō and early Shōwa periods, meteorological conditions and seemingly insignificant sounds and actions set the stage for strange events to occur. The opening of "The Sarasate Disc" captures the protagonist's unsettled state of mind and his increasing paranoia.

The wind battering the rain doors died suddenly around nightfall, and the house grew quiet. The silence gave me a strange sinking sensation. I sat with my elbows resting on the desk, my mind a blank. My thoughts cleared and my mood improved, but I grew sleepy. Then

> I heard a small, hard noise from up on the roof. Must be stones rolling down the tiles, I thought. The rolling accelerated and the sound of them hitting the eaves sent a shiver down my spine. Whether they dropped into the garden or not I don't know, for in that instant my hair stood on end, and I couldn't sit still. I moved toward the living room, as my wife, who also heard the noise, opened the sliding door with a startle, "What is it? You're white as a ghost!" (6: 125)[7]

This opening scene is reminiscent of the atmosphere in *Realm of the Dead* and *Triumphant March into Port Arthur*. The unsettling sound of battering rain doors evokes images of a prewar Tokyo, where windows and doors rattled in the late autumn wind.[8] The eerie atmosphere is one of the many characteristics of Hyakken's prewar fiction that feature in this story.

In addition to the actual record that Hyakken received from Sōseki, there are other aspects that cross over into Hyakken's real life. Critic Sakai Hideyuki has compared the story with sections of Hyakken's diary and *zuihitsu*, written before and after "The Sarasate Disc." He culled information from the following *zuihitsu* that mention a trip to Sendai and other relevant details about the food and lodgings: "An Earlier Visit" ("Sōyū," 1934); "Okaru" ("Okaru," 1936); "Waves" ("Nami," 1938); "The Eel" ("Meso," 1951); "The Riverbank" ("Dote," 1966); and "Iconoclasm" ("Aikonokurasumu," 1967). There are intimations that Hyakken was the model for Nakasago, and that the geisha was Hyakken's second wife, Satō Koi. Hyakken retells the same story in various places and in different literary styles, a method not unique to this incident. He employed a similar method in *zuihitsu* written between 1934 and 1951, in which he describes a series of meetings with Akutagawa Ryūnosuke in the last year of his life.[9] The most moving of these presage his suicide from a drug overdose, describing Akutagawa in a barely conscious state from having taken too much sleeping medication. Similar scenes also appear in "The Bowler Hat," Hyakken's fictional story thought to be about his friendship with Akutagawa.[10] The shifting perspective represented in these textual variants comments on the impossibility of fully grasping or expressing the past, the irrepressibility of such potent memories, and on the slippery line between public fact and personal memory, themes prevalent in Hyakken's fiction and *zuihitsu*.

Repetition is another prewar feature of Hyakken's "Sarasate no ban" that lends the story its eerie quality and is used to effect in the description of Ofusa's repeated visits to the protagonist's house. Ofusa makes her first appearance in the second section, as the protagonist is entertaining his former students. He remarks that little more than a month has passed since Nakasago's death, yet Ofusa has already come twice for his books. Her visits are odd not only because she knows the titles of books of which the protagonist is certain Nakasago would not have kept records, but also because she always comes at dusk and refuses to go further into the house than the entryway. She also occasionally brings along Kimiko, who also refuses to enter the house at all and instead plays outside. Suzuki masterfully captures the eerie nature of Hyakken's scenes, as the actress playing Ofusa stands in the shadows of the protagonist's door.

The most disturbing of these visits involves the Sarasate record. After the visit by Ofusa, the protagonist turns in early, and amidst the rattling of the howling wind, he hears a faint rapping in the entryway. Still in his bedclothes, he is startled to find Ofusa at his front door. The protagonist is shocked not only by the lateness of her visit, but also by the fact that sufficient time has not passed for her to have made the round trip. She asks for the Sarasate record, but the protagonist is unable to find it. When she returns for her final visit in the tenth section, she is still in search of the Sarasate. Coming at the usual hour, she asks this time to see the protagonist's wife (Shūko). When the protagonist explains his wife is not home, Ofusa relates the details of Kimiko's nightly dream conversations with her dead father. The ghostly nature of Ofusa's presence at this late night visit is echoed in the unsettling return of Nakasago's voice from the beyond.

The ghosts populating Hyakken's story are present in the film in the form of doubles. Suzuki manipulates the cinematic medium to reproduce visually the textual repetition found in Hyakken's writing. He uses the same actress, Ōtani Naoko, to play the role of Nakasago's first and second wives, Sono and Ofusa (Oine). This creates confusion for both the viewer and the other characters in the film. Suzuki also reuses or doubles images, scenes, dialogue, and sounds, at times replaying the same visual images multiple times, yet in a slightly altered fashion. This happens in scenes of an affair between Nakasago and Aochi's wife. These images are first included as part of a sequence beginning with a visit by Nakasago and Shūko to see her sister Taeko in the hospital. The scene shifts to Aochi's house where Nakasago pursues Shūko from room to room. The images are later shown on the screen a second time, as part of a dream that Aochi and Taeko are said to have shared, only now they are in a black-and-white, silent, edited form inconsistent with the original order of events. History becomes shuffled and suspect.

Suzuki's intention to play with the theme of doubling is made clear in the opening of the film. The credits are first superimposed over white and blue screens, and then over an image of falling cherry blossom petals, intercut with close-ups of a spinning record on an old-style player. The raspy gramophone noise of "Zigeunerweisen" on the soundtrack leads the viewer to think the music is coming from the spinning disc.[11] The camera cuts back and forth between images of the disc and the falling petals as the credits continue to roll. When the camera returns for a third time to a shot of the record, the director's name appears on the screen. This time, however, the record is no longer spinning, but the music continues to play on the soundtrack. A hand enters the frame from the front right and starts the gramophone, placing the needle on the record, indicating that the music should have stopped and restarted, but there is no such break in the soundtrack. Suzuki is deliberately playing with the conventions of film music, shifting back and forth between the diegetic and the nondiegetic. And given the timely placement of his directorial credit, he all but claims responsibility for this disconnect between visual and auditory.

As the music plays on, the audience hears the voice-over of Aochi and Nakasago, who are attempting to decipher garbled words they hear on the record, words thought to have been spoken by Sarasate himself. The hand reaches in a second time to lift the needle, and this time the music stops. The silence designates that we are back in the diegetic mode, and, in fact, the credits have long since ended with Suzuki's name. When the needle is again placed on the record, the music starts and the two men continue their conversation about the strange voice, commenting that they cannot understand what is being said.

This opening sequence highlights the gap between the auditory and the visual, or otherwise stated, the gap between what we see and what we think we see, and later, what we are told will happen and what really does happen. This disunity is a basic feature of *Zigeunerweisen*, which is experienced by both the characters in the film and the viewing audience. The dialogue from this scene is used again later in the film in one of the many instances of doubling in *Zigeunerweisen*. These replications, be they false or true, tie the film together in place of a formal plot, and comment on the nature of history, nostalgia, and prewar culture.

The inability to create a linear account of history is due to the disruptions of an uninvited past, which intrudes into both "The Sarasate Disc" and *Zigeunerweisen*. This past is seen in Ofusa's repeated visits to collect her dead husband's items, the doubling, and the various incomprehensible voices: Nakasago talks to Kimiko, Sarasate speaks on the record, and Aochi hears a voice of unexplained origin.

Ofusa has a connection with the past that the protagonist cannot comprehend. As mentioned earlier, she knows the names of Nakasago's specialized dictionaries and linguistics books, despite her lack of academic training. She is also acting as his messenger from the other world, retrieving his remaining items. Suzuki plays on her connection to the past by using one actress for the role of both wives, making the second wife an incarnation of the first. In *Zigeunerweisen*, Aochi is confused when he pays his final visit to Ofusa to return the Sarasate record. She changes appearance, oscillating back and forth between the two women. This is so effective that Aochi starts to doubt himself, thinking Sono has come back from the dead. It is implied later in the scene that she does so to reclaim her daughter.

In Hyakken's story, Ofusa expresses her fear of losing Kimiko when the protagonist meets them by chance in their new neighborhood. Upon parting, Ofusa remarks that she now realizes Nakasago left her to be with his dead wife, and that he was never hers to begin with. But her plans for raising his child will not be interfered with, and she will not at any cost give Kimiko back (6: 133). This comment goes unexplained in Hyakken's story, but Nakasago's nightly visits and Ofusa's strange reaction to Sarasate's voice imply that her fears may be real. Hyakken's story ends as the protagonist returns the Sarasate record. He sits on Ofusa's verandah as she offers him some beer that Nakasago had left behind. They converse about the beautiful water lily in her garden that Nakasago had cultivated, and then Ofusa remembers the record. She uncovers Nakasago's beloved phonograph and they listen together. When Sarasate's voice comes on it startles the protagonist, because it is more distinct than usual. Although it still sounds garbled to the protagonist, at the point when it seems Sarasate is saying something, Ofusa responds:

> "No, no!" Ofusa called out. She started to rise from her seat, in defiance of his incomprehensible words.
>
> "No!" she insisted, her eyes clouding over. "Kimi dear, come, quickly! Oh no, she's not here, she's at kindergarten." She pressed her apron to her face and cried as the words tumbled out of her mouth. (6: 135)

The protagonist is unable to understand anything Sarasate is saying, but Ofusa argues with him. Her emotional response is out of character, as though the record has sent her into a trance. Suzuki represents Ofusa as half-crazed in the film, as she calls out "No!" in defiance of Sarasate, or perhaps Nakasago, who seems to be saying that Kimiko is his. Ofusa cringes in fear, afraid that he will return from the dead to take the child.

There is yet another voice in *Zigeunerweisen* that Suzuki takes directly from Hyakken's "The Bowler Hat." Suzuki borrows scenes almost verbatim of a lunch between Aochi and Shūko, and a retelling of this to Nakasago. The first scene involves a strange voice heard by Aochi and his wife while eating lunch after a visit to her sister, who was dying in the hospital.

> My wife was piling the bowls up with one hand.
> "It's a pity to die at nineteen," I went on.
> "But she might get better. You never know."
> "Why do you say that?"
> "What do you mean?"
> "She's a goner, plain and simple."
> My wife startled, holding her breath in fear. The bowl in her hand broke in two.
> I blanched, sure those words hadn't come out of my mouth. (102)[12]

Aochi relates this conversation to Nakasago (Noguchi in the original story).

> "It was definitely you. But either way it's not good. Blurting out words you aren't even thinking, and then hearing your own voice as someone else's. Pretty soon it'll be all over for you."
> Noguchi rubbed his long, wriggling fingers together. He was surrounded by stacks of unwrapped magazines, picture books with unraveled bindings, and boxes of Golden Bat cigarettes scattered in between. Randomly he pulled cigarettes out and tossed the boxes back onto the mess.
> "This is scary business. You'd better watch yourself," he said again. He really looked frightened.
> "I'm fine, I'm fine. I can't talk to you about this."
> "This goes beyond the strange and mysterious. Your wife must have really been surprised. I'm getting nervous just imagining the look on your face."
> "But my frau heard the voice, too."
> "This voice you talk about was your own voice."
> "No, it wasn't. First of all, why would I be surprised by the sound of my own voice?"

"It was your expression that upset your wife. But if by some chance you didn't say what you heard, that's even scarier."

"Now do you see why I'm afraid?"

"No, no. That's not what I meant. If it really wasn't your voice, that means you're starting to hear things. You're really in trouble now. Sure scares the hell out of me."

Noguchi gave me a cold look and went to great lengths to retrieve the backscratcher that had rolled off his desk. He swung it around in the air. (102–3)

By including this scene in his film, Suzuki deepens Nakasago's character; many critics and readers believe Hyakken's enigmatic Noguchi to be a representation of Akutagawa, the literary genius whose life ended in suicide and symbolically brought the Taishō period to a close. Ghosts from the past haunt the film and the story, as both texts comment on the high cost of prewar intellectualism.[13]

In drawing freely from a variety of Hyakken's fiction, Suzuki foregoes the construction of a unitary narrative in favor of the episodic, in the process creating a confusing film.[14] Many of Hyakken's stories, especially those in *Realm of the Dead,* are fragmentary tales of strange encounters in shifting landscapes. His characters are linked only by vague memories that may have connected them in the past, but that are never fully revealed. These gaps are left open in Hyakken's texts, since the author does not provide the missing segments. Suzuki may similarly leave his viewer guessing in *Zigeunerweisen,* but he does the opposite for the reader of Hyakken. By knitting together pieces of Hyakken's fragmentary texts, Suzuki makes links across Hyakken's stories and fills in the narrative gaps in Hyakken's originals. In the process, Suzuki creates a new text, or a second version of the original, a part of the endless process of replication.

One such example is an interlude in *Zigeunerweisen* between Aochi and Sono, which is reminiscent of an unsettling encounter between Hyakken's protagonist and a strange woman from his past in "Fireworks." In the film scene, Aochi stumbles through Nakasago's house following Sono. Along the way, he passes by objects described in "Fireworks," such as the book with old, tattered pages that holds secrets the protagonist would rather not know. At the end of Hyakken's "Fireworks," the woman accuses the protagonist of cheating on her, and this latent eroticism is intensified in the film, in a scene with Aochi and Sono in which her kimono falls back to expose her naked torso. The camera cuts to Aochi's pensive face but does not visually pursue the unstated affair.

Sex is also the solution to the puzzle of the missing Sarasate disc. In Hyakken's story, Nakasago's widow asks to speak with the protagonist's wife but she never explains why. Hyakken's protagonist eventually remembers that he lent the record to another friend; in *Zigeunerweisen*, however, it is Shūko who has been hiding Nakasago's copy of the record all along. When she finally produces it, Aochi slaps her across the face, a reprimand for her infidelity. *Zigeunerweisen* confounded the average viewer in the 1980s with its confusing storyline, but Suzuki's film adds depth to Hyakken's characters and allows the reader of Hyakken's work to take pleasure in new configurations of beloved material.

In crafting this new text, Suzuki takes his inspiration from Hyakken's prewar fiction, but there is yet another layer or temporality in *Zigeunerweisen* worth considering in light of the present discussion, namely the nostalgia for the prewar in the 1980s. This nostalgia informs Suzuki's movie and is tied directly into the double structure of the film. In the same way that the song "Zigeunerweisen" moves between the diegetic and the nondiegetic in the opening credit sequence, the nostalgia functions both within the film and in the extradiagetic context of the late postwar.

## Prewar Culture as Nostalgia

Both the "Hyakken boom" and Suzuki's film occurred during an era characterized by "the production of a nostalgia for an earlier age that it was not."[15] Prewar culture functioned as a "new boundary of the exotic" for the youth of the 1980s, who were drawn to the "emergent forms of Japanese modernity and its mass culture."[16] The links between prewar and postwar culture have been addressed by a number of scholars. Marilyn Ivy discusses the mid-1980s marketing of the prewar as "vintage culture" complete with "nostalgia products" (*nosutarujī shōhin*) and Jennifer Robertson analyzes the "landscape of nostalgia" created in late postwar Japan.[17] A driving force in the creation of this nostalgia was the marketing campaigns "Discover Japan" of the 1970s and "Exotic Japan" of the 1980s, both promoted by Japan Railways.[18] These encouraged the discovery of an exotic, yet distantly familiar Japan, and provided a *furusato* or rural homeland for urbanites who had long lost any such place to which they could return.[19] This "nostalgia for the experience of nostalgia" functioned in the marketing of the prewar as vintage culture.[20] Prewar culture was sold to a generation who knew nothing of life before the war, and for whom it was truly "nostalgia for the experience of nostalgia." Suzuki's film prefigures the height of this trend, but it could very easily have been marketed as a *nosutarujī shōhin*.

*Zigeunerweisen* celebrates prewar culture as a time of decadence and moral turpitude, highlighting the mantra of "erotic grotesque nonsense" (*ero guro nansensu*) associated with early Shōwa. Suzuki creates his own version of the prewar—a decadent, nihilistic, illusory world. *Zigeunerweisen* conveys a sense of "pastness," a "1920s-ness," through images and aesthetics of fashion. But this is neither a so-called nostalgia film nor "la mode rétro."[21] Its aim is not historical realism; rather, the film questions the nature of representation and the discourse on authenticity surrounding history and culture in the 1920s and 1930s, taking it as a given that history is slippery and ultimately beyond our grasp.

Ultimately, Suzuki is not concerned with trying to reproduce the original prewar. He is actively seeking to betray that original.[22] He questions the very act of representation through the use of a false nostalgia. With its relentless doubling and slippage, the film raises the question of what in the 1920s was, in fact, original? It also questions the originality or authenticity of our own nostalgia. Suzuki shows us that nostalgia is in itself a form of doubling, "a coexistence of several pasts and the present," and that, by extension, history and memory are as elusive as his doppelgangers.[23]

The very notion of originality becomes suspect given the multiple temporalities and the jarring mix of cultures that existed in prewar Japan. As discussed in the preceding chapters, the prewar concept of culture was tied deeply into ideas of originality and authenticity. "Culture" (*bunka*) was a controversial term used to speak of the temporal, the spatial, the material, the national, and the historical. Debates raged over whether this "culture" was the constantly shifting reality as lived, or an idealized immutable that existed only in the past or in some unforeseen future.[24]

Suzuki's movement away from an original is a critique in itself. Reality in the film is only one of many possible realities, and, by extension, the Taishō of the film is only one of many possible Taishōs. By making this multiplicity apparent (and deliberate), Suzuki strips the authenticity from any possible original. In the end, the film is a movement away from any sense of an original prewar culture, because the original in *Zigeunerweisen* is like the voice on the record, ultimately indecipherable. The doubling in *Zigeunerweisen* serves to imprint a difference between the actual prewar and the nostalgia for a prewar experience.[25] It is the overlapping of history and a nostalgia for that very history. But neither is real. Both are illusions. Nostalgia is a form of memory as unreliable as the history it seeks to represent.

In representing history as an illusion, a mere repetition of a spectral past, Suzuki steps into territory that Hyakken would have found dangerous. Although Hyakken also represents history as a fragmentary, uninvited temporal intrusion, he is unwilling to go to Suzuki's postmodern extremes. Hyakken lived through the war and witnessed the active recycling and fabrication of history in the discourse of propaganda. In his stories, he warns of the danger in suturing historical ruptures and making the actual historical timeline irrelevant, as the Japanese government did in an effort to rally support for the war. Despite the historical revisionism Hyakken experienced in the 1930s, he continued to believe that history existed and that writing was a viable means for representing it. Suzuki, on the other hand, in questioning the nature of representation itself, condemns history to the realm of illusion.

Hyakken's concept of history does not allow for the unambiguous rhetoric of a return to what he sees as an inaccessible past. But Suzuki's pastiche does not allow for any rhetoric, any critical articulation, because representation itself is faulty. Suzuki's nostalgia cannot assuage the alienation of the present, but Hyakken's writing does make that alienation grounds for transformation. This absence of history is also a feature of Kurosawa's *Madadayo*, despite its setting in wartime Japan. The point of this observation is not to criticize the films for this amnesia, but to examine this forgetfulness as a function of the era in which these films were produced.

## History Moves Off Screen

*Madadayo* has the distinction of being Kurosawa Akira's final movie. This story about the life of a retired professor opens during the war in 1943 and ends in 1962, covering his daily life with his companions: his cats, wife, and devoted former students. The character of the Professor is based on Hyakken, but the film is less a depiction of Hyakken's writing than a "psychobiography" of his wartime and postwar life in Tokyo.[26] Hyakken recorded the experience of remaining in the capital during the war years 1944 and 1945 in his diary *Tokyo Burning* (*Tōkyō shōjin*, 1955), excerpts of which were adapted for a *zuihitsu* collection entitled *The New Account of My Hut* (*Shinhōjōki*, 1947). The title of this collection is a play on Kamo no Chōmei's thirteenth-century classic, *Account of My Hut* (*Hōjōki*, 1212) and refers to the small hut on neighboring property that Hyakken resided in after his house burned in the air raids. The posthumously edited *Hyakkien's Postwar Diary* (Hyakkien sengo nikki, 1982) moves into the immediate postwar, covering the year 1949.[27]

The title of the film comes from the name for the annual birthday party the Professor's students throw in his honor.

These start in 1946 and end seventeen years later when the Professor collapses at his last party and is taken home by his wife and a coterie of students. The title is also a reference to the expressions Japanese children use when playing hide-and-seek: "mō ii kai?" (are you ready?), "mada dayo" (not yet), and "mada kai?" (not yet?). In real life, Hyakken's students started the first "Maada kai" when he was 61 and continued the tradition until his death in 1971. In the film, the professor's students playfully call out "mada kai?" (you're not dead yet?), and he replies "mada dayo," with the implication that one day he will reply "mō ii yo."

Kurosawa scholars have discussed the Buddhist connotations of this game and the theme of transience present in the film.[28] Kurosawa highlights the passage of time in a montage of paired shots of the Professor and his wife in the hut during each of the four seasons. Transience is also seen in the destruction of the Professor's house. Having lost everything in the air raids, the Professor takes one item with him to his new dwelling, Chōmei's book. The inclusion of *Account of My Hut* is a clear reference to the philosophy of transience, but also to Hyakken's *zuihitsu* collection. The film ends with another nod to Chōmei and Hyakken, a dream that implies the end of the Professor's life. The Professor is brought home from his last birthday party and put to bed. He dreams of a game of hide and seek. The camera closes in on the image of a solitary child as he calls out "mada dayo" to his playmates searching in the background. He steps out of his hiding place to look at the sky and the camera tilts upward to show a beautiful painted skyscape. The film ends as the credits begin to roll and Vivaldi plays on the soundtrack.

The film is a vehicle for Kurosawa to showcase the mentoring process found in the professor-student relationship. The students revere their old professor and toast to his importance. For Kurosawa this translates into his desire to see the continuance of his directorial legacy. Although the film does draw on Hyakken's writing, the significance in Kurosawa's film lies not in his reworking of scenes from Hyakken's fiction, but in his elision of history in favor of a cultural evocation of this mentoring relationship. The episodic nature of *Madadayo* leads Kurosawa, like Suzuki, to forego plot.[29] This "attenuation of narrative" is characteristic of Kurosawa's late films and of Hyakken's works from which the director draws inspiration.[30] But in the end, the lack of a plot leads to a private, meditative narrative in which history is banished to the sidelines.

This appears clearly in Kurosawa's minimalization of exterior shots, which, if included, would provide historical and cultural context. This is unusual for Kurosawa, since the movie is not only a period film, but one focused on an era of importance to his life and directorial career.[31] Kurosawa commissioned large-scale exterior sets both on location and in the studio, sets that showcased the destruction of the Allied bombing of Tokyo. However, these sets are relegated to brief shots used to locate the Professor's house. The war appears as a background set, not as an actor. This is seen in the opening sequence of the film: after a scene of the Professor telling his students that he is retiring, the film cuts to an intertitle informing the reader of the setting—"Tokyo 1943"—followed by an exterior shot of wartime Tokyo with Japanese soldiers marching and carrying banners. However, the camera soon pans left, moving away from the soldiers to a cart carrying the Professor's belongings. His former students unload his things into his new house, and the parade quickly passes in the background. The war is displaced by the camera movement.

The subsequent destruction of the Professor's house in the air raids also happens off screen. The air raid sirens sound and the Professor's street goes dark. The camera stops on a shot of his house and a voice-over informs the viewer that it burned in the air raids, but the accompanying visuals are not provided. The next shot is of the Professor in his hut. Kurosawa establishes the time period with brief exterior shots and a voice-over, but his camera then turns to the interior spaces of the Professor's life. The end of the war and the Occupation are similarly treated. A shot of Allied jeeps and American soldiers driving past the Professor's house, combined with brief exterior shots of surrounding destruction, signal the historical movement forward, but this serves primarily to advance the timeline of the Professor's life, not that of the nation as a whole.

Kurosawa made *Madadayo* two years before the fiftieth anniversary of the end of World War II, making the absence of history in his film all the more noteworthy. Japan witnessed a deluge of print and visual productions in the early 1990s that discussed the war and its legacy. However, the vast majority of these texts focused not on the actual war, but on the experience that prevented the Japanese from "forgetting their continuing status as a defeated nation." The war itself became an experience that was impossible to represent.[32] Unlike these other texts, Kurosawa's film does depict an experience of the war: the Professor endures the hardship of living in his hut, he and his students express anxiety over the uncertainty of Occupation-era life, and he painfully imagines his beloved cat lost in the burnt ruins of the city. The background shots of destruction are used throughout the film, but this experience of war is also attenuated to the private. There is no attempt on Kurosawa's part to comment on the politics of war or the defeated nation. In his focus on the personal, Kurosawa unwittingly inscribes Hyakken to a realm detached from the era's history, echoing the postwar critique that assailed prewar writers for substituting the private for the national and standing silent as Japan invaded its Asian neighbors. The preceding chapters have been an attempt to demonstrate otherwise; Hyakken was not only aware of the increasing militarism, but he made an active critique of it through his writing.

Keiko McDonald comments on the irony of *Madadayo*'s release in the 1990s, a decade in which economic and political collapse was accompanied by disturbing new social trends. She argues that "the old professor's love for his students and pets seems a world away from all such extremes. Kurosawa's film seems a worthwhile invitation to consider the values of that world." *Madadayo* looks back to a simpler life of wartime and postwar Japan from the perspective of extreme change.[33] This sentiment is echoed by Andreas Huyssen, who writes that the contemporary obsession with memory is a means to "recover a mode of contemplation outside the universe of simulation and fast-speed information."[34] The nostalgia, seen in *Zigeunerweisen*, *Madadayo*, and such phenomena as the JR ad campaigns, is a defining feature of the cultural amnesia in late capitalism. However, this nostalgia does not serve only as a means for mitigating the whirlwind of change around us. In the case of late postwar Japan, the desire to "recollect a true past and rewrite it superficially" caused memory to act as a substitute for history.[35] This was all too apparent in the spring of 2005, as Japanese youth responded angrily to anti-Japanese riots in China, and rallied around their charismatic prime minister Koizumi Jun'ichirō, who fanned the flames of nationalism with his controversial visits to the Yasukuni Shrine. Neither Japanese nor Chinese youth had lived through the wartime experiences described in the controversial Japanese textbook that sparked the riots, and their actions exhibited a truly dangerous permutation of "nostalgia for the experience of nostalgia."[36]

On the surface, such recent social and political phenomena may seem to have little to do with the enigmatic world of a writer such as Uchida Hyakken. However, Hyakken's prewar texts allow us to see a means of responding to war, censorship, and tremendous social and cultural upheaval. Ultimately, they serve as a reminder of the dangers of historical revisionism in an "age that has forgotten how to think historically."[37]

# *Reference Matter*

# Notes

## Introduction

1. Miriam Silverberg extends the notion of the modern to cover the years between 1923 and 1938, therefore overriding the common shift from the modern to the fascist that takes place in the early 1930s. See "Introduction" in Silverberg, *Erotic Grotesque Nonsense*, especially 4–5.

2. Writers began debating the issue of war responsibility as early as 1946. See Odagiri Hideo's "Bungaku ni okeru sensō sekinin." The article is published in Odagiri's name, but he makes it clear that it was composed with the assistance of other members of the Tokyo office of the New Japanese Literature Association (Shin Nihon Bungakukai). For a summary of the Japanese position on war responsibility, see Donald Keene, "Japanese Writers and the Greater East Asia War." Jay Rubin discusses the ways in which it became increasingly difficult over the course of the 1930s to speak out against the government. For more on the Japanese Literature Patriotic Association, the final and most effective means of government coercion, see Rubin, *Injurious to Public Morals*, 272–78. For more on the postwar debates over art and politics, see Chapter 2 of Koschmann, *Revolution and Subjectivity in Postwar Japan*.

3. Harvey, *The Condition of Postmodernity*, 20.

4. Highmore, *Everyday Life and Cultural Theory*, 23.

5. Scott, "Symbolism, Decadence and Impressionism," 212.

6. Although Hyakken continued to write in the 1940s, literature had virtually come to a halt under the oppression of censorship.

7. A number of critics regard Hyakken's diaries as a Rosetta stone for *Realm of the Dead*. See Sakai, *Uchida Hyakken: "Hyakki" no yuraku*,

110–16; Masugi, *Uchida Hyakken no sekai*, 24–34; Uchida Michio, Meido *no shūhen*, 94–100; Hirayama, *Hyakkien sensei zakkichō*, especially the section titled "Meido no shūhen."

8. The biographical information in this section is indebted to Uchida Michio, ed., *Uchida Hyakken*.

9. The wide range of anthologies in which Hyakken's work appears pay testament to this: *Selected Masterpieces of Japanese Fairy Tales* (*Nihon dōwa meisaku senshū*, 1943), *Collection of Contemporary Japanese Zuihitsu* (*Gendai Nihon zuihitsushū*, 1953), *Contemporary Travel Literature* (*Gendai kikō bungaku zenshū*, 1959), *Modern Haiku* (*Gendai haiku taikei*, 1972), *Modern Japanese Comic Literature* (*Gendai Nihon no yūmoa bungaku*, 1980), *Fifty Entertaining Stories from the Shōwa Era* (*Shōwa no entateimento 50 hen*, 1989), *Japanese Tales of Poverty* (*Zen Nihon binbō monogatari*, 1991), and even something as unlikely sounding as *International Science Fiction* (*Sekai SF zenshū*, 1971).

10. Itō Sei refers to Hyakken as a perceptual homeland (*kankakuteki na kyōri*) for the Japanese, and sees in his fiction a reflection of the Japanese mentality. He argues that Hyakken recorded the "shadows of legends, sexual desires, habits, and dreams" that live in the Japanese, and his palette was "Japanese life, behavior, and landscape." Itō Sei, " 'Shōten' kaisetsu," 13.

11. The Hyakken river is a seasonal run-off of the larger Asahi river. In the prewar period, Hyakken used the characters 百間, which he changed to 百閒 after the war. He is commonly known by the latter combination. He also used the name "Hyakkien" 百鬼園, which he sometimes glossed as "Hyakken."

12. For more on the importance of Okayama in Hyakken's writing, see Uchida Michio, Meido *no shūhen*, 108–9.

13. For an analysis of Hyakken's fiction from these years, see Sakai, *Uchida Hyakken: "Hyakki" no yuraku*. *Bunshō sekai* was a springboard for up-and-coming writers.

14. The list of Sōseki disciples includes: Komiya Toyotaka, Suzuki Miekichi, Nogami Toyoichirō, Morita Sōhei, Naka Kansuke, Kume Masao, and Akutagawa Ryūnosuke.

15. Sakai, *Uchida Hyakken: "Hyakki" no yuraku*, 283–85.

16. This project began in 1917 under the aegis of the Iwanami publishing company. Hyakken had been proofreading for Sōseki since 1913.

17. Hyakken and Kiyoko would go on to have a total of five children, two boys and three girls.

18. The Military Academy was the "principal school of the Imperial Japanese Army for the study of military science and training of offi-

cers." The school was as prestigious as Tokyo Imperial University. See *Kōdansha Encyclopedia of Japan*, 1st ed., s.v. "Rikugun Shikan Gakkō."

19. One of the reasons often given for Hyakken's late entry into the literary world is that he was busy editing Sōseki's collected works after Sōseki died.

20. All descriptions of length are based on the works as they appear in Kōdansha's *Uchida Hyakken zenshū*.

21. Critics usually group together *Realm of the Dead* with *Triumphant March into Port Arthur* (*Ryojun nyūjōshiki*, 1934), Hyakken's second collection of short stories. Kawamura Jirō claims that if these two collections did not exist, he would not have been compelled to write his study of Hyakken, for these two works are the spirit and essence of Hyakken's literature. See Kawamura, *Uchida Hyakken ron*, 103.

22. See Hirayama, *Hyakkien sensei zakkichō*, 59 and Shibata, 144 on the publication of *Realm of the Dead* and its availability in bookstores.

23. Uchida Michio, "Uchida Hyakken nōto (I)," 26–27. The earliest mention of this tale is in Akutagawa's 1927 essay "Uchida Hyakken shi." Sakai, *Uchida Hyakken: "Hyakki" no yuraku*, 21, also repeats this story. Akutagawa and Satō tried to get the book reprinted earlier, but it would take the success of *Hyakkien's Miscellany* (*Hyakkien zuihitsu*) to secure the reprint. See Akutagawa, "Uchida Hyakken shi," 1.

24. Akutagawa, "Meido," 15–16.

25. I am referring to Naturalist literature and to the I-novel.

26. Chiba Kameo discusses the emergence in 1916 and 1917 of new writers he terms the New Techniques School (Shingikō-ha). This group, which included Satomi Ton, Kume Masao, Shiga Naoya, Satō Haruo, and Akutagawa Ryūnosuke, rejected the Naturalists' prescriptives against technique and their dour worldview. See Chiba, "Nihon gendai bungei shichō," 43. They would be followed by more openly modernist groups in the 1920s. For more on the inadequacy of European Naturalism to respond to modernity, see Harvey, *The Condition of Postmodernity*, 20, 265–67.

27. Akutagawa questioned the newness of the modernist Newly Arisen Artistic School (Shinkōgeijutsu-ha) in his famous 1927 "Literary, All Too Literary" ("Bungeiteki na, amari ni bungeiteki na"). He commented that he found Satō Haruo's 1914 "The House of the Spanish Dog" ("Supein inu no ie") to be just as new as the modernist fiction of this group based around the writer Yokomitsu Riichi. Akutagawa, "Bungeiteki na, amari ni bungeiteki na," 165–67. For recent scholarship on Japanese modernism see Sas, *Fault Lines* and Lippit, *Topographies of Japanese Modernism*.

28. Sas, *Fault Lines*, 1.

29. Bradbury and McFarlane, "Movements, Magazines and Manifestos," 202. See Sasaki Kiichi for more on the Newly Arisen Artistic School, and Dennis Keene for the New Sensationalist School, especially Yokomitsu Riichi.

30. Itō, "'Shōten' kaisetsu," 13.

31. The reference to Kafka is also in Shōji Hajime and Kawamura Jirō. See Mishima, "'Uchida Hyakken' kaisetsu," 40, and the discussion in Kawamura and Irokawa, "Uchida Hyakken no fukkatsu," 200–201. Shōji, *Uchida Hyakken*, 73, suggests a connection between Hyakken's "anti-realism" and the late European modernist movements of Dadaism and Surrealism.

32. Up until the mid-1920s, a writer's path into the literary establishment was clearly, if narrowly, defined through publication in certain magazines and journals. At the top of the hierarchy stood the general interest magazine (*sōgō zasshi*) *Chūō kōron*. Hyakken also published in the up-and-coming *Bungei shunjū*, the newspapers and weeklies *Asahi shinbun*, *Shūkan Asahi*, and *Sandē Mainichi*, the women's journal *Josei*, the detective fiction journal *Shinseinen*, the economics-*zuihitsu* magazine *Keizai ōrai*, Hōsei University's newspaper, and lesser-known venues such as *Tōen*. It is worth noting that 28 of the 34 *zuihitsu* eventually included in *Hyakkien's Miscellany* were published after 1930. The "Hyakkien" of the title is both the name of one of Hyakken's fictional characters and a nickname Hyakken used in real life.

33. Hyakken resigned from the Military Academy in 1925 and was living under the burden of increasing debt. His life of insolvency forms the basis of his *zuihitsu* dubbed the "poverty tales" (*binbō monogatari*), and monetary troubles may have also been the root of his marital problems. Although it is not known exactly when or why Hyakken moved out of his home in Koishikawa, by 1927 he was living in the Waseda Hotel, and two years later he had set up house with another woman, Satō Koi, whom he would officially marry only after his wife's death in 1964.

34. Classic examples include Sei Shōnagon's *The Pillow Book* (*Makura no sōshi*, ca. 1000) and Yoshida Kenkō's *Essays in Idleness* (*Tsurezuregusa*, ca. 1330).

35. See Huyssen, *After the Great Divide*.

36. One possible way to define, or more specifically, to locate the Japanese canon is by referencing the various anthologies of modern and contemporary literature, or *Kindai/Gendai Nihon bungaku zenshū*. The relationship between prestigious literary anthologies and the canon remains undefined, and one cannot unequivocally say that

inclusion in an anthology means that a work or writer has arrived at canonical status; but certainly these multivolume sets, by virtue of their existence and availability, guide who gets read and who does not. On a surface level, the physical layout of these multivolume anthologies identifies the important figures in literary history. A visual scan indicates that certain authors occupy their own volume, or multiple volumes, while others are grouped in threes, fives, eights, or even twelves. More often than not, those in the single-author volumes are major figures, such as Natsume Sōseki, Akutagawa Ryūnosuke, Tanizaki Jun'ichirō, or Shiga Naoya, authors who need no introduction. Writers such as Hyakken, however, are in what I call "bookend volumes," and are forced to share space with other understudied writers. Hyakken usually appears with Morita Sōhei, Naka Kansuke, Suzuki Miekichi, and Terada Torahiko.

37. This may not have been the case for the high modernists or the Marxists writers and theorists.

38. Huyssen, *After the Great Divide*, vii.

39. Other advertisements of note in this issue include volumes on Nietschze studies, Dostoyevsky and modern consciousness, Hegel, and an anthology of contemporary Soviet literature. Mikasa, the company that printed Hyakken's anthology, had plans to print Hoffmann's collected works (6 vols.) in 1936, which would have included one of Hyakken's translations. See Hirayama, *Hyakkien sensei zakkichō*, 53.

40. Nogami was hired to head a new preparatory course at Hōsei University in 1920, and in this capacity he hired Hyakken and Sōhei as German and English teachers. Nogami was later promoted to college dean and director. However, in November 1933, a movement began among teachers and students to oust Nogami, who was absolved of his duties as college dean and head of the preparatory course, and suspended. (He was eventually fired.) In response, 47 teachers submitted letters of resignation in an act of support for Nogami. Hyakken was one of these 47 but Sōhei was not. The details of the movement and eventual outcome are not clear, and conflicting information was reported in the press. However, it appears that Sōhei and three other professors may have incited the movement against Nogami, and although Sōhei was also to have lost his job, he was protected by higher-ups in the school administration, in an act that further incensed the Nogami supporters. Hyakken was seen as one of the core instigators and was one of the first to be officially fired. (Incidentally, Satō Haruo and Tosaka Jun were also among those who lost their jobs as lecturers.) Eventually the head of the

school quit and Sōhei was forced to resign by the new director general. For more details and excerpts of newspaper articles see Sakai, *Uchida Hyakken: "Hyakki" no yuraku*, 255–63. Hyakken fictionalized the events in *A Busy Houseboy*.

41. McDonald, *Reading a Japanese Film*, 272n6.

42. Uchida Hyakken, *Uchida Hyakken zenshū*, vol. 1, 71. All subsequent quotations of Hyakken's writing are from one of the following two sources: the English translation *Realm of the Dead* and the *Uchida Hyakken zenshū*, unless noted otherwise. Quotations from the former are given with page numbers, while those from the latter are cited by volume and page number.

43. *Tokyo Burning* covers November 1944 through August 1945, and *Hyakkien's Postwar Diary* chronicles 1949. The latter was published in two parts, appearing in March and April of 1982.

44. This parody of Sōseki's *I Am a Cat* was published as a book in April of 1950.

45. See the epilogue for more on this film.

46. *Shōsetsu shinchō* printed the work in seven installments between January 1951 and June 1952.

47. See Tada, "'Iya da kara, iya da' no otsukai o shite." Hyakken wrote out a memo and had Tada deliver the news to the Academy in his place. Kawabata Yasunari, then committee chairman, went to confirm this with Hyakken, but after roaming unsuccessfully around Hyakken's neighborhood, he returned home unable to find his house.

48. Harvey, *The Condition of Postmodernity*, 10. Harvey is referencing Baudelaire's famous essay, "The Painter of Modern Life," 403, but he altered the last word in the translation to read "immutable" rather than "immovable." Harvey's is a common translation for the original French, and I use his version. Both the characterization of modernity in this section and the emphasis on both halves of Baudelaire's conceptualization are indebted to Chapters 2 and 16 in Harvey, *The Condition of Postmodernity*.

49. See, for example, Berman, *All That Is Solid Melts Into Air* and Frisby, *Fragments of Modernity*.

50. For a discussion of Kunikida Doppo's stories *Musashino* and *Wasureenu hitobito*, both published in 1898, see Chapter 1 ("The Discovery of Landscape") in Karatani, *Origins of Modern Japanese Literature*.

51. Tokyo's population grew from 1,874,000 in 1908 to 3,699,000 in 1920. At the same time, the agricultural Niigata, Tokyo's former rival for most populated city, lost ten percent of its citizens and fell to number seven on the 1920 population scale. Kano, *Taishō demokurashī*, 298–99. Newspaper circulation rose from 1,630,000 in 1905 to 6,250,000

in 1924, and the number of journals registered with the state more than tripled between 1918 and 1932. Silverberg, "Constructing a New Cultural History of Prewar Japan," 123–24. Along with this growth came a rise in readership. The number enrolled in higher education rose from between 40,000 and 80,000 in 1910 to between 180,000 and 200,000 in 1930. See Sakada, "Modanizumu no jidai sō," 461. For similar developments in the West, see Harvey, *The Condition of Postmodernity*, 23.

52. Kōno, *Tōki toshite no bungaku*, 258–61.

53. Kornicki, *The Book in Japan*, 5–7. For more on literature as a commodity, see Gardner, *Advertising Tower*.

54. Silverberg, *Erotic Grotesque Nonsense*, 19.

55. For more on the connection between the *bundan* (literary establishment) and print capitalism, see Mack, "The Value of Literature," 46–47 and his forthcoming book *Manufacturing Modern Japanese Literature*. For more on the expansion of literary venues, see Silverberg, "Constructing a New Cultural History," 123–24.

56. For discussion of the one-yen book, see Minami, *Shōwa bunka*, 287–302; Nagamine, "Enpon būmu to dokusha."

57. Silverberg, *Erotic Grotesque Nonsense*, 14–15.

58. See Silverberg, *Erotic Grotesque Nonsense*.

59. Miriam Silverberg notes that the press was not brought fully under government control until the 1940s. Well into the 1930s their ideology was not fully reconciled with the state. Ibid., 37.

60. Doak, *Dreams of Difference*, 48.

61. David Harvey calls this myth, in the context of Nazi Germany, "reactionary modernism." He is citing Jeffery Herf's *Reactionary Modernism: Technology, Culture, and Politics in Weimar and the Third Reich*. Harvey, *The Condition of Postmodernity*, 30–31.

62. Ida Nozomi recites one such argument by Tsubouchi Yūzō in his book *Yasukuni*. See Ida, "Uchida Hyakken 'Yūshūkan' ron," 16; Tsubouchi, *Yasukuni*, 30.

63. On Hyakken's refusal to join the group, see Hirano, *Shōwa bungakushi*, 242. The other writer Hirano mentions is Nakazato Kaizan. This is also noted in Yoshimoto, *Kurosawa*, 221. The quotation from the group's charter appears in Jay Rubin, *Injurious to Public Morals*, 274. Membership included the likes of leftist writers Nakano Shigeharu and Miyamoto Yuriko.

64. See DiNitto, "Return of the *zuihitsu*," 285–89.

65. Although prewar censorship was severe, it was also an inconsistent process. See Jay Rubin, *Injurious to Public Morals*.

66. Unno, *Modan toshi Tōkyō*, 8, 236. Unno extends the Western concept of "the 1920s" to the years 1918 to 1932 in Japan.

67. This is Unno's argument in Chapter 12, *Toshi e no wakare* (Farewell to the City), in *Modan toshi Tōkyō*. Some writers willingly turned away from their works of the previous decade, while others, specifically proletarian writers, were forced to denounce these works as part of a renunciation of their political beliefs.

68. Smith, "Tokyo as an Idea," 73.

69. See Odagiri Hideo, "Bungaku ni okeru sensō sekinin."

70. Doak, *Dreams of Difference*, xxix–xxx. For a discussion of Tanizaki's "aesthetic nostalgia," see Najita and Harootunian, "Japan's Revolt Against the West," 247.

71. Akutagawa refers to Sōseki's 1908 collection of mysterious vignettes, each of which opens with the line, "I had such a dream." See Akutagawa, "Meido," 15. He is referring to the following six stories published in the January 1921 issue of *Shinshōsetsu*: "Realm of the Dead," "Santō Kyōden," "Fireworks" ("Hanabi"), "Kudan," "The Companion" ("Michizure"), and "The Leopard" ("Hyō").

72. Itō Sei, "'Shōten' kaisetsu" and "Daiichi ahō ressha," 358; Takahashi Yoshitaka, "Kaisetsu," 130. Writing in the 1950s, Takahashi Yoshitaka unquestioningly imported Itō's characterization and even commended the expert dream writing in other of Hyakken's works. This interpretation carries over into the work of 1980s and 1990s critics, such as Takahashi Hideo, who describes *Realm of the Dead* and Hyakken's second fictional collection *Triumphant March into Port Arthur* as a realm in which "all is a dream," and there is no outside, no escape from the all-pervasive reverie. Takahashi Hideo, *Mugen keiretsu*, 180–81.

73. Critic Uchida Michio has suggested that Hyakken crafted *Realm of the Dead* by grafting his own dreams onto this model set by Sōseki. Uchida Michio, Meido *no shūhen*, 108.

74. Upton, "Architecture in Everyday Life," 711.

75. Harootunian, *Overcome by Modernity*, 95.

76. Silverberg, *Erotic Grotesque Nonsense*, 19.

77. See Silverberg, "Constructing the Japanese Ethnography," for more on Kon and Gonda. Silverberg labels these two cultural critics "ethnographers." It is worth noting Gonda's shift in the early 1940s away from the modern to advocate for the "forced representation of a unitary national culture outside of time." See Silverberg, *Erotic Grotesque Nonsense*, 45–46.

78. Harootunian, *Overcome by Modernity*, xxxii.

79. Ibid., 37.

80. Singer, *Melodrama and Modernity*, 35.

81. See Georg Simmel's famous essay, "The Metropolis and Mental Life."

82. Silverberg, "Constructing the Japanese Ethnography," 31.

83. On the "blasé outlook" of the city dweller, see Simmel, "Metropolis and Mental Life," 14.

84. Harootunian, *Overcome by Modernity*, 100.

85. The term *nichijō kūkan* was used in the sense of "everyday space" by Tosaka Jun. See Tosaka, "Shisō to shite no bungaku," 99.

86. Interest in the outmoded arose in Europe during the 1920s and 1930s, when the second technological revolution penetrated everyday life. See Hal Foster, *Compulsive Beauty*, 165.

87. Alice Kaplan and Kristin Ross provided an introduction to everyday theory in a special issue of *Yale French Studies* in 1987. As Kaplan and Ross duly note, everyday theory is contemporary with structuralism, but it did not come to the United States from France. Although both theories came out of the same period in French postwar history—namely the intellectual and political critique of the 1950s and 1960s—structuralism succeeded overseas because it was not dependent upon a knowledge of French culture or history. Unlike its more successful counterpart, the theory of everyday life has only recently begun making headway into American scholarship. The past few years have seen a flurry of books, special journal issues, and translations on theories of the everyday including such examples as: *New Literary History*, special issue, Autumn 2002; Harris and Berke, eds., *Architecture of the Everyday*; Gardiner, *Critiques of Everyday Life*; and Highmore, *Everyday Life and Cultural Theory* and *The Everyday Life Reader*. Everyday theory encompasses a range of disciplines including architecture, cultural studies, anthropology, and sociology, and surfaces in the work of Walter Benjamin, Georg Simmel, Sigmund Freud, Martin Heidegger, Georg Lukács, the Surrealists, and others.

## *Chapter One*

EPIGRAPH: Uchida Hyakken, *Realm of the Dead*, 3. All subsequent citations will appear in parentheses in the text.

1. Here I am thinking of the work of Georg Simmel, specifically the essay "The Metropolis and Mental Life." See Frisby, *Fragments of Modernity*, 72–86.

2. Pollock, *Vision and Difference*, 66.

3. Crary, *Techniques of the Observer*, 10.

4. Critics have traditionally read this story autobiographically. Hyakken lost his father at age sixteen, and wrote in his diaries about his dreams, fear of death, and longing for this lost parent. His diaries cover the years during which *Realm of the Dead* was written, and critics such as Hirayama Saburō, Uchida Michio, Sakai Hideyuki, and Masugi Hideki regard the diaries as a Rosetta stone for *Realm of the Dead*. For a discussion of death and fatherhood as motifs in Hyakken's diaries, and the relationship of the diaries to *Realm of the Dead*, see Hirayama, *Hyakkien sensei zakkichō*, 48–59; Sakai, *Uchida Hyakken: "Hyakki" no yuraku*, 110–16; Masugi, *Uchida Hyakken no sekai*, 24–34; Uchida Michio, Meido *no shūhen*, 94–100.

5. The Portuguese is *candeja*, which may have originated from the Dutch *kandelaar*. The connection to candlelight is clear. This *kantera* also appears in the story "Fireworks."

6. The barrier that Hyakken's protagonist experiences is similar in function to the barrier that exists between "sensitive and nervous" residents in the modern metropolis. Georg Simmel theorized that this barrier is "indispensable for the modern form of life." See Simmel's essay "Sociological Aesthetics," as discussed in Frisby, *Fragments of Modernity*, 73.

7. Screech, *The Western Scientific Gaze and Popular Imagery in Later Edo Japan*, 1.

8. See Introduction and Chapter 4 of Screech, *The Western Scientific Gaze and Popular Imagery in Later Edo Japan*.

9. Ibid., 106.

10. Early films were shown in sites used for magic lantern shows, alongside other media productions. Komatsu, "Japan," 177.

11. Gerbert, "A New Look," 20–21.

12. Crary, *Techniques of the Observer*, 138.

13. High, "The Dawn of Cinema in Japan," 36.

14. Walter Benjamin defines aura as distance: "What is aura? A strange web of time and space: the unique appearance of a distance, however close at hand." Benjamin, "A Short History of Photography," 209. Cited in Hal Foster, *Compulsive Beauty*, 282*n*43.

15. This word *utsuru* (映る) is the same as the first Sino-Japanese character in the word *eiga* (映画; film). The italics are my own. Despite the linguistic connection here to film, Hyakken is not employing the language of the cinema in this story. A much clearer use of cinematic language can be found in his "Triumphant March into Port Arthur" (as discussed in Chapter 3 of the present study).

16. Screech highlights the connection between lanterns (by extension magic lanterns) and the supernatural, specifically ghosts and

ghouls in traditional Japanese folklore. Screech, *The Western Scientific Gaze and Popular Imagery in Later Edo Japan*, 109.

17. For more on the other world (Sai no kawara) and spirits of children, see Hardacre, *Marketing the Menacing Fetus in Japan*, 30.

18. This is reminiscent of "The Echo," in which the protagonist is similarly guided by the auditory.

19. This repetition, or doubling, was a common feature of Taishō-era texts, which made full use of doppelganger imagery.

20. Hyakken was named after his maternal grandfather. He didn't begin using the pen name Hyakken until high school.

21. Uchida Michio discusses the connections to Sōseki, specifically to "Ten Nights of Dreams." Uchida, Meido *no shūhen*, 47–57.

22. Natsume Sōseki, "Yume jūya," 108. See also Itō and Wilson's translation *Ten Nights of Dream*.

23. Ibid., 108–9.

24. The story appeared as "The Embankment" in a minor journal titled *Tōa no hikari* in January 1917, and was rewritten as "The Companion" for publication in both *Shinshōsetsu* (January 1921) and *Realm of the Dead*. See Sakai, *Uchida Hyakken: "Hyakki" no yuraku*, 84.

25. "The Embankment" in Uchida Hyakken, *Shinshū Uchida Hyakken zenshū*, vol. 1, 350.

26. Translations of these plays appear in Tyler, *Japanese Nō Dramas*.

27. A number of stories in *Realm of the Dead* draw on folkloric images. "The Short Night" ("Mijikayo") opens with a reference to a common figure in Japanese folklore, the fox: "I left the house to see for myself the place known for fox bewitching" (45). The protagonist watches a fox turn into a woman and make a baby out of dry leaves. In his attempts to expose the fox, he kills the baby and is taken to a temple to do penance. However, he wakes in the morning to find it was all an illusion. In Hyakken's stories, folklore plays itself out on the body, changing the very physicality of his characters. The animal-like transformations of women into dogs, cats, and cows in some of Hyakken's later stories from the *Port Arthur* collection—"Envoy to Tang China" ("Kentōshi,"), "Magnolia" ("Mokuren,"), and "Wisteria" ("Fuji no hana")—are reminiscent of the "non-human wives" of folklore. The alluring woman in "Jintōshi" unnerves the protagonist when he notices her foxlike hands and animal-like behavior, and the young wife in "The Short Night" is in reality a fox. A number of Hyakken's female characters have qualities akin to the folkloric *yama-uba*, or mountain crone. The old woman in "Seaweed" ("Ryūsō"), who is killed by the protagonist and reborn as a young girl, provides one such example. The transformational process is not,

however, limited to women. Other examples include the small guest who is actually an ant in "Santō Kyōden," and the animal herbalist's brother in "Jintōshi," whose face is transformed into a horse at the conclusion of the story. For more on folklore in Hyakken, see Akiyama, "Semarikuru mizu to kaze," 112. For more on folklore and women, see Chapters 2 and 6 of Kawai, *The Japanese Psyche*.

28. Benjamin, *Illuminations*, 83, 88–89.

29. For more discussion of the origins and uses of the *kudan* story, see Gensō bungaku kikakushitsu, ed. *Tokushū: kudan, minotaurosu, gyū-yō densetsu*.

30. Cited in Kataoka, "Uchida Hyakken 'Kudan' o yonde," 98.

31. Kawamura dedicated a chapter to this story. See Kawamura, *Uchida Hyakken ron*, 136–39.

32. See Takahashi Hideo, *Mugen keiretsu*, 189; Kawamura, *Uchida Hyakken ron*, 142.

33. Figal, *Civilization and Monsters*, 4.

34. Benjamin, *Illuminations*, 88–89. For more on the government's abolishment of local folkways in Meiji, and on the coexistence of mythical animals and modern technology, see Michael Foster's articles, "Strange Games and Enchanted Science" and "Walking in the City with Natsume Sōseki."

35. The protagonist never arrives at the Ushimado harbor in "Fireworks," or at the police station in "Driftwood." In "The Companion" he travels in circles. See Kōno, *Tōki toshite no bungaku*, 271.

36. For more on fragmentation as a feature of the modern experience, see Frisby, *Fragments of Modernity*.

37. The echo of his footsteps in this passage reverberates with the title of the story, although different Sino-Japanese characters are used for the two words. The title of the story is "Kodama," as in the two character combination for "tree spirit" (木霊), whereas the verb used for the echo of his footsteps is from the single character (谺) with the *tani* or valley radical, pronounced *kodamasu* (谺す) or *ka* in the Chinese reading.

38. Highmore, *Everyday Life and Cultural Theory*, 67. See Benjamin's essay "On Some Motifs in Baudelaire" in *Illuminations*. See Frisby, *Fragments of Modernity*, 61–68 for more on Simmel and the difference between his and Benjamin's conceptualizations of experience. This concept of experience is not unique to Benjamin and Simmel, and has been taken up by a number of other German thinkers.

39. Benjamin, *Illuminations*, 184.

40. Highmore, *Everyday Life and Cultural Theory*, 67–68. This idea of repetition is also central to notions of the everyday as theorized by

Lefebvre. See Highmore, *Everyday Life and Cultural Theory*, 128. Baudelaire was also concerned with the transitory, passing moment, as discussed in his essay, "The Painter of Modern Life." For more on Baudelaire, see Frisby, *Fragments of Modernity*, 14–20, 45.

41. Yamaguchi, "Meido ni sasurau kotoba," 70.

42. Ibid., 73.

43. Ibid., 74.

44. Morita Sōhei, " 'Meido' sono ta," 101–2.

45. Kawamura and Tanemura, "Meiseki naru seishin hakujaku," 68–69.

46. Waki, "Monogatari no nai fūkei," 83.

47. The argument in this section is indebted to the chapter on Hyakken in Kōno, *Tōki toshite no bungaku*.

48. As discussed above, there are extratextual references such as those to Sōseki's "Ten Nights of Dreams" or Hyakken's "The Embankment," but the links have been severed such that the protagonist cannot follow them back to the source.

49. Kōno refers to a line from a Hyakken story called "The Dragonfly Marble" ("Tonbodama," 1929) which opens with the following line: "The word I here refers to the I of the story, not to the author himself" (Watashi to iu no wa bunshōjō no watashi desu. Hissha jishin no koto de wa arimasen) (1: 288). I discuss this in Chapter 2 in relation to the narrative stance of the I-novel.

50. For more on the unnatural use of pronouns, see Chapter 5 of Indra Levy, *Sirens of the Western Shore*.

51. Ten of the eighteen stories in *Realm of the Dead* have the explicit first-person pronoun *watashi* in the opening sentence.

52. Kōno, *Tōki toshite no bungaku*, 269.

53. Despite his awareness of Hyakken's unnatural emphasis on the first-person pronoun, Kōno is consciously breaking with a tradition of reading Hyakken's stories as thinly veiled autobiography, and clearly distinguishing Hyakken's texts from those of the I-novelists. Kōno, *Tōki toshite no bungaku*, 269.

54. There are examples of children and/or a wife in "The Echo," "Kudan," "Driftwood," "The Companion," "The Smallpox Demon," and "The Pier." Both "Realm of the Dead" and "The Companion" mention a father who is assumed to be dead. The last story also mentions an unborn brother.

55. Kōno, *Tōki toshite no bungaku*, 269–70, 282.

56. This extreme indeterminacy does not translate well into English, and hence most references were removed from the translation. For more on language, see Kōno, *Tōki toshite no bungaku*, 276–78.

57. See Simmel, "The Metropolis and Mental Life"; Benjamin's comments on the everyday in "The Work of Art in the Age of Mechanical Reproduction," *Illuminations*; and Felski, "Introduction," 608.

58. Kōno, *Tōki toshite no bungaku*, 276.

59. Frisby, *Fragments of Modernity*, 80.

60. This story is mentioned in Kōno, *Tōki toshite no bungaku*, 281.

61. See "Jintōshi" in *Uchida Hyakken zenshū*, vol. 1, 18.

62. Kōno, *Tōki toshite no bungaku*, 268–69. These are Kōno's words to describe Hyakken's style.

63. Ibid., 269; Lefebvre, *Everyday Life in the Modern World*, 37.

64. Masugi, *Uchida Hyakken no sekai*, 51; Shōji, *Uchida Hyakken*, 47, 75; Mishima, "'Uchida Hyakken' kaisetsu," 38.

65. Felski, 609–10. For de Certeau, they are "gestures" from the "multifarious and silent 'reserve' of procedures" hidden in the everyday (*The Practice of Everyday Life*, 48).

66. Here I am thinking of Benjamin, Lefebvre, and de Certeau, who, unlike Hyakken, saw the possibility of change on the level of practice.

67. Kōno, *Tōki toshite no bungaku*, 268. When Kōno says Hyakken returns magic to the language, he is referring to Hyakken's use of the Sino-Japanese character for the word *kudan* (件). However, his observation can encompass a larger sense as noted above.

68. Any evaluation of the contemporary reaction to *Realm of the Dead* in 1922 must take into account that the experience of reading the original text is qualitatively different than one based on subsequent reprints (*bunko*, *zenshū*, thematic anthologies, etc.).

69. Peter Kornicki describes the prominence of cover designs from the seventeenth century onward (Kornicki, *The Book in Japan*, 56–57). I have not been able to determine how much of a role, if any, Hyakken had in the cover design for *Realm of the Dead*. Modern authors designed covers themselves, worked closely with famous artists, or turned the design decisions completely over to the artist. Regardless of who made the decision in Hyakken's case, the fact that the cover of *Realm of the Dead* is so spare can be read as a conscious act to reject more detailed cover art.

70. Hirayama, *Hyakkien sensei zakkichō*, 56. According to Hirayama, the publisher misaligned the pages and Hyakken was embarrassed and disappointed with the poor presentation (ibid., 59).

71. Cited in Kōno, *Tōki toshite no bungaku*, 266. A version of this story also appears in Hirayama, *Hyakkien sensei zakkichō*, 59.

72. Kōno, *Tōki toshite no bungaku*, 266.

73. Ibid., 267.

74. Kornicki, *The Book in Japan*, 27.

75. Benjamin, *Illuminations*, 186.

76. Kornicki, *The Book in Japan*, 29.

77. Kōno, *Tōki toshite no bungaku*, 258–61.

78. Benjamin, *Illuminations*, 223.

79. Nagamine, *Zasshi to dokusha no kindai*, 8–9.

80. Hirayama, *Hyakkien sensei zakkichō*, 59. Hirayama relates a story about two of Hyakken's students who found *Realm of the Dead* in a bookstore and were surprised at the lack of page numbers. They bought a copy and went to visit Hyakken for an explanation.

81. Genette, *Paratexts*, 34.

82. Huyssen, *Twilight Memories*, 3.

83. This contrasts with the spirits of the *nō* theatre (or the priest in "The Embankment"), who are freed from the karmic cycle by narrating their past.

84. For another instance of this, see "The Albino" ("Shirako"). The protagonist is walking down the street mentally affirming his belief that there is no God, when a woman walks up to him and says, "That's not right. God does exist" (62).

85. Other than the crying of the woman and her child in "The Echo," there are no verbalizations that occur within the present tense of the story. When the protagonist remembers the sound of his footsteps, it is the voice of the woman in his memory that corrects his unspoken assumption.

86. Huyssen, *After the Great Divide*, 52.

87. Examples of such works include Tayama Katai's "Futon" and Tanizaki Jun'ichirō's *Naomi*. See Levy, *Sirens of the Western Shore* for more on these female representations.

88. For more on this process, see "The Work of Art in the Age of Mechanical Reproduction," in Benjamin, *Illuminations*.

89. For more on Benjamin's optimism, see Huyssen, *After the Great Divide*, 14; Highmore, *Everyday Life and Cultural Theory*, 68. Highmore discusses this in relation to Benjamin's *One-Way Street* and "The Work of Art in the Age of Mechanical Reproduction."

90. Hyakken did continue to write fiction, but the vast majority of his work is in the *zuihitsu*.

## *Chapter Two*

EPIGRAPH: Tosaka, "Shisō to shite no bungaku," 27.

1. During these years, Hyakken continued to write and publish stories in the vein of *Realm of the Dead*. These were subsequently

included in his second collection *Triumphant March into Port Arthur.* He also actively began to write the *zuihitsu* that would form the collection *Hyakkien's Miscellany.*

2. Tosaka, "Shisō to shite no bungaku," 27–28.

3. Silverberg analyzes the choices and interpretations made by consumers that she reads as modern, specifically the mixing of native and foreign "gestures, objects and words." Silverberg, *Erotic Grotesque Nonsense,* 32. See Looser, "From Edogawa to Miyazaki" for a discussion on intermedia.

4. It is ironic that the Akutagawa Prize ended up excluding the *zuihitsu,* given the prominent role played by Kikuchi Kan, creator of the prize, and his magazine *Bungei shunjū* in promoting the *zuihitsu* in the 1920s.

5. The establishment of new critical criteria for evaluating the modern *zuihitsu* is an issue that needs to be addressed, but this is a project beyond the bounds of this book.

6. For more on the separate placement in journals of *zuihitsu* and literature, and on the *zuihitsu*'s connection to censorship, see DiNitto, "Return of the *zuihitsu.*" Miriam Silverberg discusses Tosaka Jun's reaction to the government's fascist control of mores as a form of censorship. See Silverberg, *Erotic Grotesque Nonsense,* 34–35.

7. See Chapter 3 for more on militarism in the 1930s.

8. Huyssen uses the term "Great Divide" to describe the distinction between high art and mass culture.

9. See Kōno, *Tōki toshite no bungaku,* 261–62, for more on Hyakken's use of different Sino-Japanese characters to write his own surname. For further examples, see Uchida Hyakken, *Uchida Hyakken zenshū,* vol. 1, 243.

10. Kawamura and Irokawa, "Uchida Hyakken no fukkatsu," 186; Morita Sakan, *Oboegaki Hyakkien nōto,* 4.

11. Contemporary critic Takada Mizuho acknowledged Hyakken, along with Akutagawa, as one of the elite *zuihitsu* writers. Takada, "Kindai no zuihitsu," 121.

12. Miki, "Zuihitsu jidai."

13. Almost two-thirds of Hyakken's total production is *zuihitsu.*

14. The above list is representative of the types of writing featured in the *zuihitsu* column in issues of the journal *Bungei shunjū* dating from the 1920s and early 1930s.

15. See DiNitto, "Return of the *zuihitsu.*"

16. There is no systematic study of the *zuihitsu* as a modern literary genre. However, the following scholars do refer to the *zuihitsu* within their discussions of modern literature, which are usually

focused around the I-novel (*shishōsetsu*): Marleigh Ryan, "Modern Japanese Fiction" 249–66; Tomi Suzuki, *Narrating the Self*, 205n29; Fowler, *The Rhetoric of Confession*, 84–86. The primary scholarship on premodern *zuihitsu* has been written by Yoshida Seiichi, Hasegawa Izumi, and Linda Chance. Chance's *Formless in Form* is the most recent. She notes that Hasegawa's and Yoshida's are the only monograph-length reconsiderations of the genre, and they are now outdated (both were originally published in 1965). Yoshida, *Zuihitsu no sekai*; Hasegawa, *Zuihitsu dokkai no riron*.

17. There are fewer instances of the reverse situation, a *zuihitsu* being included in a short story collection, but examples do exist.

18. Page length and numbers are from Kōdansha's *Uchida Hyakken zenshū*.

19. Chiba made this comment in an essay titled "Zenki zuihitsuka raisan" in the inaugural issue of the second incarnation of the journal *Zuihitsu* (June 1926). Cited in Wada, "Kindai no zuihitsu to zuihitsu no 'kindai,'" 286–87. The *zuihitsu* appealed to readers who were burdened by the weighty offerings in intellectual journals such as *Chūō kōron* and *Kaizō*, as well as by dense political writing and the experimental and often convoluted modernist productions published in other journals of the era. See DiNitto, "Return of the *zuihitsu*," 265.

20. Chiba, "Zenki zuihitsuka raisan," as cited in Wada,"Kindai no zuihitsu to zuihitsu no 'kindai,'" 286–87.

21. This match between protagonist and author is also the case in "The Memoirs of Professor Hyakkien."

22. The story is in the *Port Arthur* collection and originally dates from 1929.

23. The quotation is from Hirayama's *Waga Hyakkien sensei* and is cited in Uchida Michio, Meido *no shūhen*, 149. Hirayama mentions Hyakken's resistance to this theory in his afterword to Hyakken's *Watashi no "Sōseki" to "Ryūnosuke,"* 266–67.

24. Sakai, *Uchida Hyakken: "Hyakki" no yuraku*, 208–14.

25. See Sakai, *Uchida Hyakken: "Hyakki" no yuraku*, 216n14. See also "The Nightingale" in *The Bumpy Road* (*Dekoboko michi*), Uchida Hyakken, *Uchida Hyakken zenshu*, vol. 2, 185.

26. Philippe Lejeune uses the concept of an "autobiographical pact" to indicate a contractual agreement between consumer and producer, an affirmation in the text that the identity of the character in the story refers back to the name of the author on the cover. When the author invites the reader to extend this pact to everything he has written, even fictional works, Lejeune describes the opening of an "autobiographical space." Lejeune, *On Autobiography*, 13, 26.

27. See Lejeune, *On Autobiography*, and also Odagiri Susumu, *Kindai Nihon no nikki*, who claims other modern authors, such as Higuchi Ichiyō, Ishikawa Takuboku, and Shiga Naoya, used their diaries as testing grounds or springboards for their fiction. Odagiri Susumu, *Kindai Nihon no nikki*, 17–18.

28. The word *tonbodama* refers to a small, round glass bead or marble often of a deep blue color with yellow specks, so called because it resembles a dragonfly's eye. They are often found in ancient Japanese burial mounds dating back as far as the third century. The object in this story comes from Taiwan and is light green with white lines.

29. The original Japanese of the prefatory line reads: "Watashi to iu no wa bunshōjō no watashi desu. Hissha jishin no koto de wa arimasen." The first line of the text proper reads: "Sate, watashi wa iroiro no kōto ga ki ni kakatte komaru."

30. Kōno, *Tōki toshite no bungaku*, 270–71.

31. This can be seen as an instance of Philippe Lejeune's "phantasmic pact": "This has meaning in relation to me, but is not I" (Lejeune, *On Autobiography*, 33).

32. This essay, "Terada Torahiko hakase," appeared in *Chūō kōron*, and was later included in Hyakken's collection *Rapture* (*Uchōten*) published in July 1936. Terada died in December 1935.

33. Genette argues that a book title asks the reader to "look on the book" as a certain genre. He terms this expectation as "illocutionary force." Genette, *Paratexts*, 10–11, 94. Genette is drawing on the work of speech act theorists J. L. Austin and John Searle.

34. This is volume ten in the series *Library of Zuihitsu and Impressionistic Writing* (*Zuihitsu kansō sōsho*), one of the many *zuihitsu* anthologies that Tosaka mentioned in his essay. See the original advertisement for the series in DiNitto, "Return of the *zuihitsu*," 261.

35. By "paratext," Genette refers to the accompanying productions of the text—author's name, title, preface, illustrations—that enable it to become a book. Genette argues that "a text without a paratext does not exist and never has existed." See Genette, *Paratexts*, 1, 3.

36. Chance, *Formless in Form*, 32.

37. Ibid., 28. Chance goes on to argue otherwise in her book.

38. Yoshida, *Zuihitsu no sekai*, 9.

39. Ibid., 9. Hasegawa Izumi also defines the *zuihitsu* as "a literary genre that manifests the self," Hasegawa, *Zuihitsu dokkai no riron*, 77. He argues, compared to the novel and drama, which incorporate fictional material, the *zuihitsu*, because it is based on raw experience, requires that more attention be given to the construction of the author's experience and thought. Hasegawa, *Zuihitsu dokkai no riron*, 80.

40. Murō, "*Hyakkien zuihitsu*," 152.

41. Lejeune, *On Autobiography*, 13.

42. Yoshida, *Zuihitsu no sekai*, 9.

43. Hasegawa, *Zuihitsu dokkai no riron*, 80.

44. Cited in Wada, "Kindai no zuihitsu to zuihitsu no 'kindai,'" 187.

45. Chiba, "Zuihitsu ni tsuite," 288; Yoshida, "Akutagawa Ryūnosuke shū kaisetsu," 37.

46. Nakaya, "Terada Torahiko no tsuisō," 425.

47. The translation is from Tomi Suzuki, *Narrating the Self*, 49. See also Suzuki's Chapter 3 on the I-novel and authenticity.

48. Ibid., 51.

49. The quotation is from a preface to *Koi kara ai e*, an anthology of Chikamatsu's works. The translation is from Fowler, *The Rhetoric of Confession*, 154.

50. Lejeune, *On Autobiography*, 27.

51. Itō Sei, *Shōsetsu no hōhō* (1948), as cited in Hijiya-Kirschnereit, *Rituals of Self-Revelation*, 83. Also see remarks on Itō and Hirano in Hijiya-Kirschnereit, *Rituals of Self-Revelation*, 299. Marleigh Ryan also discusses the connection between premodern *zuihitsu*, diaries, and modern literature, although not exclusively the I-novel. See Ryan, "Modern Japanese Fiction."

52. Keene, *Seeds in the Heart*, 9.

53. Chance, *Formless in Form*, 27.

54. Toyama Shigehiko comments on the shared features of the two genres, interestingly noting that the popularity of the *zuihitsu* seems tied to the popularity of the I-novel (Toyama, "Zuihitsuteki naru mono no han'i," 13).

55. Tosaka, "Shisō to shite no bungaku," 28.

56. Tomi Suzuki, *Narrating the Self*, 7.

57. Ujita Hyakugen appears in *I Am a Cat: The Fake Version* (*Gansaku wagahai wa neko de aru*, 1950).

58. Nakamura Mitsuo, as quoted in Cohn, *Studies in the Comic Spirit in Modern Japanese Fiction*, 25. The original is from Nakamura, "Warai no sōshitsu," 113–15.

59. For more on *zuihitsu* and literary journals in the 1920s and 1930s, see DiNitto, "Return of the *zuihitsu*."

60. Takeuchi Michinosuke, "*Hyakkien zuihitsu* gaiden," 304–5.

61. Mack, "The Value of Literature," 190–91.

62. Ibid., 192.

63. Nagamine, "Enpon būmu to dokusha," 202–3.

64. Morita Sakan, *Oboegaki Hyakkien nōto*, 4.

65. Iwanami had made its name on classic bestsellers such as Natsume Sōseki's collected works, and on *bunko*, smaller sized and less expensive books on the humanities and natural and social sciences. Unlike the subscription one-yen book series, which forced consumers to purchase all volumes in the set, Iwanami *bunko* could be sold individually, allowing the reader to choose topics of interest to them. The publishing house made its reputation for selling high-quality texts, unlike rival Kaizōsha, who sought to publish widely from the highbrow and popular realms. For more in English, see Mack, "The Value of Literature," 175–90.

66. Hagiwara, "Suisenbun," 445.

67. Murō, *Tsuru*, 338.

68. Uchida Hyakken, *Uchida Hyakken zenshū*, vol. 2, 323.

69. See, for example, the critical roundtable (*gappyōkai*) in the April 1924 issue of *Shinchō*. The participants, including Kume Masao, Uno Kōji, and Nakamura Murao, discuss whether a recent story by Kume can be classified as a novel (*shōsetsu*). The issue becomes complicated when Kume admits he intended to write a *zuihitsu shōsetsu*. For more on mixed terminology, see Imai, "Zuihitsu hanran to zuihitsuteki shōsetsu."

70. Murō's sentiments were echoed in the 1980s and 1990s by scholars who felt a similar need to validate Hyakken. One prominent Hyakken scholar, Sakai Hideyuki, describes Hyakken's *zuihitsu* as "novelistic *zuihitsu*" (*Uchida Hyakken: "Hyakki" no yuraku*, 205). Shōji Hajime also dubs the works I-novels (*Uchida Hyakken*, 183).

71. Wada Toshio comments on the low status of the modern *zuihitsu* ("Kindai no zuihitsu to zuihitsu no 'kindai,'" 278). Tomi Suzuki asserts the I-novel was always a "value-laden concept" (*Narrating the Self*, 3). See also Mack, "The Value of Literature."

72. Hagiwara, "Zuihitsu to wa nan zo ya," 313.

73. Murō's review is reprinted in Murō, "*Hyakkien zuihitsu*," 153. Despite his early criticism, Murō went on to try his hand at the *zuihitsu* and even published his own collections.

74. Strecher, "Purely Massive or Massively Pure?" 362.

75. Huyssen, *After the Great Divide*, viii.

76. For more on these attempts, see Strecher, "Purely Massive or Massively Pure?"; Suzuki Sadami, "Junbungaku to taishū bungaku"; and Chapter 4 of Mack, "The Value of Literature."

77. Kikuchi Kan, editor and writer for the literary journal *Bungei shunjū*, complained that the rival journal *Zuihitsu* was out-pricing the competition with their high manuscript fees. For more, see DiNitto, "Return of the *zuihitsu*," 260–63.

78. The situation changed somewhat for *zuihitsu* when Kikuchi Kan further solidified the pure/popular divide and changed the face of literary history by creating two prizes in 1935: the Akutagawa Prize for pure literature and the Naoki Prize for popular literature. The prize committees were filled with members of the literary elite and the winners of the former had their work published in *Bungei shunjū* and the latter in *Ōru yomimono*, the popular *Bungei shunjū* spin-off. In this way, Kikuchi established the boundary via literary and commercial means. In doing so, he limited the definition of literature to the novel (and by extension the short story), and excluded other genres such as the *zuihitsu*. For more on this argument, see Chapter 5 of Mack, "The Value of Literature."

79. The term popular literature (*taishū bungaku*) does not necessarily indicate only lowbrow literature, nor was popular literature always a reflection of popular culture. The popularization of literature and truly popular literature are two different things. Suzuki Sadami, "Junbungaku to taishū bungaku," 175.

80. DiNitto, "Return of the *zuihitsu*," 267.

81. The information in the following section is based on entries for the separate magazines and weeklies in Nihon kindai bungakukan, ed., *Nihon kindai bungaku daijiten*, vol. 5, s.v. *shinbun, zasshi*.

82. Hyakken's *zuihitsu* were featured regularly in both national and local papers; between 1933 and 1936, Hyakken published one-third to one-half of his *zuihitsu* in newspaper weeklies and dailies.

83. Another venue in which Hyakken published was the *Sandē Mainichi*. Originally created by the *Mainichi shinbun* as an American-style Sunday paper, the *Sandē Mainichi* debuted alongside *Shūkan Asahi*. In its first year, the *Sandē Mainichi* published a special quarterly issue devoted to fiction, and in 1924 added serialized novels at the beginning of each regular issue. This was a turning point in the history of the weeklies, marking them as a popular, fiction-based medium. In 1926, the *Mainichi*'s weekly initiated a prize contest for popular literature, and was tremendously influential in the promotion of this literature and its new authors. This was mainly through the efforts of its fourth editor, Chiba Kameo, a great supporter of the *zuihitsu*.

84. *Keizai ōrai* mimicked Kikuchi Kan's formula for success and the strategy yielded results: within one year, circulation rose from 28,000 to 100,000 copies per issue. Surveys from the bookstore at Tokyo Station, in the business district, show that sales of *Keizai ōrai* were solid with this group of readers, ranking between the literary journal *Shinchō* and the general interest magazine *Chūō kōron*. By publishing established writers, the editors were able to raise the prestige level of

the magazine. In addition to fiction, the magazine is noteworthy for important critical essays, including Tanizaki Jun'ichirō's tongue-in-cheek paean on Japanese aesthetics, "In Praise of Shadows" ("In'ei raisan," 1933) and Kobayashi Hideo's critique, "Discourse on the I-novel" ("Watakushi shōsetsu ron," 1935). This combination of literature and economics seems eclectic, but given the careers and lifestyles of middle-class readers, it proved to be a smart marketing decision. See Nagamine, *Modan toshi*, 213, 215.

85. Despite its status as a literary journal, the magazine distinguished itself from more prestigious sites by nature of its readership. *Josei* regularly glossed the Sino-Japanese characters, providing a reading aid not present in the elite journals. The use of this glossing signals the journal's recognition of and desire to cater to a less educated consumer. This is interesting since *Josei*'s audience is usually considered to be the intellectual female. Women constituted a new reading class in this period, and although the educated professional numbered among them, magazines such as *Josei* could not, or would not, take the risk of alienating its audience by eliminating the reading guides.

86. *Josei* featured Tanizaki Jun'ichirō's novel *Naomi* (*Chijin no ai*, 1924–25), which captured the new, modernist "simple lifestyle" (*shinpuru raifu*) of the 1920s. Readers lived vicariously through Tanizaki's heroine Naomi, who resembled the famous American movie star Mary Pickford. *Naomi* began as a serial piece in the *Ōsaka Asahi shinbun* on March 20, 1924, but due to increasing pressure from the censors, the newspaper ended serialization on June 14. Tanizaki resumed publication in the November issue of *Josei* and finished it in July of the following year. Writers such as Tanizaki used women's magazines as a venue for middle-length stories and serialized novels, forms that were not featured in the literary and general interest magazines due to their over-emphasis on the short story. See Nagamine, *Modan toshi*, 97, 249n1; Jay Rubin, *Injurious to Public Morals*, 236; Minami, "Sōsetsu—Ningen seken," 494; Maeda, *Kindai dokusha no seiritsu*, 167.

87. See Maeda, *Kindai dokusha no seiritsu*, 162 on the high manuscript fees paid by women's journals. Maeda notes that manuscript fees rose dramatically after the Great Kantō Earthquake.

88. The earliest of the Professor Hyakkien stories, "The Memoirs of Professor Hyakkien" and "Documentary Proof of the Existence of Half-Wits" were both published in *Shinseinen*, the former in serial installments in July, September, and December 1928, and the latter in March 1929.

89. *Shinseinen* is generally classified as a *yomimono zasshi*, a magazine of light reading selections. The term *yomimono*, literally, something to read, does not imply literary craft on the level of the novel. However, *Shinseinen* writers did catch the attention of and garner praise from the *bundan*. One such example is Edogawa Ranpo (a creative transliteration of Edgar Allan Poe), the father of Japanese detective fiction, and arguably the most famous contributor to *Shinseinen*. The detective genre marks this literature as a popular mode, but the stories by Ranpo and fellow contributor Yumeno Kyūsaku are not so readily categorized as mass fiction. In addition to the gritty sleuthing of Ranpo, the magazine decided to focus on experimental modernist writing in 1927 under the direction of a new editor. But the purely modernist platform did not work well as a vehicle for their mainstay of detective novels, and as a result, the popular flavor returned in the following years.

90. Nagamine, *Modan toshi*, 213.

91. Ibid.

92. Ibid., 211–12. Nagamine notes that a household would subscribe to a variety of magazines aimed at the interests of each family member. Reading was no longer a group activity.

93. Unlike the other literary venues, the largest of the dailies, the *Asahi* and the *Mainichi*, were not based in Tokyo but in Osaka. In this sense, many newspapers were able to escape the dictates of the Tokyo-centered publishing world and cater to their regional and national following. Other smaller papers based in Tokyo relied on a niche readership to survive in the competitive news world.

94. Hagiwara, "Suisenbun," 445–46. Hagiwara's essay originally appeared in *Zenshū Hyakken zuihitsu*.

95. For more on Tosaka and the role of criticism in everyday life, see DiNitto, "Return of the *zuihitsu*," 285–89.

96. Modern *zuihitsu* writers made few visibly conscious efforts to base their *zuihitsu* on premodern examples. Those who did, like Hagiwara, found their work out of tune with the contemporary expectations of *zuihitsu* journals. See DiNitto, "Return of the *zuihitsu*," 255.

97. Furukawa Roppa read Hyakken's *zuihitsu* before filming began on February 6, 1939. Furukawa, *Furukawa Roppa Shōwa nikki*, 525, 527.

98. I have been unable to acquire a copy of the film. Hyakken's family does not own a copy and inquiries indicate it may have been lost in the war. The information in the section is based on the screenplay in Hatta Naoyuki, *Hatta Naoyuki sakuhinshū*, vol. 2.

99. The "Hoojiro" in the title of the film is a near homophone for the given name of the character Aoji Hōjirō.

100. Hatta, *Hatta Naoyuki sakuhinshū*, 132.

101. Ibid., 136.

102. See entry for February 14, Furukawa, *Furukawa Roppa Shōwa nikki*, 529.

103. For the former, see Taki, "Kaisetsu," 812, and the latter, Sakurai, "20-seiki nikki shō," 268.

104. This is printed in English in Hyakken's original text.

105. This is my paraphrase of the *Mencius*: "The way of the people is this: If they have a certain livelihood they will have a fixed heart; if they have not a certain livelihood, they have not a fixed heart." The translation is from Legge, *The Works of Mencius*, 239–40.

106. Hatta, *Hatta Naoyuki sakuhinshū*, 135.

107. Ibid., 158.

108. Ibid., 150.

109. His family does not have a copy of the film, nor do they seem to have much interest in it. Personal communication, Okuno Kikumi, June 2002.

110. In an interesting aside, Roppa comments that he was not surprised to find Hyakken a bit of an odd bird.

111. Furukawa, *Furukawa Roppa Shōwa nikki*, 541.

112. Satō, *Nihon eigashi*, vol. 1, 391. Satō's comment is curious given the literary basis and the lack of vaudevillian gags and music in *The Pale Faced Professor*. Roppa mentions meeting to discuss the screenplay at its untitled stage, and remarks that there were hardly any jokes (*hotondo warai ga nai*). Furukawa, *Furukawa Roppa Shōwa nikki*, 524.

113. Information on Roppa comes from Sakurai, "20-seiki nikki shō"; Taki, "Kaisetsu."

114. For more on Kobayashi and his involvement in theater and film, see Anderson and Richie, *The Japanese Film*, 82–84.

115. These Chaplin-style films boosted the reputation of the studios, as commercial hits such as the "Enoken mono" (Enoken films) helped keep the industry afloat. Tōhō officially added a number of these live theater troupes, including those of Roppa and Enoken, as well as the Takarazuka Girls Opera, to their company in 1938. For more on Enoken, see Satō, *Nihon eigashi*, vol. 1, 382, 388–90.

116. Richie, *A Hundred Years of Japanese Film*, 94.

117. Tōkyō Hassei was only in business for six years (1935–41) before collapsing due to poor management. The company produced high-quality films and helped raise the profile of the larger corporation Tōhō, under whose contract their films were distributed.

118. Satō, *Nihon eigashi*, vol. 1, 396, 401.

119. Ibid., 200; Richie, 45.

120. Satō, *Nihon eigashi*, vol. 1, 253.

121. For a summary of the film see Anderson and Richie, 52. For more on the film and Abe's career, see Satō, *Nihon eigashi*, vol. 1, 253–56.

122. Anderson and Richie, *The Japanese Film*, 89.

123. This introduction is discussed in Uchida Michio ed., *Uchida Hyakken*, 94–95.

124. This is Huyssen's term in *After the Great Divide.*

125. See Murphy, "Economies of Culture."

## Chapter Three

EPIGRAPH: Uchida Hyakken, *Realm of the Dead*, 165.

1. For more on these incidents, see the "March Incident," "October Incident," "May 15th Incident," and also the "February 26th Incident" of 1926 in the *Kodansha Encyclopedia of Japan*; Chapter 8 of Skya, *Japan's Holy War.*

2. Young, *Japan's Total Empire*, 55.

3. The Communist leaders, Sano Manabu and Nabeyama Sadachika, were jailed in 1927 and sentenced to life in prison in 1932. Hoston, "Tenkō," 96–98. For more on *tenkō* literature, see Chapter 22 of Keene, *Dawn to the West.* For more on the high mark of proletarian literature and its downfall, see Doak, *Dreams of Difference*, 23–24.

4. Both stories are in the *Triumphant March into Port Arthur* collection. The dates above are those for the original publication of the stories in literary journals.

5. Young, *Japan's Total Empire*, 91.

6. This is my translation of the Japanese term *jissha eiga*. The word "documentary" was not in use in Japan at the time these films were made.

7. *Kodansha Encyclopedia of Japan*, s.v. Manchurian Incident.

8. Young, *Japan's Total Empire*, 89; Wilson, "The Russo-Japanese War and Japan," 185.

9. At one such riot on September 5, 1905, a crowd of some 30,000 people overwhelmed the police and rushed Hibiya Park shouting "Port Arthur 203 Meter Hill fell. *Banzai*!" For more on these rallies, see Okamoto, "The Emperor and the Crowd," 260. The incident described here is the famous Hibiya Riot, one of the best known of the anti-peace rallies organized to repudiate the Portsmouth Treaty that ended the Russo-Japanese War, because the nation felt it was cheated of its wartime efforts. The crowd was further angered by police attempts to ban the rally.

10. Young, *Japan's Total Empire,* 73, 77–78, 92. The "three human bullets" refers to soldiers who died in the line of duty in the assault on Shanghai. They were reputed to have blown themselves up to explode a section of wire fence blocking the army's advance. Rumors circulated at the time that their deaths were actually attributable to a miscalculation on the part of their commanding officer, but these rumors were suppressed by the state and ignored by the mass media eager to capitalize on the boom.

11. Ibid., 74.

12. Ibid., 71–72.

13. The information here is from Minami, *Shōwa bunka,* 269–71. Also see Young, *Japan's Total Empire,* 65–68 for more on mass media productions of the war.

14. This term *kiroku eiga* came into use around the time of the 1923 earthquake to indicate films with larger scale and more of a story line than newsreels. The term *dokyumentarī* also came into use in the 1920s. See Tsuchimoto, "Jissha eiga o miru," 321.

15. See Young, *Japan's Total Empire.*

16. See Tsuchimoto, "Jissha eiga o miru."

17. For more on Nogi's life and death, see Lifton, Katō, and Reich, *Six Lives, Six Deaths.*

18. For more on reactions to Nogi's death, see Rubin, *Injurious to Public Morals,* 222–24.

19. The play was titled *Omoi okosu Nogi shōgun* and the film *Omoi okose Nogi shōgun.* Young, *Japan's Total Empire,* 90.

20. Tsuchimoto does not provide a date for *Immortal Nogi,* just a comment that it was made in early Shōwa ("Jissha eiga o miru," 325). For a discussion of these films, see "Jissha eiga o miru," 331–33.

21. Nogi is held up as a symbol of heroism, a good commander and loyal subject, somewhere between a god and a man. The *benshi* (performers who narrated silent films) narrates scenes from the original actuality film and explains Nogi's motivations. As one would expect, the film ends with a shot of the room in which he and his wife Shizuko committed suicide. Nogi's loyalty served to make the figure of the Emperor all the more important. Tsuchimoto comments that this film is a classic right-wing picture, which appears to have been produced by a nongovernmental company. Judging from the documents Nogi left behind, he was unaware that his wife intended to die with him. She stabbed herself and died after he had already committed the ritual suicide of *seppuku.* See Lifton, Katō, and Reich, *Six Lives, Six Deaths,* 34.

22. Tsuchimoto, "Jissha eiga o miru," 325.

23. Ibid., 333.

24. According to one estimate, as many as 80 percent of the films released between 1904 and 1905 were on the Russo-Japanese War. These were a combination of actuality and staged dramatizations or "fake documentaries" made by both Japanese and foreign film crews. See Komatsu, "Some Characteristics," 236–39 for more on early war documentary filming. Satō Tadao mentions a catalog from 1910 that lists 93 films on the Russo-Japanese War, with titles such as *The Great Naval Battle at Port Arthur* (*Ryojun no daikaisen*) and *The Humorous Aftermath of the Beheading of Russian Soldiers* (*Rohei zanzai no kokkei*). The perplexingly gruesome title of the latter film refers to disturbing gags played by drunken soldiers with the dead bodies and severed heads of their former comrades. The fact that such material could be considered a comedy is telling of the mood of the era and of the Japanese perception of the Russians. It is unclear if these films were shot by the Japanese or purchased from foreign studios. From the titles, it is equally difficult to ascertain whether they are documentaries or fictionalized versions of the war. Satō warns that even thought these films were termed *jissha,* meaning actuality, many were likely staged, something common to war films of the 1930s as well. Satō Tadao, *Nihon eigashi,* vol. 1, 107–10.

25. The war was of particular importance to Japanese cinema, as the nascent film industry built its foundation on celluloid reels of the Russo-Japanese War. High, "The Dawn of Cinema in Japan," 38.

26. Satō Tadao, *Nihon eigashi,* vol. 1, 107–10. Although these early films may be termed documentaries, Tsuchimoto comments that the use of "documentary" (*dokyumentarī*) is misleading since it was not current at the time, only coming into use in the 1920s. The preferred term was *jissha katsudō shashin* (actual photographic moving picture, or actuality film).

27. Young, *Japan's Total Empire,* 13.

28. It is surprising that the book was not censored, but there does not appear to be evidence to the contrary.

29. For more on construction of early movie theaters in every "substantial sized town" in Japan, see High, "The Dawn of Cinema in Japan," 32, 49–50. According to Miriam Silverberg, there were 1,056 movie theatres in Japan by 1926 ("Constructing a New Cultural History," 124).

30. Tsuchimoto, "Jissha eiga o miru," 321.

31. Gunning, "The Cinema of Attraction," 64.

32. Sergei Eisenstein, as cited in Gunning, "The Cinema of Attraction," 66.

33. See "The Work of Art in the Age of Mechanical Reproduction" in Benjamin, *Illuminations*.

34. Wilson and Wells, "Introduction," 15. David Levy notes that more than the difficulty of filming on-site, the main reason that fake documentaries were often made was because "there was no guarantee of obtaining sufficiently thrilling footage" when filming during the actual events. These re-enactment films provided the drama lacking in on-site footage. See Levy, "Re-constituted Newsreels," 260*n*11.

35. See Young, *Japan's Total Empire*, 72, 91 for more on these war songs, and 91 for the lyrics of the popular tune "Comrade" ("Sen'yū").

36. The italics are my own.

37. Wilson and Wells, "Introduction," 10.

38. Film critic Satō Tadao quotes from "Films from the Russo-Japanese War Era" ("Nichi-Ro sensō jidai no eiga"), a 1937 essay from the *Sandē Mainichi*, in which the author reminisces about watching a 1904 war film. He mentions images of a Russian Vice Admiral walking and waving his hands in anger. When an aide approaches to speak with him, the content is relayed to the audience by the *benshi*, who most likely ad-libbed the lines to the crowd's liking. Not only would *benshi* narrate the films with snippets of poetry and the like, but they would present the piece with an inspired introduction accompanied by the martial tunes of a live band. High, "The Dawn of Cinema in Japan," 34–36. In his article, High recreates the viewing of a Russo-Japanese War actuality film.

39. For more on the *benshi* or *katsuben*, see Anderson, "Spoken Silents in the Japanese Cinema," 259.

40. The essay is reprinted in *Uchida Hyakken zenshū*, vol. 4, 63–66.

41. By one count there were eight versions made of this film between 1908 and 1932. I do not know which one Hyakken saw.

42. David Levy, "Re-constituted Newsreels," 250.

43. High, "The Dawn of Cinema in Japan," 36.

44. The Sino-Japanese character Hyakken uses here for *utsuru* is 写る, the first character in the word for "photograph," *shashin* (写真).

45. Rikusenshi kenkyū fukyūkai, ed., *Nichi-Ro sensō Ryojun yōsai kōryakusen*, 202.

46. Wilson and Wells, "Introduction," 11; Lifton, Katō, and Reich, *Six Lives, Six Deaths*, 51–52. Lifton notes that Nogi was replaced as commander of Japanese forces at Port Arthur for the final, successful military operation for control of the hill.

47. Lifton, Katō, and Reich, *Six Lives, Six Deaths*, 51.

48. The following account by a correspondent from the *London Daily Mail* describes one of Nogi's unsuccessful attempts in which

the Japanese soldiers were unexpectedly hit by the fire of Russian Maxim machine gunners: "The Japanese were sitting huddled together in the narrow space, quite unconcernedly, when the avalanche of lead was poured into them. Within a few seconds the trench was turned into a veritable pandemonium, a seething mass of humanity, where men were fighting wildly to get away, trampling on the wounded, climbing over the piles of corpses which blocked the entrance, or trying to escape over the edge of the parallel down the coverless hillside. But the Maxims did their work as only Maxims can." Bowring and Kornicki, eds., *Cambridge Encyclopedia of Japan*, 87.

49. Natsume Sōseki, *Ten Nights of Dream*, 138–40.

50. Ibid., 145.

51. Lifton, Katō, and Reich, *Six Lives, Six Deaths*, 60. This quotation is also cited in Jay Rubin, *Injurious to Public Morals*, 223.

52. Since so many of these films were made during the war it is difficult to know if Hyakken is referring to a specific documentary or commenting on the genre in general. However, Tsuchimoto mentions the actuality *The Fall of Port Arthur and General Nogi* (*Ryojun kaijō to Nogi shōgun*, 1905), which bears a strong resemblance to the film in Hyakken's story. The representative scenes Tsuchimoto mentions are similar to those in Hyakken's fictional film: battleships headed to the Japan Sea, warship bombardments, the blockade at Port Arthur, the battles on 203 Meter Hill, and the meeting between Generals Nogi and Stessel. The similarities are striking. Tsuchimoto also discusses a scene in which a group of soldiers pull a 28-centimeter cannon up a mountain—an important image in Hyakken's story—and other images of the daily life of the average enlisted man. Like the film in Hyakken's story, *The Fall of Port Arthur and General Nogi* is reputed to have been shot by a foreign cameraman. This may account for Tsuchimoto's remark that there is no room for nationalistic sentiment in *The Fall of Port Arthur and General Nogi*. Faces of important people and battle scenes are shot like scenery. The meeting of Nogi and Stessel is filmed such that the camera keeps equal distance between the two generals. There are no images of Nogi as victor or Stessel as vanquished, and if it were not for the difference in uniforms, it would be hard to tell the Japanese from the Russians. Tsuchimoto, "Jissha eiga o miru," 326. Peter High also comments on the unbiased representations of Russians in these films ("The Dawn of Cinema in Japan," 37–38). Although Satō Tadao includes in his study of Japanese cinema history a still for this film and one for another titled *General Nogi's Triumphal Return* (*Nogi shōgun no gaisen*, 1905), he does not include any discussion of these films (*Nihon eigashi*, vol. 1, 107, 109).

53. A similar literary scene occurs in the short story "Professor Fujino" ("Tengye xiansheng," 1926) by the Chinese novelist Lu Xun, who also experienced the shocking impact of photographic images while studying to be a medical doctor in Japan between 1904 and 1906. One day, when his lecture ended early, the teacher showed his class some lantern slides of the Russo-Japanese War. One in particular—an image of a Chinese spy about to be killed in front of a crowd of Chinese onlookers—caught his attention and compelled him to change his career and take up writing.

> In our second year of study, we took classes on bacteriology. The bacteria were all shown on lantern slides and sometimes when the class ended early, the teacher would show us news slides. Of course, they were all scenes of the Japanese victory over Russia. But one time, a Chinese person appeared on the screen. Arrested as a Russian spy, [the Chinese person] was about to be shot to death by the Japanese. The crowd gathered around to observe him was also Chinese. And then there was me, here in the classroom. . . . *Banzai!*—rang the heavy thunder of applause and cheers. . . . It was customary for cheers to regularly follow each slide, but never before had these sounds of joy so assaulted my ears. Later, after I'd returned to China, when I saw such observers, casually watching prisoner executions and cheering like drunks, I couldn't make sense of it. But that day in Japan completely changed my way of thinking.

In Lu Xun's story we see the same patterns of conflation present in Hyakken. When Lu Xun's character says, "And then there was me, here in the classroom," his protagonist identifies with the image on screen, with both the condemned spy and the cheering crowds. There is yet another level of identification in which a connection forms between the author, former medical student Lu Xun, and the fictional protagonist. There are fictional and nonfictional versions of this incident in Lu Xun's oeuvre. Lu Xun's lantern slides and the film in "Triumphant March into Port Arthur" are both originally part of the narratives of the Russo-Japanese War, which are later incorporated into the discourse of the Manchurian conquest. Both also derive their power from photographic images (*shashin*), which are dangerously left open to interpretation. Neither Lu Xun's nor Hyakken's protagonist "correctly" interprets the images via the national discourse. Lu Xun is assaulted and overpowered by the cheers of his nationalistic Japanese classmates and his foolish Chinese countrymen. Hyakken is equally ill at ease with the images of distressed and disoriented soldiers. Neither author accepts a patriotic, glorified reading of the war. The passage above is translated from Takeuchi Yoshimi's Japanese translation of Lu Xun's story, cited in Satō, *Nihon eigashi*, vol 1, 110–11. I also consulted Lu Xun, "Mr. Fujino."

54. Wilson, "Russo-Japanese War and Japan," 184.
55. Wilson, "Past in the Present," 179.
56. Young, *Japan's Total Empire*, 3–4.
57. Wilson, "Past in the Present," 173.
58. Ibid., 180*n*31.
59. The journal regularly published articles on politics, philosophy, art, and culture. It did not always feature fiction, but often had a few *zuihitsu* selections. *Shisō* produced important special issues on Hegel, race and tradition, political philosophy, and personal and intellectual freedom. Hyakken's story appeared in one such special issue on dialectics alongside dense articles on Hegel and the role of dialectics in freedom and nature, which were written by such intellectual heavyweights as Nishida Kitarō and Miki Kiyoshi. The editor's notes in the back of the issue explain the centrality of dialectics to the philosophical world and welcome this look back to what some mistakenly consider an outmoded way of thinking. The issue contains advertisements for the collected works of Tolstoy and Dante, economics, psychology and philosophy texts, and is conspicuously lacking in advertisements for department stores, soap, and fountain pens so common in the middle-class and lowbrow journals. If it is hard to imagine the average, middle-class consumer reading this magazine, it would be next to impossible for the lower-class reader to comprehend its contents. There are no reading guides on any of the articles, and the editor's comments are aimed at a specific, educated audience. This is not surprising, since the journal revolved around philosopher Watsuji Tetsurō who studied in Germany with Heidegger, and academic-turned-entrepreneur Iwanami Shigeo, famous for his publishing company Iwanami, and his reputation for printing intellectual material.
60. The shrine is located in the Kudan district at the top of Kudanzaka, as approached from the east. The name of the district comes from the name of the hill, which dates back to 1709. Yasukuni dōri (street) divides the northern and southern parts of the Kudan district.
61. See the following chapter for more on modernization and urban planning in Tokyo.
62. Everett, *Exciting Experiences in the Japanese-Russian War*, 513.
63. For a brief history of the shrine see Tsubouchi and Yoshida, "Yasukuni Shrine as a Symbol of Japan's Modernization" and Masugi, *Uchida Hyakken no sekai*, 99–100. For more detailed information, see Yasukuni Jinja, *Yasukuni Jinja hyakunenshi*. The name of the annex "Yūshūkan" is derived from a passage of the Xunzi titled "Encouragement to Learning." The Xunzi passage is translated in Knoblock,

*Xunzi*, 137: "Accordingly, where the gentleman resides is sure to be a carefully chosen neighborhood, and when he travels, it is certain to be in the company of scholars" (君子居必擇鄰遊必就士). The word *yūshū* is derived from the second half of the above phrase. The Tsubouchi and Yoshida article cited here is a translated version that appeared in *Japan Echo*. The original is in the journal *Ronza* (April 1999): 76–87.

64. Seidensticker, *Low City, High City*, 69. The Rokumeikan was designed by British architect Josiah Condor, and opened a year after the War Museum.

65. Yasukuni Jinja, *Yasukuni no inori*, 240.

66. A temporary structure was erected the following year and was in use until the new building was ready.

67. Ida, "Uchida Hyakken 'Yūshūkan' ron," 26*n*6.

68. Ibid., 14.

69. Yasukuni Jinja, *Yasukuni no inori*, 246.

70. Ibid., 246–47.

71. Kashiwagi, "On Rationalization and the National Lifestyle," 71.

72. Tsubouchi and Yoshida, "Yasukuni Shrine as a Symbol of Japan's Modernization," 50.

73. By "overcome modernity" I am referring to the Conference on Overcoming Modernity (Kindai no chōkoku) of 1942, during which a number of prominent critics and thinkers discussed the meaning of the war within a global context of the modern. A number of scholars have written on this conference. For an overview and analysis in English, see Harootunian, *Overcome by Modernity*, 34–94. In Japanese, see Takeuchi Yoshimi, *Kindai no chōkoku*.

74. After the Sino-Japanese War of 1894–95, people came in great numbers from all over Japan to worship at Yasukuni. Attendance soared at the War Museum, from one million in 1893 to seven million in 1894. It rose again during the Russo-Japanese War, peaking in 1905 at eleven million. Fujitani, *Splendid Monarchy*, 126–27.

75. Ida, "Uchida Hyakken 'Yūshūkan' ron," 14.

76. Young, *Japan's Total Empire*, 67.

77. Ibid., 33.

## *Chapter Four*

EPIGRAPH: Uchida Hyakken, *Uchida Hyakken zenshū*, vol. 3, 211.

1. "Tokyo Diary" was first published in the *sōsaku* (creative writing) column of the general interest magazine *Kaizō*. The quotation in the epigraph is from episode seventeen.

2. Seidensticker describes this neighborhood as home to the "artist and the intellectual, and to an increasing extent the manager and the magnate." Seidensticker, *High City, Low City*, viii. Although the low city is often celebrated, Haga Noboru argues that the history of modern Tokyo is centered in the middle-class residential areas opened up in the Yamanote region. See Burton, 239.

3. Highmore, *Everyday Life and Cultural Theory*, 139. Highmore is referring to the Situationist's practice of *dérive*.

4. Hyakken never fled Tokyo, even choosing to stay during the bombing raids of the Second World War. See his *Shinhōjōki* (The New Account of My Hut, 1947), which covers this period, in Uchida Hyakken, *Uchida kyakken zenshū*, vol. 5.

5. For more on this combination, and on the many voices within the Japan Romantic School, see Doak, *Dreams of Difference*.

6. Ōgai resided in Germany in the mid-1880s, and Sōseki in London in the early 1900s. Ōgai created his fictional alter ego in a short story titled "Dancing Girl" ("Maihime," 1890). The protagonist, Toyotarō, is a young diplomat sent to Germany by the Japanese government, only to fall in love with a local cabaret girl and risk losing his future career. Whereas Ōgai describes the brilliance of the grand German thoroughfares, Sōseki in "The Tower of London" ("Rondon-tō," 1906) could not see beyond the chaos of the British crowds and trains that threatened to unhinge his mind. Tokyo often featured as a backdrop in Sōseki's later novels; the city was less menacing than London, but was depicted as a landscape scarred by modernization. In the 1910s, one member of the White Birch Society (Shirakaba-ha), Mushanokōji Saneatsu, found his model community not in the city, but in the "new villages" (*atarashiki mura*) he established on the southern island of Kyushu and in other areas removed from Tokyo. For more on Sōseki, see Burton, "The Image of Tokyo in Sōseki's Fiction"; for the Naturalists, see Smith, "Tokyo as an Idea," 57, 67.

7. For more on the city in Japanese scholarship, see: Maeda, *Toshi kūkan no naka no bungaku*; Jinnai, *Tokyo: A Spatial Anthropology* (Tōkyō no kūkan jinruigaku, originally published in 1983); Unno, *Modan toshi Tōkyō*. In English, see Karan and Stapleton, eds., *The Japanese City* and Fiévé and Waley, eds., *Japanese Capitals in Historical Perspective*. For more on the modern identities constructed within the urban locale, see also Silverberg, *Erotic Grotesque Nonsense*; Sand, "The Cultured Life as Contested Space" and *House and Home in Modern Japan*; and Tipton, "The Café: Contested Space of Modernity in Interwar Japan." For Unno, the Western concept of the 1920s can be applied to the years 1918 to 1932 in Japan. Unno, *Modan toshi Tōkyō*, 8, 236.

8. Watanabe, "Metropolitanism as a Way of Life," 416–17.

9. Jinnai, *Tokyo*, 6.

10. Watanabe, "Metropolitanism as a Way of Life," 422. See Watanabe's article for more on Tokyo's urban planning laws, influence, and history.

11. Yoshimi, *Toshi no doramaturugī*, 244–50.

12. Both stories are by Ryūtanji. The second story is included in Yoshiyuki and Saitō, eds., *Yoshiyuki Eisuke to sono jidai*, the title of which indicates the connection to the city. Stories from other contemporaries are included.

13. See Chapters 2 and 3 of Lippit, *Topographies*.

14. Hirabayashi commented that: "Modernism . . . is born of the factories, exchanges, radio, the sound of engines, taxis, working women, labor unions, salaried employees, movies and Communism. It comes from jazz and the sound of machines. Cafes and apartments rise out of the ruins of the family, driven by the increase of salaried workers. Women's western dress and hairstyles are a direct result of their needs in the workplace. Behind it all is the machine, the womb of Modernism." Shimada, "Bungaku ni arawareta modanizumu," 76.

15. Smith, "Tokyo as an Idea," 73.

16. See Chapter 3 and the Introduction for more about *tenkō*.

17. Unno, *Modan toshi Tōkyō*, 243–44; Silverberg, *Changing Song*, 198–99.

18. This is Unno Hiroshi's argument in "Toshi e no wakare" (Farewell to the City), Chapter 12 of *Modan toshi Tōkyō*.

19. Doak, *Dreams of Difference*, 37–40.

20. For more on Hagiwara's concept of the wanderer, see his "Song of the Wanderer" ("Hyōhakusha no uta") in *The Iceland* (*Hyōtō*, 1934). See also Chapter 2 of Doak, *Dreams of Difference*.

21. Najita and Harootunian, "Japan's Revolt against the West," 253.

22. Doak, *Dreams of Difference*, xxxvi.

23. Najita and Harootunian, "Japan's Revolt against the West," 264.

24. This is Najita and Harootunian's argument. See ibid., 231–32.

25. Doak, *Dreams of Difference*, 48.

26. Hagiwara, "Nihon e no kaiki," 487; as cited in Doak, *Dreams of Difference*, 48.

27. Najita and Harootunian, "Japan's Revolt against the West," 266.

28. See Chapters 4 and 5 in Doak, *Dreams of Difference*.

29. Ibid., xix.

30. Crary, *Techniques of the Observer*, 11.

31. Highmore, *Everyday Life and Cultural Theory*, 139–40. Established in 1957, the Situationist International was an avant-garde group whose members were spread across Europe.

32. Hal Foster, *Compulsive Beauty*, 159.

33. Hirose was posthumously appointed the rank of Commander. See *Kōdansha Encyclopedia of Japan*, 1st ed., s.v. "Hirose Takeo."

34. Jinnai, *Tokyo*, 113.

35. Ibid., 197.

36. Itō Takashi, *Tōkyō saihakken*, 42.

37. Jinnai, *Tokyo*, 196.

38. Marukawa, "Uchida Hyakken to teito," 201.

39. Hal Foster, *Compulsive Beauty*, 165.

40. Young, *Japan's Total Empire*, 91. The paper set was included in the magazine's May 1932 issue.

41. de Certeau, Giard, and Mayol, *The Practice of Everyday Life*, 133, 135.

42. Jinnai, *Tokyo*, 18.

43. de Certeau, Giard, and Mayol, *The Practice of Everyday Life*, 133.

44. Marukawa, "Uchida Hyakken to teito," 201–2.

45. Mishima, "'Uchida Hyakken' kaisetsu," 38.

46. Horikiri Naoto suggests that Hyakken may have gotten the idea for the movement of the water from the mattress on which he was sleeping at the Tokyo Tetsudō Hotel. See Masugi, *Uchida Hyakken no sekai*, 65*n*11. In "Rambling Notes from the Tetsudōkan" ("Tetsudōkan manki"), Hyakken compares sleeping on the Western mattress to sleeping in the swaying branches of a tree (3: 150–53). Mishima, "'Uchida Hyakken' kaisetsu," 39, says this scene is so realistically described it is like watching the television news.

47. Marukawa, "Uchida Hyakken to teito," 202.

48. Itō Takashi, *Tōkyō saihakken*, 3–10.

49. For more on Kafū's story, see Seidensticker, *Low City, High City*, 45–47.

50. Barthes, *Empire of Signs*, 30–32.

51. Nagamine, *Modan toshi*, 208.

52. Kawahigashi, "Maru biru, ōrubakku, musan seitō," 12. The second term is Japanese for "all-back," a reference to a Western men's hairstyle popular in Taishō among the new intellectual class.

53. Doak, *Dreams of Difference*, xxxvi.

54. Mishima, "'Uchida Hyakken' kaisetsu," 38.

55. Watanabe, "Metropolitanism as a Way of Life," 412.

56. Ibid.

57. Seidensticker, *Low City, High City*, 78.

58. Takahama Kyoshi, cited and translated in Seidensticker, *Low City, High City*, 76.

59. The first term is from Minami, "Sōsetsu—Ningen seken," 498, and the second two from Sata, "Shinkeibyō jidai," 292, 297.

60. Najita and Harootunian, "Japan's Revolt against the West," 257.

61. Crary, *Techniques of the Observer*, 10.

62. Seidensticker, *Low City, High City*, 199.

63. Tipton, "The Café," 123.

64. Yoshimi, *Toshi no doramaturugī*, 222.

65. Yoshimi Shun'ya describes Ginza as an island and Asakusa as the ocean, but this relationship reversed as Asakusa lost out to Ginza by the end of the 1930s (*Toshi no doramaturugī*, 252); Tipton, "The Café," 124.

66. For more on Asakusa as a place of refuge and escape from modern life in Tokyo, see Yoshimi, *Toshi no doramaturugī*, 244–45.

67. A decision was reached to accommodate the downtown and open a back entrance in 1920, but due to the local bickering of neighboring wards, the entrance was not constructed until after the earthquake.

68. Seidensticker, *Low City, High City*, 78–80.

69. Mackie, "Modern Selves and Modern Spaces," 195.

70. Ibid.

## *Epilogue*

1. The first two volumes of a new 33-volume series of collected works were printed in 1986. The love letters date from 1905 and 1906 and were published by Fukutake in 1989 as *Love Letters, Love Diaries* (*Koibumi, koinikki*). Six reprints of Hyakken's original publications were issued in the 1980s and sixteen between 1990 and 1994. Hyakken's fiction was also reprinted in anthologized versions, with eighteen appearing in the 1980s and sixteen between 1990 and 1994. This implies that the resurgence of interest was not limited to the 1980s. This publication history is from Morita Sakan, *Oboegaki Hyakkien nōto*, which only covers up to 1994.

2. Kawamura, *Uchida Hyakken ron* was awarded the Yomiuri literary prize in 1984. The *Asahi Journal* published an article titled, "Uchida Hyakken ga naze ka yominaosarete iru" (July 24, 1981). For other reconsiderations, see, for example, Uchida Michio, "Hyakkien būmu kō"; Kawamura and Irokawa, "Uchida Hyakken no fukkatsu."

3. Huyssen, *Twilight Memories*, 5.

4. The story was originally published in the journal *Shinchō* in November 1948, and later included in Hyakken's third fictional collection (*sōsakushū*), *The True Story of Sōhei* (*Jissetsu Sōheiki*, 1950). It is often included in anthologies of his fiction.

5. For a detailed analysis of Suzuki's film and a commentary on its relevance to the postwar film industry and prewar culture, see DiNitto, "Translating Prewar Culture into Film."

6. Itō Mino, "Chichi, Uchida Hyakken," 16–17; Uchida Hyakken, "Sōseki chikuonki," in *Uchida Hyakken zenshū*. For comments by Sōseki's son, Natsume Shinroku, see Sakai Hideyuki, *Hyakken*, 216–17.

7. Compare this to the opening of "The Reflection" ("Eizō") from *Triumphant March into Port Arthur*: "The gale-force winds that had been blowing all afternoon suddenly died down around ten o'clock at night. Somewhere in the distance a dog howled with a humanlike cry. All else was silent. It felt as though the desk I was leaning on, the cushion underneath me, the room, and the entire house itself were quietly slipping to the bottom of an abyss" (143).

8. Okaya, "Yume no shikaku," 137.

9. The seven *zuihitsu* are: "Story of the Bamboo Cane" ("Chikujōki," 1934); "The Kappa Memorial" ("Kappaki," 1934); "The Fan from Hunan" ("Konan no ōgi," 1934); "The Wild Boar's Nap" ("Inoshishi no hirune," 1935); "Memories of Instructor Akutagawa"("Akutagawa kyōkan no omoide," 1935); "The Shirahama Reunion" ("Shirahama-kai," 1937); and "The Turtle Cries" ("Kame naku ya," 1951).

10. Similar versions of this episode appear in the following works: "The Bowler Hat" (1: 105–6); "The Fan from Hunan" (2: 70); "The Kappa Memorial" (1: 526); and "The Turtle Cries" (6: 153).

11. Suzuki Kōichi reminisces about listening to this legendary record as a grammar school student. He describes the scratchy gramophone noise as the very sound of late Taishō and early Shōwa itself. Suzuki Kōichi, "Miwataseba hana mo arashi mo," 234.

12. This and the following scene are translations from the Hyakken story.

13. For more on references to prewar intellectuals in *Zigeunerweisen*, see DiNitto, "Translating Prewar Culture into Film," 56–57.

14. The majority of reviews remark on the confusing nature of *Zigeunerweisen*. See, for example, Izumiya, "Tsigoineruwaizen," 138; Kanai, "Eiga jihyō," 183.

15. Treat, ed., *Contemporary Japan and Popular Culture*, 10.

16. Ivy, *Discourses of the Vanishing*, 47, 55.

17. Ibid., 55; Robertson, "Hegemonic Nostalgia," 99.

18. Both Ivy and Robertson address the JR campaigns.

19. This is unlike the Japan Romantic School writers who experienced firsthand the alienation of both city and country in the prewar era.

20. Robertson, "Hegemonic Nostalgia," 92.

21. Fredric Jameson discusses postmodern nostalgia and images of "pastness" in film in *Postmodernism,* 19–20.

22. This interpretation draws on Rey Chow's discussion of translation and the concept of an original within a cultural context. See Part 3 of Chow, *Primitive Passions.*

23. Harootunian, *Overcome by Modernity,* xvii.

24. For an examination of culture via various thinkers of the prewar, see Harootunian, *Overcome by Modernity.*

25. The "imprinting of difference" refers to the following quotation by Harry Harootunian: "Thinkers and writers responded to Japan's modernity by describing it as a *doubling* that imprinted a difference between the new demands of capitalism and the market and the force of received forms of history and cultural patterns." Ibid., xvii.

26. Stephen Prince applies this term to Kurosawa's last three films. Prince, *The Warrior's Camera,* 296. Kurosawa cites *Shinshū Uchida Hyakken zenshū*, published in the late 1980s, and he focuses on writings from the 1940s through the 1960s.

27. Kurosawa also draws on Hyakken's *Nora* and *Kuru, Is That You?* for the scenes with the Professor and his runaway cats.

28. Prince, *The Warrior's Camera,* 332–35; McDonald, *Reading a Japanese Film.*

29. For more on the episodic nature of this film, see Prince, *The Warrior's Camera,* 331.

30. Ibid., 329.

31. The discussion of historical absence here is indebted to Stephen Prince's analysis of *Madadayo*. See ibid., 328–32.

32. Harootunian, "Japan's Long Postwar," 101, 107–8.

33. McDonald, *Reading a Japanese Film,* 197.

34. Huyssen, *Twilight Memories,* 7.

35. Harootunian, "Japan's Long Postwar," 98, 107.

36. The revisionist text *Atarashii rekishi kyōkasho* was one of the many underlying causes of the riots, including Japan's bid for permanent membership to the United Nations Security Council and drilling rights for oil in the East China Sea.

37. Jameson, *Postmodernism,* ix. For more on the loss of history and obsession with memory in the contemporary West and East, see Jameson, *Postmodernism;* Huyssen, *Twilight Memories;* and the essays in Yoda and Harootunian, *Japan After Japan.*

# Works Cited


Akiyama Satoko. "Semarikuru mizu to kaze." *Yuriika* (February 1984): 105–15.

Akutagawa Ryūnosuke. "Bungeiteki na, amari ni bungeiteki na." In *Akutagawa Ryūnosuke shū*. Tokyo: Kadokawa shoten, 1970.

——. "Meido." In *Kaisō Uchida Hyakken*, ed. Hirayama Saburō. Tokyo: Tsugaru shobō, 1975.

——. "Uchida Hyakken shi." In *Uchida Hyakken: yume to warai*. Vol. 22 of *Nihon bungaku kenkyū shiryō shinshū*, ed. Sakai Hideyuki. Tokyo: Yūseidō, 1986.

Anderer, Paul. "Tokyo and the Borders of Modern Japanese Fiction." In *Visions of the Modern City: Essays in History, Art and Literature*, ed. William Sharpe and Leonard Wallock. New York: Columbia University Press, 1983.

Anderson, J. L. "Spoken Silents in the Japanese Cinema: or, Talking to Pictures: Essaying the Katsuben, Contextualizing the Texts." In *Reframing Japanese Cinema: Authorship, Genre, History*, ed. Arthur Nolletti, Jr. and David Desser. Bloomington, IN: Indiana University Press, 1992.

Anderson, Joseph L. and Donald Richie. *The Japanese Film: Art and Industry (Expanded Edition)*. Princeton, NJ: Princeton University Press, 1982.

Barthes, Roland. *Empire of Signs*. Translated by Richard Howard. New York: Hill and Wang, 1982.

Baudelaire, Charles. *Selected Writings on Art & Artists*. Translated by P. E. Charvet. Cambridge, UK: Cambridge University Press, 1981.

Benjamin, Walter. *Illuminations*. New York: Harcourt, Brace & World Inc., 1968.

——. *One-Way Street, and Other Writings*. London: Verso, 1997.

——. *Reflections: Essays, Aphorisms, Autobiographical Writings*. New York: Harcourt Brace Jovanovich, 1978.

——. "A Short History of Photography." In *Classic Essays on Photography*, ed. Alan Trachtenberg. New Haven, CT: Leete's Island Books, 1980.

Berman, Marshall. *All That Is Solid Melts Into Air: The Experience of Modernity*. New York: Penguin Books, 1988.

Bowles, Scott. "An Intro to the Deliriously Lurid Cinema of Seijun Suzuki: Welcome to Wicked, Wonderful World of Japanese Auteur Seijun Suzuki." *iF Magazine*, 27 August 1999. http://www.ifmagazine.com/common/ArticlePrint.asp?ArticleID=333.

Bowring, Richard and Peter F. Kornicki, eds. *Cambridge Encyclopedia of Japan*. Cambridge, UK: Cambridge University Press, 1993.

Bradbury, Malcolm and James McFarlane. "Movements, Magazines and Manifestos: The Succession from Naturalism." In *Modernism: A Guide to European Literature 1890–1930*, ed. Malcolm Bradbury and James McFarlane. London: Penguin, 1991.

Bungei shunjū shinsha. *Bungei shunjū 35-nen shikō*. Tokyo: Bungei shunjū shinsha, 1959.

Burton, William. "The Image of Tokyo in Sōseki's Fiction." In *The Japanese City*, ed. P. P. Karan and Kristin Stapleton. Lexington, KY: University of Kentucky Press, 1997.

Chance, Linda. "Constructing the Classic: *Tsurezuregusa* in Tokugawa Readings." *Journal of the American Oriental Society* 111.1 (January–March 1997): 39–56.

——. *Formless in Form: Kenkō, Tsurezuregusa, and the Rhetoric of Japanese Fragmentary Prose*. Stanford, CA: Stanford University Press, 1997.

Chiba Kameo. "Nihon gendai bungei shichō." In *Hyōron I*. Vol. 1 of *Chiba Kameo chosakushū*. Tokyo: Yumani shobō, 1991.

——. "Zuihitsu ni tsuite." In *Hyōron I*. Vol. 1 of *Chiba Kameo chosakushū*. Tokyo: Yumani shobō, 1991.

*Chō daitokushū = waido kōsei,* Tsigoineruwaizen *Suzuki Seijun: sono bigaku tetsuri no shinkotchō kanpeki naru shintenkai*. Special Issue. *Eiga geijutsu* 333 (April–June 1980).

Chow, Rey. *Primitive Passions: Visuality, Sexuality, Ethnography, and Contemporary Chinese Cinema*. New York: Columbia University Press, 1995.

Chute, David. "Branded to Thrill." In *Branded to Thrill: The Delirious Cinema of Suzuki Seijun*, ed. Simon Field and Tony Rayns. London: Institute of Contemporary Arts, 1994.

Cohn, Joel. *Studies in the Comic Spirit in Modern Japanese Fiction*. Cambridge, MA: Council on East Asian Studies, Harvard University, 1998.

Crary, Jonathan. *Techniques of the Observer: On Vision and Modernity in the Nineteenth Century*. Cambridge, MA: The MIT Press, 1990.

Crawford, Margaret. "Introduction" to *Everyday Urbanism*, ed. John Chase, Margaret Crawford, and John Kaliski. New York: Monacelli Press, 1999.

Dai Jinhua. "Imagined Nostalgia." In *Postmodernism and China*, ed. Arif Dirlik and Xudong Zhang. Durham, NC: Duke University Press, 2000.

de Certeau, Michel. *The Practice of Everyday Life*. Translated by Steven Rendall. Berkeley, CA: University of California Press, 1984.

de Certeau, Michel, Luce Giard, and Pierre Mayol. *The Practice of Everyday Life, Volume II: Living and Cooking*. Translated by Timothy J. Tomasik. Minneapolis, MN: University of Minnesota Press, 1998.

DiNitto, Rachel. "Return of the *zuihitsu*: Print Culture, Modern Life, and Heterogeneous Narrative in Prewar Japan." *Harvard Journal of Asiatic Studies* 64, no. 2 (December 2004): 251–90.

——. "Translating Prewar Culture into Film: The Double Vision of Suzuki Seijun's *Zigeunerweisen*." *Journal of Japanese Studies* 30, no. 1 (2004): 35–63.

Doak, Kevin. *Dreams of Difference: The Japan Romantic School and the Crisis of Modernity*. Berkeley, CA: University of California Press, 1994.

Everett, Marshall. *Exciting Experiences in the Japanese-Russian War*. N.p., c1904.

Felski, Rita. "Introduction." *New Literary History* 33.4 (Autumn 2002): 607–22.

Fiévé, Nicholas and Paul Waley, eds. *Japanese Capitals in Historical Perspective: Place, Power, and Memory in Kyoto, Edo, and Tokyo*. London: Routledge, 2003.

Figal, Gerald. *Civilization and Monsters: Spirits of Modernity in Meiji Japan*. Durham, NC: Duke University Press, 1999.

Foster, Hal. *Compulsive Beauty*. Cambridge, MA: The MIT Press, 1993.

Foster, Michael Dylan. "Strange Games and Enchanted Science: The Mystery of Kokkuri." *Journal of Asian Studies* 65, no. 2 (May 2006): 251–75.

——."Walking in the City with Natsume Sōseki: The Metaphorical Landscape in 'Koto no sorane'." *PAJLS: Proceedings of the Association for Japanese Literary Studies* 6 (Summer 2005): 137–46.

Fowler, Edward. *The Rhetoric of Confession: Shishōsetsu in Early Twentieth-Century Japanese Fiction*. Berkeley, CA: University of California Press, 1988.

Frisby, David. *Fragments of Modernity: Theories of Modernity in the Work of Simmel, Kracauer, and Benjamin*. Cambridge, MA: The MIT Press, 1986.

Fujikawa Yoshiyuki. "Hyakken no onna oboegaki." *Yuriika* (February 1984): 123–27.

Fujitani, Takashi. *Splendid Monarchy: Power and Pageantry in Modern Japan*. Berkeley, CA: University of California Press, 1996.

Furukawa Roppa. *Furukawa Roppa Shōwa nikki*. Vol. 1: *Senzen hen*. Tokyo: Shōbunsha, 1987–88.

Gardiner, Michael. *Critiques of Everyday Life*. London: Routledge, 2000.

Gardner, William O. *Advertising Tower: Japanese Modernism and Modernity in the 1920s*. Cambridge, MA: Harvard University Asia Center, 2006.

Genette, Gérard. *Paratexts: Thresholds of Interpretation*. Cambridge, UK: Cambridge University Press, 1997.

Gensō bungaku kikakushitsu, ed. *Tokushū: kudan, minotaurosu, gyūyō densetsu*. Special issue. *Gensō bungaku* 56 (October 1999).

Gerbert, Elaine. Introduction to *Beautiful Town: Stories and Essays*, by Satō Haruo. Honolulu, HI: University of Hawai'i Press, 1996.

——. "A New Look: The Influence of Vision Technology on Narrative in Taishō." In *New Trends and Issues in Teaching Japanese Language and Culture*, ed. Haruko M. Cook, Kyoko Hijirida, and Mildred Tahara. Honolulu, HI: University of Hawai'i Press, 1997.

Gomez, Edward. "When Japan Tried on the Modernist Mantle." *New York Times*, 27 January 2002, Arts & Leisure section.

Gordon, Andrew. *A Modern History of Japan: From Tokugawa Times to the Present*. Oxford, UK: Oxford University Press, 2003.

Greimel, Hans. "From Kamikazes to Suicide Subs, Japanese Museum Paints a Different World War II History." *Associated Press*, 15 August 2002. International News.

Gunning, Tom. "The Cinema of Attraction: Early Film, Its Spectator and the Avant-Garde." *Wide Angle* 8, nos. 3/4 (Fall 1986): 63–70.

Haga Noboru. *Dai-Tōkyō no shisō*. Tokyo: Yūzankaku, 1992.

Hagiwara Sakutarō. "Nihon e no kaiki." In *Hagiwara Sakutarō zenshū*, vol. 10. Tokyo: Chikuma shobō, 1975.

——. "Suisenbun." In *Kaisō Uchida Hyakken*, ed. Hirayama Saburō. Tokyo: Tsugaru shobō, 1975.

——. "Zuihitsu towa nanzo ya." In *Hagiwara Sakutarō zenshū*, vol. 5. Tokyo: Chikuma shobō, 1975.

Hardacre, Helen. *Marketing the Menacing Fetus in Japan*. Berkeley, CA: University of California Press, 1997.

Harootunian, Harry. "Japan's Long Postwar: The Trick of Memory and the Ruse of History." In *Japan After Japan: Social and Cultural Life from the Recessionary 1990s to the Present*, ed. Tomiko Yoda and Harry Harootunian. Durham, NC: Duke University Press, 2006.

——. *Overcome by Modernity: History, Culture, and Community in Interwar Japan*. Princeton, NJ: Princeton University Press, 2000.

Harris, Steven and Deborah Berke, eds. *Architecture of the Everyday*. New York: Princeton Architectural Press, 1997.

Harvey, David. *The Condition of Postmodernity: An Enquiry into the Origins of Cultural Change*. Cambridge, UK: Blackwell, 1990.

Hasegawa Izumi. *Zuihitsu dokkai no riron*. Tokyo: Meiji shoin, 1965.

——, ed. *Kindai bungaku zasshi jiten*. Tokyo: Shibundō, 1966.

Hasumi Shigehiko. "Yūrei wa kawaita oto o hibikaseru." In *Chō daitokushū = waido kōsei,* Tsigoineruwaizen *Suzuki Seijun: sono bigaku tetsuri no shinkotchō kanpeki naru shintenkai*. Special Issue. *Eiga geijutsu* 333 (April–June 1980): 31–36.

Hatta Naoyuki. *Hatta Naoyuki sakuhinshū*, vol. 2. Tokyo: Engeki shuppansha, 1972.

High, Peter B. "The Dawn of Cinema in Japan." *Journal of Contemporary History* 19, no. 1 (January 1984): 23–57.

Highmore, Ben. *Everyday Life and Cultural Theory: An Introduction*. New York: Routledge, 2002.

——. *Everyday Life Reader*. New York: Routledge, 2002.

Hijiya-Kirschnereit, Irmela. *Rituals of Self-Revelation: Shishōsetsu as Literary Genre and Socio-Cultural Phenomenon*. Cambridge, MA: Council on East Asian Studies, Harvard University, 1996.

Hirano Ken. *Shōwa bungakushi*. Tokyo: Chikuma shobō, 1963.

Hirayama Saburō. *Hyakkien sensei zakkichō*. Tokyo: Mikasa shobō, 1969.

——. *Waga Hyakkien sensei*. Tokyo: Rokkō shuppan, 1979.

Hosten, Germaine A. "Tenkō: Marxism & the National Question in Prewar Japan." *Polity* 16, no. 1 (Autumn 1983): 96–118.

Huyssen, Andreas. *After the Great Divide: Modernism, Mass Culture, Postmodernism*. Bloomington, IN: Indiana University Press, 1986.

——. *Twilight Memories: Marking Time in a Culture of Amnesia*. New York: Routledge, 1995.

Ida Nozomi. "Uchida Hyakken 'Yūshūkan' ron: sei to shi no hazama de yōyō suru 'watakushi.'" *Nihon bungaku kenkyū* 53, no. 3 (December 2001): 13–29.

Imai Tatsuo. "Zuihitsu hanran to zuihitsuteki shōsetsu." *Jiji shinpō*, 12–14 August 1934.

Isoda Tsutomu, ed. *Seijun sutairu*. Tokyo: Waizu shuppan, 2001.

Itō Mino. "Chichi, Uchida Hyakken: dai yon kai." Interview by Nonomura Saburō. *Bungei hiroba* (July 1982): 14–25.

Itō Sei. "Daiichi ahō ressha." In *Kaisō Uchida Hyakken*, ed. Hirayama Saburō. Tokyo: Tsugaru shobō, 1975.

——. "'Shōten' kaisetsu." In *Uchida Hyakken: yume to warai*. Vol. 22 of *Nihon bungaku kenkyū shiryō shinshū*, ed. Sakai Hideyuki. Tokyo: Yūseidō, 1986.

Itō Takashi. *Tōkyō saihakken: doboku isan wa kataru*. Tokyo: Iwanami shoten, 1993.

Ivy, Marilyn. *Discourses of the Vanishing: Modernity, Phantasm, Japan*. Chicago, IL: University of Chicago Press, 1995.

Izumiya Shigeru. "Tsigoineruwaizen." *Kinema junpō* (June 1980): 138.

Jackson, Rosemary. *Fantasy: The Literature of Subversion*. New York: Routledge, 1981.

Jameson, Fredric. *Postmodernism; or, The Cultural Logic of Late Capitalism*. Durham, NC: Duke University Press, 1983.

Jinnai Hidenobu. *Tokyo: A Spatial Anthropology*. Translated by Kimiko Nishimura. Berkeley, CA: University of California Press, 1985.

Kaizōsha, ed. *Kikō zuihitsu shū*. Vol. 36 of *Gendai Nihon bungaku zenshū*. Tokyo: Kaizōsha, 1929.

Kamuro Tōru. "Zuihitsusho no kōzui." *Jiji shinpō*, 13–15 December 1934.

Kanai Mieko. "Eiga jihyō." *Bungei* (June 1980): 182–85.

Kano Masanao. *Taishō demokurashī*. Vol. 27 of *Nihon no rekishi*. Tokyo: Shogakukan, 1976.

Kaplan, Alice and Kristin Ross. "Introduction." *Everyday Life*, special issue of *Yale French Studies* 73 (1987): 1–4.

Karan, P. P. and Kristin Stapleton, eds. *The Japanese City*. Lexington, KY: University of Kentucky Press, 1997.

Karatani Kōjin. *Origins of Modern Japanese Literature*. Durham, NC: Duke University Press, 1993.

Kashiwagi Hiroshi. "On Rationalization and the National Lifestyle: Japanese Design of the 1920s and 1930s." In *Being Modern in Japan: Culture and Society from the 1910s to the 1920s*, ed. Elise K. Tipton and John Clark. Honolulu, HI: University of Hawai'i Press, 2000.

Kataoka Shigeru. "Uchida Hyakken 'Kudan' o yonde." *Komazawa Kokubun* 25 (February 1988): 97–104.

Kawahigashi Hekigotō. "Maru biru, ōrubakku, musan seitō." In *Shūkan Asahi no Shōwashi*, vol. 1. Tokyo: Asahi shinbunsha, 1990.

Kawai, Hayao. *The Japanese Psyche: Major Motifs in the Fairy Tales of Japan*. Woodstock, CT: Spring Publications, 1996.

Kawamoto Saburō. *Taishō gen'ei*. Tokyo: Shinchōsha, 1990.

Kawamura Jirō. *Uchida Hyakken ron: muimi no namida*. Tokyo: Fukutake shoten, 1983.

Kawamura Jirō and Irokawa Takeō. "Uchida Hyakken no fukkatsu." *Bungakukai* (March 1985): 186–204.

Kawamura Jirō and Tanemura Suehiro. "Meiseki naru seishin hakujaku: aruiwa Hyakken ni okeru 'jiga.'" In *Uchida Hyakken: yume to warai*. Vol. 22 of *Nihon bungaku kenkyū shiryō shinshū*, ed. Sakai Hideyuki. Tokyo: Yūseidō, 1986.

Keene, Dennis. *Yokomitsu Riichi: Modernist*. New York: Columbia University Press, 1980.

Keene, Donald. *Dawn to the West: Japanese Literature of the Modern Era – Fiction*. New York: Columbia University Press, 1998.

——. "Japanese Writers and the Greater East Asia War." In *Landscapes and Portraits: Appreciations of Japanese Culture*. Tokyo: Kodansha International, 1971.

——. *Seeds in the Heart: Japanese Literature from Earliest Times to the Late Sixteenth Century*. New York: Henry Holt and Company, 1993.

Klein, Andy. "Give It the Gas: Nuart Series Highlights the Legacy That Was Seijun Suzuki's Thrill Ride." *New Times Los Angeles*, 13 March 1997, sec. movies.

Knoblock, John. *Xunzi: A Translation and Study of the Complete Works*. Vol. 1, Books 1–6. Stanford, CA: Stanford University Press, 1988.

Kōdansha Encyclopedia of Japan. New York: Kodansha, 1983.

Komatsu Hiroshi. "Japan: Before the Great Kanto Earthquake." In *The Oxford History of World Cinema*, ed. Geoffrey Nowell-Smith. Oxford, UK: Oxford University Press, 1996.

——. "Some Characteristics of Japanese Cinema before World War I." Translated by Linda C. Ehrlich and Yuko Okutsu. In *Reframing Japanese Cinema: Authorship, Genre, History*, ed. Arthur Nolletti, Jr. and David Desser. Bloomington, IN: Indiana University Press, 1992.

Konaka Yōtarō. "Tsigoineruwaizen." *Ushio* (July 1980): 210.

Kōno Kensuke. *Tōki toshite no bungaku: katsuji, kenshō, media*. Tokyo: Shin'yōsha, 2003.

——. "Zadankai: shuppan bunka to kindai bungaku." *Bungaku* 9, no. 1 (Winter 1998): 4–28.

Kōno Toshirō, Tanizawa Eiichi, Nishigaki Tsutomu, Sukegawa Noriyoshi, and Takahashi Haruo. *Taishō bungaku*. Volume 17 of *Shinpojiumu Nihon bungaku*. Tokyo: Gakuseisha, 1976.

Kornicki, Peter. *The Book in Japan: A Cultural History from the Beginnings to the Nineteenth Century*. Leiden: Brill, 1998.

Koschmann, J. Victor. *Revolution and Subjectivity in Postwar Japan*. Chicago, IL: University of Chicago Press, 1996.

Kusamori Shinichi and Wada Makoto. "Kantoku no shiken made uketa eiga seinen jidai no omoide." *Kinema junpō* (March 1981): 119–27.

Lefebvre, Henri. *Critique of Everyday Life: Volume I*. Translated by John Moore. London: Verso, 1991.

——. *Everyday Life in the Modern World*. Translated by Sacha Rabinovitch. New Brunswick, NJ: Transaction Publishers, 1984.

Legge, James. *The Works of Mencius*. New York: Dover Publications, 1970.

Lejeune. Philippe. *On Autobiography*. Translated by Katherine Leary. Minneapolis, MN: University of Minnesota Press, 1989.

Levy, David. "Re-constituted Newsreels, Re-enactments and the American Narrative Film." In *Cinema 1900–1906*, ed. Roger Holman. Brussels, Belgium: Fiaf, 1982.

Levy, Indra. *Sirens of the Western Shore: The Westernesque Femme Fatale, Translation, and Vernacular Style in Modern Japanese Literature*. New York: Columbia University Press, 2006.

Lifton, Robert Jay, Shūichi Katō, and Michael R. Reich. *Six Lives, Six Deaths: Portraits from Modern Japan*. New Haven, CT: Yale University Press, 1979.

Lippit, Seiji. "The Disintegrating Machinery of the Modern: Akutagawa Ryūnosuke's Late Writings." *Journal of Asian Studies* 58, no. 1 (February 1999): 27–50.

——. *Topographies of Japanese Modernism.* New York: Columbia University Press, 2002.

Looser, Thomas. "From Edogawa to Miyazaki: Cinematic and *Anime*-ic Architectures of Early and Late Twentieth Century Japan." *Japan Forum* 14, no. 2 (2002): 297–327.

Lu Xun. "Mr. Fujino." In *Dawn Blossoms Plucked at Dusk*, translated by Yang Xianyi and Gladys Yang. Beijing: Foreign Languages Press, 2000.

Mack, Edward T. "The Value of Literature: Cultural Authority in Interwar Japan." Ph.D. dissertation, Harvard University, 2002.

Mackie, Vera. "Modern Selves and Modern Spaces: An Overview." In *Being Modern in Japan: Culture and Society from the 1910s to the 1920s*, ed. Elise K. Tipton and John Clark. Honolulu, HI: University of Hawai'i Press, 2000.

Maeda Ai. *Kindai dokusha no seiritsu.* Tokyo: Chikuma shobō, 1989.

——. *Toshi kūkan no naka no bungaku.* Tokyo: Chikuma shobō, 1982.

Marukawa Tetsushi. "Uchida Hyakken to teito." *10+1* 22 (2000): 201–9.

Masugi Hideki. *Uchida Hyakken no sekai.* Tokyo: Kyōiku shuppan sentā, 1993.

Matsuura Sōzō. *Genkōryō no kenkyū: sakka jānarisuto no keizaigaku.* Tokyo: Miki shobō, 1978.

——, ed. *Bungei shunjū no kenkyū: takaha jānarizumu to shisō no ronri.* Tokyo: Banseisha, 1977.

McDonald, Keiko I. *Reading a Japanese Film: Cinema in Context.* Honolulu, HI: University of Hawai'i Press, 2006.

McLeod, Mary. "Henri Lefebvre's Critique of Everyday Life: An Introduction." In *Architecture of the Everyday*, ed. Steven Harris and Deborah Berke. New York: Princeton Architectural Press, 1997.

Mes, Tom. "Seijun Suzuki." *Midnight Eye.* 11 October 2001. http://www.midnighteye.com/interviews/seijun_suzuki.shtml.

Miki Kiyoshi. "Zuihitsu jidai." In *Miki Kiyoshi zenshū,* vol. 16. Tokyo: Iwanami shoten, 1968.

Minami Hiroshi. *Shōwa bunka.* Tokyo: Keisō shobō, 1987.

——. "Sōsetsu—Ningen seken." In *Ningen seken.* Vol. 1 of *Kindai shomin seikatsu shi.* Tokyo: San'ichi shobō, 1985.

——. *Taishō bunka.* Tokyo: Keisō shobō, 1965.

Mishima Yukio. "'Uchida Hyakken' kaisetsu." In *Uchida Hyakken: yume to warai*. Vol. 22 of *Nihon bungaku kenkyū shiryō shinshū*, ed. Sakai Hideyuki. Tokyo: Yūseidō, 1986.

Mori Ōgai. "Dancing Girl." Translated by Ivan Morris. In *Youth and Other Stories: Mori Ōgai*, ed. J. Thomas Rimer. Honolulu, HI: University of Hawai'i Press, 1994.

Morita Sakan. Oboegaki Hyakkien nōto: shoshi Uchida Hyakken chō. Tokyo: Shōnandō shoten, 1994.

Morita Sōhei. "'Meido' sono ta." In *Uchida Hyakken: yume to warai*. Vol. 22 of *Nihon bungaku kenkyū shiryō shinshū*, ed. Sakai Hideyuki. Tokyo: Yūseidō, 1986.

Murō Saisei. "Hyakkien zuihitsu." In *Uchida Hyakken: yume to warai*. Vol. 22 of *Nihon bungaku kenkyū shiryō shinshū*, ed. Sakai Hideyuki. Tokyo: Yūseidō, 1986.

——. "*Tsuru* to Hyakken Sensei." In *Kaisō Uchida Hyakken*. Tokyo: Tsugaru shobō, 1975.

Murphy, Joseph. "Economies of Culture: The Taishō *Bundan* Dallies with the Movies." *Japan Forum* 11, no. 1 (1999): 5–22.

Nagamine Shigetoshi. "Enpon būmu to dokusha." In *Taishū bunka to masu media*, ed. Aoki Tamotsu et al. Tokyo: Iwanami shoten, 1999.

——. *Modan toshi no dokusho kūkan*. Tokyo: Nihon editā sukūru shuppanbu, 2001.

——. *Zasshi to dokusha no kindai*. Tokyo: Nihon editā sukūru shuppanbu, 1997.

Najita, Tetsuo and H. D. Harootunian. "Japan's Revolt against the West." In *Modern Japanese Thought*, ed. Bob Tadashi Wakabayashi. Cambridge, UK: Cambridge University Press, 1998.

Nakamura Mitsuo. "Warai no sōshitsu." In *Nakamura Mitsuo zenshū*, vol. 10. Tokyo: Chikuma shobō, 1972.

Nakano Shigeharu. "Zuihitsu en'o." In *Nakano Shigeharu zenshū*, vol. 26. Tokyo: Chikuma shobō, 1978.

Nakaya Ukichirō. "Terada Torahiko no tsuisō." In *Suzuki Miekichi, Morita Sōhei, Terada Torahiko, Uchida Hyakken, Naka Kansuke shū*. Vol. 29 of *Gendai Nihon bungaku taikei*. Tokyo: Chikuma shobō, 1974.

Napier, Susan. *The Fantastic in Modern Japanese Literature: The Subversion of Modernity*. New York: Routledge, 1996.

Natsume Sōseki. "London Tower." In *The Tower of London*. Translated by Peter Milward and Kii Nakano. Brighton, UK: In Print Publishing, 1992.

——. *Ten Nights of Dream, Hearing Things, The Heredity of Taste.* Translated by Aiko Ito and Graeme Wilson. Rutland, VT: Charles E. Tuttle, 1974.

——. "Yume jūya." In *Sōseki zenshū*, vol. 12. Tokyo: Iwanami shoten, 1994.

*Nihon Eiga 1981: '80-nen kōkai Nihon eiga zenshū.* Tokyo: Haga shoten, 1981.

Nihon kindai bungakukan, ed. *Nihon kindai bungaku daijiten.* 6 Vols. Tokyo: Kōdansha, 1977–78.

Odagiri Hideo. "Bungaku ni okeru sensō sekinin." *Shin Nihon bungaku* 3, no. 3 (June 1946): 64–65.

Odagiri Susumu. *Kindai Nihon no nikki.* Tokyo: Kōdansha, 1984.

Okamoto Shumpei. "The Emperor and the Crowd: The Historical Significance of the Hibiya Riot." In *Conflict in Modern Japanese History: The Neglected Tradition*, ed. Tetsuo Najita and J. Victor Koschmann. Princeton, NJ: Princeton University Press, 1982.

Okaya Kōji. "Yume no shikaku: watakushi no Uchida Hyakken." *Yuriika* (February 1984): 134–40.

Pollock, Griselda. *Vision and Difference: Femininity, Feminism, and Histories of Art.* New York: Routledge, 1988.

Prince, Stephen. *The Warrior's Camera: The Cinema of Akira Kurosawa.* Princeton, NJ: Princeton University Press, 1991.

Radway, Janice. *A Feeling for Books: The Book-of-the-Month Club, Literary Taste, and Middle-Class Desire.* Chapel Hill, NC: University of North Carolina Press, 1997.

Rayns, Tony. "The Kyoka Factor: The Delights of Suzuki Seijun." In *Branded to Thrill: The Delirious Cinema of Suzuki Seijun*, ed. Simon Field and Tony Rayns. London: Institute of Contemporary Arts, 1994.

Rayns, Tony and Simon Field, eds. *Branded to Thrill: The Delirious Cinema of Suzuki Seijun.* London: Institute of Contemporary Arts, 1994.

Richie, Donald. *A Hundred Years of Japanese Film.* New York: Kodansha International, 2001.

Rikusenshi kenkyū fukyūkai, ed. *Nichi-Ro sensō Ryojun yōsai kōryakusen.* Tokyo: Hara shobō, 1969.

Robertson, Jennifer. "Hegemonic Nostalgia, Tourism, and Nation-Making in Japan." In *Japanese Civilization in the Modern World*, ed. Tadao Umesao, Harumi Befu, and Shuzo Ishimori. Senri Ethnological Studies no. 38. Osaka: National Museum of Ethnology, 1995.

Rubin, Jay. *Injurious to Public Morals: Writers and the Meiji State*. Seattle, WA: University of Washington Press, 1984.

Rubin, Joan Shelley. *The Making of Middlebrow Culture*. Chapel Hill, NC: University of North Carolina Press, 1992.

Ryan, Marleigh. "Modern Japanese Fiction: 'Accommodated Truth.'" *Journal of Japanese Studies* 2, no. 2 (Summer 1976): 249–66.

Sakada Minoru. "Modanizumu no jidai sō." In *Ningen seken*. Vol. 1 of *Kindai shomin seikatsu shi*. Tokyo: San'ichi shobō, 1985.

Sakai Hideyuki. *Hyakken: Ai no ayumi, bungaku no ayumi*. Tokyo: Yūseidō, 1995.

——. *Uchida Hyakken: "Hyakki" no yuraku*. Tokyo: Yūseidō, 1993.

——, ed. *Uchida Hyakken: yume to warai*. Vol. 22 of *Nihon bungaku kenkyū shiryō shinshū*. Tokyo: Yūseidō, 1986.

Sakurai Tetsuo, "20-seiki nikki shō: *Furukawa Roppa Shōwa nikki*." *THIS IS yomimono* (September 1996): 266–71.

Sand, Jordan. "The Cultured Life as Contested Space: Dwelling and Discourse in the 1920s." In *Being Modern in Japan: Culture and Society from the 1910s to the 1920s*, ed. Elise K. Tipton and John Clark. Honolulu, HI: University of Hawai'i Press, 2000.

——. *House and Home in Modern Japan: Architecture, Domestic Space, and Bourgeois Culture, 1880–1930*. Cambridge, MA: Harvard University Asia Center, 2005.

Sas, Miryam. *Fault Lines: Cultural Memory and Japanese Surrealism*. Stanford, CA: Stanford University Press, 1999.

Sasaki Kiichi. "Kaitai ka, atarashii riariti no hakken ka." In *Hōhō no jikken*. Vol. 2 of *Zenshū: gendai bungaku no hakken*. Tokyo: Gakugei shorin, 1968.

Sata Yoshihisa. "Shinkeibyō jidai." In *Ningen seken*. Vol. 1 of *Kindai shomin seikatsu shi*. Tokyo: San'ichi shobō, 1985.

Satō Haruo. "The Fingerprint." In *Beautiful Town: Stories and Essays*. Translated by Francis B. Tenny. Honolulu, HI: University of Hawai'i Press, 1996.

——. "House of the Spanish Dog." Translated by George Saitō. In *Modern Japanese Stories: An Anthology*, ed. Ivan Morris. Rutland, VT: Charles E. Tuttle, 1993.

——. "Kubi kukuri no heya." *Chūō kōron* 38, no. 5 (1923): 180–82.

Satō Tadao. *ATG eiga o yomu: 60-nendai ni hajimatta meisaku no ākaibu*. Tokyo: Film Art, 1991.

——. *Nihon eigashi*. Vol. 1, *1896–1940*. Tokyo: Iwanami shoten, 1995.

——. "Tsigoineruwaizen." *Shinario* (June 1980): 154–55.

Scott, Clive. "Symbolism, Decadence, and Impressionism." In *Modernism: A Guide to European Literature 1890–1930,* ed. Malcolm Bradbury and James McFarlane. London: Penguin, 1991.

Screech, Timon. *The Western Scientific Gaze and Popular Imagery in Later Edo Japan: The Lens Within the Heart.* Cambridge, UK: Cambridge University Press, 1996.

Seidensticker, Edward. *Low City, High City: Tokyo from Edo to the Earthquake.* New York: Alfred A. Knopf, 1983.

Shibata Hisaki. *Shibata Hisaki bunshū,* vol. 7. Tokyo: Ozawa shoten, 1993.

Shields, Rob. *Lefebvre, Love and Struggle: Spatial Dialectics.* New York: Routledge, 1999.

Shimada Atsushi. "Bungaku ni arawareta modanizumu." In *Nihon modanizumu no kenkyū: shisō, seikatsu, bunka,* ed. Minami Hiroshi. Tokyo: Bureen shuppan, 1982.

Shinario sakka kyōkai, ed. *Nenkan daihyō shinarioshū: 1980-nen ban.* Tokyo: Daviddosha, 1981.

Shirane, Haruo. "Curriculum and Competing Canons." In *Inventing the Classics: Modernity, National Identity, and Japanese Literature,* ed. Haruo Shirane and Tomi Suzuki. Stanford, CA: Stanford University Press, 2000.

——. "Introduction: Issues in Canon Formation." In *Inventing the Classics: Modernity, National Identity, and Japanese Literature,* ed. Haruo Shirane and Tomi Suzuki. Stanford, CA: Stanford University Press, 2000.

Shirane, Haruo and Tomi Suzuki, eds. *Inventing the Classics: Modernity, National Identity, and Japanese Literature.* Stanford, CA: Stanford University Press, 2000.

Shishido Jō. "Seijun-san wa Taishō roman no senchimentarisuto." In *Seijun Sutairu,* ed. Isoda Tsutomu. Tokyo: Waizu shuppan, 2001.

Shōji Hajime. *Uchida Hyakken: hitoripotchi no piero.* Tokyo: Chūsekisha, 1993.

Silverberg, Miriam. "The Café Waitress Serving Modern Japan." In *Invented Traditions of Modern Japan,* ed. Stephen Vlastos. Berkeley, CA: University of California Press, 1998.

——. *Changing Song: The Marxist Manifestos of Nakano Shigeharu.* Princeton, NJ: Princeton University Press, 1990.

——. "Constructing a New Cultural History of Prewar Japan." In *Japan in the World,* ed. Masao Miyoshi and H. D. Harootunian. Durham, NC: Duke University Press, 1993.

——. "Constructing the Japanese Ethnography of Modernity." *Journal of Asian Studies* 51, no. 1 (February 1992): 30–54.

——. *Erotic Grotesque Nonsense: The Mass Culture of Modern Times.* Berkeley, CA: University of California Press, 2006.

——. "The Modern Girl as Militant." In *Recreating Japanese Women: 1600–1945,* ed. Gail Lee Bernstein. Berkeley, CA: University of California Press, 1991.

Simmel, Georg. "The Metropolis and Mental Life." In *The Blackwell City Reader,* ed. Gary Bridge and Sophie Watson. Oxford, UK: Blackwell, 2002.

Singer, Ben. *Melodrama and Modernity: Early Sensational Cinema and Its Contexts.* New York: Columbia University Press, 2001.

Skya, Walter. *Japan's Holy War: The Ideology of Radical Shinto Ultranationalism.* Durham, NC: Duke University Press, 2009.

Smith, Henry D. "Tokyo as an Idea: An Exploration of Japanese Urban Thought Until 1945." *Journal of Japanese Studies* 4, no. 1 (Winter 1978): 45–80.

Strecher, Matthew C. "Purely Massive or Massively Pure? The Division Between 'Pure' and 'Mass' Literature." *Monumenta Nipponica* 51, no. 3 (Autumn 1966): 357–74.

Suzuki Kōichi. "Miwataseba hana mo arashi mo. . . ." *Tsukuru* (July 1980): 234–37.

Suzuki Sadami. "Junbungaku to taishū bungaku." *Bungakukai* (October 1993): 170–92.

Suzuki, Tomi. "Gender and Genre: Modern Literary Histories and Women's Diary Literature." In *Inventing the Classics: Modernity, National Identity, and Japanese Literature,* ed. Haruo Shirane and Tomi Suzuki. Stanford, CA: Stanford University Press, 2000.

——. *Narrating the Self: Fictions of Japanese Modernity.* Stanford, CA: Stanford University, 1996.

Tada Motoi. "'Iya da kara, iya da' no otsukai o shite." In *Uchida Hyakken: yume to warai.* Vol. 22 of *Nihon bungaku kenkyū shiryō shinshū,* ed. Sakai Hideyuki. Tokyo: Yūseidō, 1986.

Takada Mizuho. "Bungeiteki na, amari ni bungeiteki na." In *Akutagawa Ryūnosuke,* ed. Nihon bungaku kenkyū shiryō kankōkai. Tokyo: Yūseidō shuppan, 1970.

——. "Kindai no zuihitsu." *Kokubungaku kaishaku to kyōzai no kenkyū* 10, no. 9 (July 1965): 116–22.

Takahashi Hideo. *Mugen keiretsu: Sōseki, Ryūnosuke, Hyakken.* Tokyo: Ozawa shoten, 1989.

Takahashi Yoshitaka. "Kaisetsu." In *Shōwa bungaku zenshū*, vol. 42. Tokyo: Kadokawa shoten, 1954.

Takeuchi Michinosuke. "*Hyakkien zuihitsu* gaiden." In *Kaisō Uchida Hyakken*, ed. Hirayama Saburō. Tokyo: Tsugaru shobō, 1975.

Takeuchi Yoshimi. *Kindai no chōkoku*. Tokyo: Chikuma shobō, 1979.

Taki Daisaku, "Kaisetsu." In *Furukawa Roppa Shōwa nikki*. Vol. 1, *Senzen hen*. Tokyo: Shōbunsha, 1987–88.

Tanizaki Jun'ichirō. "Longing for Mother." Translated with an Afterword by Edward Fowler. *Monumenta Nipponica* 35, no. 4 (Winter 1980): 467–78.

Teo, Stephen. "Seijun Suzuki: Authority in Minority." Spotlight on 49th Melbourne International Film Festival. July 2000. http://www.sensesofcinema.com/contents/00/8/miff/suzuki.html.

Tipton, Elise K. "The Café: Contested Space of Modernity in Interwar Japan." In *Being Modern in Japan: Culture and Society from the 1910s to the 1920s*, ed. Elise K. Tipton and John Clark. Honolulu, HI: University of Hawai'i Press, 2000.

Tosaka Jun. "Shisō to shite no bungaku." In *Tosaka Jun zenshū*, vol. 4. Tokyo: Keisō shobō, 1966.

Toyama Shigehiko. "Zuihitsuteki naru mono no han'i." *Kokubungaku kaishaku to kyōzai no kenkyū* 10, no. 9 (July 1965): 12–17.

Trebitsch, Michel. Preface to *Critique of Everyday Life: Volume I*, by Henri Lefebvre. London: Verso, 1991.

Treat, John Whittier, ed. *Contemporary Japan and Popular Culture*. Honolulu, HI: University of Hawai'i Press, 1996.

Tsubouchi Yūzō. *Yasukuni*. Tokyo: Shinchōsha, 1999.

Tsubouchi Yūzō and Yoshida Tsukasa. "Yasukuni Shrine as a Symbol of Japan's Modernization." *Japan Echo* 26, no. 3 (June 1999): 48–51.

Tsuchimoto Noriaki. "Jissha eiga o miru." In *Nihon eiga no tanjō*. Vol. 1 of *Kōza Nihon eiga*. Tokyo: Iwanami shoten, 1985.

Tyler, Royall. *Japanese Nō Dramas*. London: Penguin Books, 1992.

Uchida Hyakken. *Realm of the Dead*. Translated by Rachel DiNitto. Normal, IL and London: Dalkey Archive Press, 2006.

——. *Shinshū Uchida Hyakken zenshū*. 33 vols. Tokyo: Fukutake shoten, 1986–89.

——. *Uchida Hyakken zenshū*. 10 vols. Tokyo: Kōdansha, 1971–73.

——. *Watashi no "Sōseki" to "Ryūnosuke."* Tokyo: Chikuma sōsho, 1965.

Uchida Michio. "Hyakkien būmu kō." *Mainichi Shinbun*, 13 June 1983, evening edition.

——. Meido *no shūhen*. Tokyo: Kanrin shobō, 1997.

———. "Uchida Hyakken nōto (I)." In *Uchida Hyakken: yume to warai*. Vol. 22 of *Nihon bungaku kenkyū shiryō shinshū*, ed. Sakai Hideyuki. Tokyo: Yūseidō, 1986.

———, ed. *Uchida Hyakken*. Vol. 42 of *Shinchō Nihon bungaku arubamu*. Tokyo: Shinchōsha, 1993.

Ueno Kōshi. "Suzuki Seijun no undō." *Yuriika* (June 1980): 170–77.

———, ed. *Suzuki Seijun zen'eiga*. Tokyo: Rippū shobō, 1986.

Unno Hiroshi. *Modan toshi Tōkyō: Nihon no 1920 nendai*. Tokyo: Chūō kōronsha, 1983.

Upton, Dell. "Architecture in Everyday Life." *New Literary History* 33, no. 4 (Autumn 2002): 707–23.

Uranishi Kazuhiko. "Dōjin zasshi no jidai." In *Toshi to kigō: Shōwa shonendai no bungaku*. Vol. 1 of *Kōza Shōwa bungakushi*. Tokyo: Yūseidō, 1988.

Wada Toshio. "Kindai no zuihitsu to zuihitsu no 'kindai.'" In *Nikki, zuihitsu, kiroku*. Vol. 7 of *Nihon bungaku kōza*. Tokyo: Taishūkan, 1989.

Waki Teruko. "Monogatari no nai fūkei: Hyakken to Kyōka." *Yuriika* (February 1984): 79–83.

Watanabe, Shun-ichi J. "Metropolitanism as a Way of Life: The Case of Tokyo, 1868–1930. In *Metropolis 1890–1940*, ed. Anthony Sutcliffe. Chicago, IL: University of Chicago Press, 1984.

Watts, Jonathan. "Japan's Revisionists Turn Emperor into a God Once More." *The Guardian*, 21 August 2002. http://www.guardian.co.uk/world/2002/aug/21/japan.jonathanwatts.

White, Steven K. *Sustaining Affirmation: The Strengths of Weak Ontology in Political Theory*. Princeton, NJ: Princeton University Press, 2000.

Wilson, Sandra. "The Past in the Present: War in Narratives of Modernity in the 1920s and 1930s." In *Being Modern in Japan: Culture and Society from the 1910s to the 1930s*, ed. Elise K. Tipton and John Clark. Honolulu, HI: University of Hawai'i Press, 2000.

———. "The Russo-Japanese War and Japan: Politics, Nationalism and Historical Memory." In *The Russo-Japanese War in Cultural Perspective, 1904–05*, ed. David Wells and Sandra Wilson. New York: St. Martin's Press, 1999.

Wilson, Sandra and David Wells. "Introduction." In *The Russo-Japanese War in Cultural Perspective, 1904–05*, ed. David Wells and Sandra Wilson. New York: St. Martin's Press, 1999.

Yamaguchi Tōru. "Meido ni sasurau kotoba." *Nihon kindai bungaku* 62 (May 2000): 70–83.

Yamamoto Taketoshi. *Kindai Nihon no shinbun dokushasō*. Tokyo: Hōsei Daigaku shuppankyoku, 1981.

Yamamura, Kozo. "The Japanese Economy, 1911–1930: Concentration, Conflicts, and Crises." In *Japan in Crisis*, ed. Bernard S. Silberman and H. D. Harootunian. Princeton, NJ: Princeton University Press, 1974.

Yasukuni Jinja. *Yasukuni Jinja hyakunenshi*. 4 vols. Tokyo: Yasukuni Jinja, 1984.

———. *Yasukuni no inori: me de miru Meiji, Taishō, Shōwa, Heisei*. Tokyo: Sankei Shinbun nyūsu sābisu, 1999.

Yoda, Tomiko and Harry Harootunian, eds. *Japan After Japan: Social and Cultural Life from the Recessionary 1990s to the Present*. Durham, NC: Duke University Press, 2006.

Yoshida Seiichi. "Akutagawa Ryūnosuke shū kaisetsu." In *Akutagawa Ryūnosuke shū*. Vol. 38 of *Nihon kindai bungaku taikei*. Tokyo: Kadokawa shoten, 1970.

———. *Zuihitsu no sekai*. Vol. 25 of *Yoshida Seiichi chosakushū*. Tokyo: Ōfūsha, 1980.

Yoshimi Shun'ya. *Toshi no doramaturugī: Tōkyō, sakariba no shakaishi*. Tokyo: Kōbundō, 1987.

Yoshimoto, Mitsuhiro. *Kurosawa: Film Studies and Japanese Cinema*. Durham, NC: Duke University Press, 2000.

Yoshiyuki Kazuko and Saitō Masaya, eds. *Yoshiyuki Eisuke to sono jidai: modan toshi no hikari to kage*. Tokyo: Tōkyō shiki shuppan, 1997.

Young, Louise. *Japan's Total Empire: Manchuria and the Culture of Wartime Imperialism*. Berkeley, CA: University of California Press, 1998.

———. "Marketing the Modern: Department Stores, Consumer Culture, and the New Middle Class in Interwar Japan." *International Labor and Working-Class History* 55 (Spring 1999): 52–70.

# List of Characters

Abe Yutaka 阿部豊
Ahō ressha 阿房列車
Aikonokurasumu 偶像破壊
Akutagawa Ryūnosuke
芥川龍之介
Aochi Toyojirō 青地豊二郎
Aoji Hōjirō 青路法二郎
Asakusa kurenaidan
浅草紅団
Atsumori 敦盛

binbō monogatari 貧乏物語
Bokutō kitan 濹東綺譚
bundan 文壇
bungei eiga 文芸映画
Bungei shunjū 文芸春秋
Bunshō sekai 文章世界
bushidō 武士道

Chiba Kameo 千葉亀雄
Chikamatsu Shūkō
近松秋江
chōchin 提灯
chōtsugai 蝶番
Chūgaku sekai 中学世界
Chūō kōron 中央公論

Dote 土手

Eiga jidai 映画時代
Eizō 映像
Enomoto Ken'ichi (Enoken)
榎本健一（エノケン）

Fuji no hana 藤の花
Fujita Hyakkien 藤田百鬼園
Fujita Hyakuan 藤田百庵
Fukagawa no uta 深川の唄
Fumetsu Nogi 不滅乃木
Furokku kōto フロックコート
Furukawa Roppa 古川緑波
(ロッパ)

Gansaku wagahai wa neko de
aru 贋作吾輩は猫である
ginbura 銀ブラ
Ginza 銀座
Gochisōchō 御馳走帖
gokoku no oni 護国の鬼
Gonda Yasunosuke
権田保之助
gunka 軍歌
gunshin 軍神

hageyama 禿山
Hagiwara Sakutarō 萩原朔太郎
Hana 鼻
Hanabi 花火
Hatoba 波止場
Hatta Naoyuki 八田尚之
Hayashi Fumiko 林芙美子
Hayashi Fusao 林房雄
Hibiya 日比谷
Hirabayashi Hatsunosuke 平林初之輔
Hirano Ken 平野謙
Hirose Takeo 広瀬武夫
Hori Tatsuo 堀辰雄
Horino Yutaka 堀野寛
Hōsōshin 疱瘡神

Hyakkien haiku 百鬼園俳句
Hyakkien sengo nikki 百鬼園戦後日記
Hyakkien sensei genkōroku 百鬼園先生言行録
Hyakkien sensei genkōyoroku 百鬼園先生言行余録
Hyakkien shinsō 百鬼園新装
Hyakkien zuihitsu 百鬼園随筆
hyōhakusha 漂泊者

Ibuse Masuji 井伏鱒二
Ichigaya 市ヶ谷
itchō Rondon 一丁ロンドン
Itō Sei 伊藤整
Ittōsha 一等車
Iwanami Shoten 岩波書店

Jigoku no mon 地獄の門
Jiji shinpō 時事新報
Jintōshi 尽頭子
Jissetsu Sōheiki 実説艸平記
jissha eiga 実写映画
Josei 女性
Jūgonen sensō 十五年戦争
junbungaku 純文学
junshi 殉死
junsui bunshō 純粋文章

Kagayaku kōgun 輝く皇軍
kage-e 影絵
Kaigun Kikan Gakkō 海軍機関学校
Kaizō 改造
Kamei Katsuichirō 亀井勝一郎
Kanda 神田
Karasu 烏
Katō Hiroyuki 加藤弘之
Kawabata Yasunari 川端康成
Kawaguchi Matsutarō 川口松太郎
Kawahigashi Hekigotō 河東碧梧桐
Keizai ōrai 経済往来
Kentōshi 遣唐使
Kikuchi Kan 菊池寛
kindai tōyōshiki 近代東洋式
Kinema junpō キネマ旬報
Kingu キング
kiroku eiga 記録映画
Kishida Kunio 岸田國士
Kobayashi Ichizō 小林一三
Kobayashi Takiji 小林多喜二
Kōbu 甲武
Kodama 木霊
Kohaku 琥珀
Kokumin Daigaku 国民大学
Kon Wajirō 今和次郎
Korera 虎列刺
Kudan (short story) 件
Kudan (district) 九段

kukaku seiri 区画整理
Kuki Shūzō 九鬼周造
Kume Masao 久米正雄
Kuru ya omae ka クルやお前か
Kyōrinki 梟林記

Maada kai 摩阿陀会
Mamore manmō 守れ満蒙
Manseibashi 万世橋
Manuke no jitsuzai ni kansuru bunken 間抜けの実在に関する文献
Marunouchi 丸の内
Meido 冥途
Meso めそ
Michizure 道連
Mijikayo 短夜
Mikasa Shobō 三笠書房
Miki Kiyoshi 三木清
Miokuri 見送り
Mishima Yukio 三島由紀夫
mobo モボ
Modan Nihon モダン日本
Modori michi 戻り道
moga モガ
Mokuren 木蓮
Mokuyōkai 木曜会
monogatari 物語
Mori Ōgai 森鴎外
Morita Sōhei 森田草平
mugen shōsetsu 夢幻小説
Mukō saisha mukō shin 無恒債者無恒心
Mura no ie 村の家
Murō Saisei 室生犀星

Nagai Kafū 永井荷風
Nakamura Mitsuo 中村光夫
Nakamura Murao 中村武羅夫
Nakano Shigeharu 中野重治
Nami 浪
Natsume Sōseki 夏目漱石
Nichibotsu heimon 日没閉門
nichijō kūkan 日常空間
nichijōsei 日常性
Nihon Bungaku Hōkokukai 日本文学報国会
Nihon Geijutsuin 日本藝術院
Nihon Kaiki 日本回帰
Nihon Roman-ha 日本浪漫派
nō 能
Nogi Maresuke 乃木希典
Nogi shōgun 乃木将軍
Nonomiya 野宮
Nora ya ノラや
nosutarujī shōhin ノスタルジー商品

Ōhashi Chōichirō 大橋長一郎
Okaru おかる
Oki no inazuma 沖の稲妻
Omoi okose Nogi shōgun 憶ひ起せ乃木将軍
oni tōrō 鬼灯篭
Ōru yomimono オール讀物

Rikugun Shikan Gakkō 陸軍士官学校
Rōbyō monogatari 老猫物語
Rokumeikan 鹿鳴館
Roppa no Hoojiro sensei ロッパの頬白先生
Ryojun kaijō to Nogi shogun 旅順開城と乃木将軍
Ryojun nyūjōshiki 旅順入城式
Ryūboku 流木
Ryūsō 柳藻
Ryūtanji Yū 龍胆寺雄

Saiki 債鬼
sakariba 盛り場
Samushiro 狭筵
Sandē Mainichi サンデー毎日
Sangatsu tōka 三月十日
Sanshirō 三四郎
Santō Kyōden 山東京伝
Sarasāte no ban
サラサーテの盤
Satō Haruo 佐藤春夫
Satō Koi 佐藤こひ
Satomi Ton 里見弴
shiden 市電
Shinajin 支那人
Shinbashi 新橋
Shinchō 新潮
Shinhōjōki 新方丈記
Shinkankaku-ha 新感覚派
Shinkōgeijutsu-ha
新興芸術派
shinkyō shōsetsu 心境小説
Shinseinen 新青年
Shirako 白子
shishōsetsu 私小説
Shisō 思想
Shōkonsha 招魂社
Shōnen kurabu 少年倶楽部
Shōsetsu shinchō 小説新潮
Shuju no kotoba 侏儒の言葉
Shūkan Asahi 週刊朝日
Shūkō zuihitsu 秋江随筆
Shumi no iden 趣味の遺伝
Shun'yōdō 春陽堂
sōsaku 創作
Sōyū 曽遊
Sudachō 須田町
Suishiei no kaiken
水師営の会見
Suzuki Seijun 鈴木清順
Taishō 大正
taishū shōsetsu 大衆小説
Takahama Kyoshi 高浜虚子
Takarazuka 宝塚
Takayama Chogyū 高山樗牛
Takeuchi Michinosuke
竹内道之助
Tamanoi 玉の井
Tanaka Yōzō 田中陽造
Tanizaki Jun'ichirō
谷崎潤一郎
teikan yōshiki 帝冠様式
tenkō 転向
Terada Torahiko 寺田寅彦
Tokage 蜥蜴
Tokubetsu ahō ressha
特別阿房列車
Tōkyō Asahi shinbun
東京朝日新聞
Tōkyō Hassei 東京発声
Tōkyō nikki 東京日記
Tōkyō shōjin 東京焼尽
Tōmondō 稲門堂
Tonbodama 蜻蛉玉
Tosaka Jun 戸坂潤
toshi keikaku 都市計画
toshi shōsetsu 都市小説
Toyoda Shirō 豊田四郎
Toyoshima Yoshio
豊島与志雄
Tsuru 鶴

Uchida Hyakken
内田百閒 (百間)
Uchida Kiyoko 内田清子
Ujita Hyakugen 蛆田百減
Ukatōsen 羽化登仙
Uno Kōji 宇野浩二
Utsukushii mura 美しい村

Wagahai wa neko de aru
吾輩は猫である
Warai no sōshitsu 笑いの喪失
Watsuji Tetsurō 和辻哲郎
Yamamoto Yūzō 山本有三
Yamanote 山の手
Yamataka bōshi 山高帽子
yama-uba 山姥
Yanagita Kunio 柳田国男
Yasuda Yojūrō 保田與重郎
Yasukuni Jinja 靖国神社
Yōkyoshū 漾虚集
Yokomitsu Riichi 横光利一
Yoshiyuki Eisuke
吉行エイスケ
Yume jūya 夢十夜
Yume miru heya 夢見る部屋
Yūshūkan 遊就館

zuihitsu 随筆
zuihitsu hanran 随筆氾濫
zuihitsuka 随筆家

# *Index*

*Harvard East Asian Monographs*
(*out-of-print)

*1. Liang Fang-chung, *The Single-Whip Method of Taxation in China*

*2. Harold C. Hinton, *The Grain Tribute System of China, 1845–1911*

3. Ellsworth C. Carlson, *The Kaiping Mines, 1877–1912*

*4. Chao Kuo-chün, *Agrarian Policies of Mainland China: A Documentary Study, 1949–1956*

*5. Edgar Snow, *Random Notes on Red China, 1936–1945*

*6. Edwin George Beal, Jr., *The Origin of Likin, 1835–1864*

7. Chao Kuo-chün, *Economic Planning and Organization in Mainland China: A Documentary Study, 1949–1957*

*8. John K. Fairbank, *Ching Documents: An Introductory Syllabus*

*9. Helen Yin and Yi-chang Yin, *Economic Statistics of Mainland China, 1949–1957*

10. Wolfgang Franke, *The Reform and Abolition of the Traditional Chinese Examination System*

11. Albert Feuerwerker and S. Cheng, *Chinese Communist Studies of Modern Chinese History*

12. C. John Stanley, *Late Ching Finance: Hu Kuang-yung as an Innovator*

13. S. M. Meng, *The Tsungli Yamen: Its Organization and Functions*

*14. Ssu-yü Teng, *Historiography of the Taiping Rebellion*

15. Chun-Jo Liu, *Controversies in Modern Chinese Intellectual History: An Analytic Bibliography of Periodical Articles, Mainly of the May Fourth and Post-May Fourth Era*

*16. Edward J. M. Rhoads, *The Chinese Red Army, 1927–1963: An Annotated Bibliography*

*17. Andrew J. Nathan, *A History of the China International Famine Relief Commission*

*18. Frank H. H. King (ed.) and Prescott Clarke, *A Research Guide to China-Coast Newspapers, 1822–1911*

*19. Ellis Joffe, *Party and Army: Professionalism and Political Control in the Chinese Officer Corps, 1949–1964*

*20. Toshio G. Tsukahira, *Feudal Control in Tokugawa Japan: The Sankin Kōtai System*

*21. Kwang-Ching Liu, ed., *American Missionaries in China: Papers from Harvard Seminars*

*22. George Moseley, *A Sino-Soviet Cultural Frontier: The Ili Kazakh Autonomous Chou*

23. Carl F. Nathan, *Plague Prevention and Politics in Manchuria, 1910–1931*

*24. Adrian Arthur Bennett, *John Fryer: The Introduction of Western Science and Technology into Nineteenth-Century China*

*25. Donald J. Friedman, *The Road from Isolation: The Campaign of the American Committee for Non-Participation in Japanese Aggression, 1938–1941*

*26. Edward LeFevour, *Western Enterprise in Late Ching China: A Selective Survey of Jardine, Matheson and Company's Operations, 1842–1895*

27. Charles Neuhauser, *Third World Politics: China and the Afro-Asian People's Solidarity Organization, 1957–1967*

*28. Kungtu C. Sun, assisted by Ralph W. Huenemann, *The Economic Development of Manchuria in the First Half of the Twentieth Century*

*29. Shahid Javed Burki, *A Study of Chinese Communes, 1965*

30. John Carter Vincent, *The Extraterritorial System in China: Final Phase*

31. Madeleine Chi, *China Diplomacy, 1914–1918*

*32. Clifton Jackson Phillips, *Protestant America and the Pagan World: The First Half Century of the American Board of Commissioners for Foreign Missions, 1810–1860*

*33. James Pusey, *Wu Han: Attacking the Present Through the Past*

*34. Ying-wan Cheng, *Postal Communication in China and Its Modernization, 1860–1896*

35. Tuvia Blumenthal, *Saving in Postwar Japan*

36. Peter Frost, *The Bakumatsu Currency Crisis*

37. Stephen C. Lockwood, *Augustine Heard and Company, 1858–1862*

38. Robert R. Campbell, *James Duncan Campbell: A Memoir by His Son*

39. Jerome Alan Cohen, ed., *The Dynamics of China's Foreign Relations*

40. V. V. Vishnyakova-Akimova, *Two Years in Revolutionary China, 1925–1927,* trans. Steven L. Levine

41. Meron Medzini, *French Policy in Japan During the Closing Years of the Tokugawa Regime*

42. Ezra Vogel, Margie Sargent, Vivienne B. Shue, Thomas Jay Mathews, and Deborah S. Davis, *The Cultural Revolution in the Provinces*

43. Sidney A. Forsythe, *An American Missionary Community in China, 1895–1905*

*44. Benjamin I. Schwartz, ed., *Reflections on the May Fourth Movement.: A Symposium*

*45. Ching Young Choe, *The Rule of the Taewŏngun, 1864–1873: Restoration in Yi Korea*

46. W. P. J. Hall, *A Bibliographical Guide to Japanese Research on the Chinese Economy, 1958–1970*

47. Jack J. Gerson, *Horatio Nelson Lay and Sino-British Relations, 1854–1864*

48. Paul Richard Bohr, *Famine and the Missionary: Timothy Richard as Relief Administrator and Advocate of National Reform*
49. Endymion Wilkinson, *The History of Imperial China: A Research Guide*
50. Britten Dean, *China and Great Britain: The Diplomacy of Commercial Relations, 1860–1864*
51. Ellsworth C. Carlson, *The Foochow Missionaries, 1847–1880*
52. Yeh-chien Wang, *An Estimate of the Land-Tax Collection in China, 1753 and 1908*
53. Richard M. Pfeffer, *Understanding Business Contracts in China, 1949–1963*
*54. Han-sheng Chuan and Richard Kraus, *Mid-Ching Rice Markets and Trade: An Essay in Price History*
55. Ranbir Vohra, *Lao She and the Chinese Revolution*
56. Liang-lin Hsiao, *China's Foreign Trade Statistics, 1864–1949*
*57. Lee-hsia Hsu Ting, *Government Control of the Press in Modern China, 1900–1949*
*58. Edward W. Wagner, *The Literati Purges: Political Conflict in Early Yi Korea*
*59. Joungwon A. Kim, *Divided Korea: The Politics of Development, 1945–1972*
60. Noriko Kamachi, John K. Fairbank, and Chūzō Ichiko, *Japanese Studies of Modern China Since 1953: A Bibliographical Guide to Historical and Social-Science Research on the Nineteenth and Twentieth Centuries, Supplementary Volume for 1953–1969*
61. Donald A. Gibbs and Yun-chen Li, *A Bibliography of Studies and Translations of Modern Chinese Literature, 1918–1942*
62. Robert H. Silin, *Leadership and Values: The Organization of Large-Scale Taiwanese Enterprises*
63. David Pong, *A Critical Guide to the Kwangtung Provincial Archives Deposited at the Public Record Office of London*
*64. Fred W. Drake, *China Charts the World: Hsu Chi-yü and His Geography of 1848*
*65. William A. Brown and Urgrunge Onon, translators and annotators, *History of the Mongolian People's Republic*
66. Edward L. Farmer, *Early Ming Government: The Evolution of Dual Capitals*
*67. Ralph C. Croizier, *Koxinga and Chinese Nationalism: History, Myth, and the Hero*
*68. William J. Tyler, tr., *The Psychological World of Natsume Sōseki,* by Doi Takeo
69. Eric Widmer, *The Russian Ecclesiastical Mission in Peking During the Eighteenth Century*
*70. Charlton M. Lewis, *Prologue to the Chinese Revolution: The Transformation of Ideas and Institutions in Hunan Province, 1891–1907*
71. Preston Torbert, *The Ching Imperial Household Department: A Study of Its Organization and Principal Functions, 1662–1796*
72. Paul A. Cohen and John E. Schrecker, eds., *Reform in Nineteenth-Century China*
73. Jon Sigurdson, *Rural Industrialism in China*
74. Kang Chao, *The Development of Cotton Textile Production in China*

75. Valentin Rabe, *The Home Base of American China Missions, 1880–1920*
*76. Sarasin Viraphol, *Tribute and Profit: Sino-Siamese Trade, 1652–1853*
77. Ch'i-ch'ing Hsiao, *The Military Establishment of the Yuan Dynasty*
78. Meishi Tsai, *Contemporary Chinese Novels and Short Stories, 1949–1974: An Annotated Bibliography*
*79. Wellington K. K. Chan, *Merchants, Mandarins and Modern Enterprise in Late Ching China*
80. Endymion Wilkinson, *Landlord and Labor in Late Imperial China: Case Studies from Shandong by Jing Su and Luo Lun*
*81. Barry Keenan, *The Dewey Experiment in China: Educational Reform and Political Power in the Early Republic*
*82. George A. Hayden, *Crime and Punishment in Medieval Chinese Drama: Three Judge Pao Plays*
*83. Sang-Chul Suh, *Growth and Structural Changes in the Korean Economy, 1910–1940*
84. J. W. Dower, *Empire and Aftermath: Yoshida Shigeru and the Japanese Experience, 1878–1954*
85. Martin Collcutt, *Five Mountains: The Rinzai Zen Monastic Institution in Medieval Japan*
86. Kwang Suk Kim and Michael Roemer, *Growth and Structural Transformation*
87. Anne O. Krueger, *The Developmental Role of the Foreign Sector and Aid*
*88. Edwin S. Mills and Byung-Nak Song, *Urbanization and Urban Problems*
89. Sung Hwan Ban, Pal Yong Moon, and Dwight H. Perkins, *Rural Development*
*90. Noel F. McGinn, Donald R. Snodgrass, Yung Bong Kim, Shin-Bok Kim, and Quee-Young Kim, *Education and Development in Korea*
*91. Leroy P. Jones and Il SaKong, *Government, Business, and Entrepreneurship in Economic Development: The Korean Case*
92. Edward S. Mason, Dwight H. Perkins, Kwang Suk Kim, David C. Cole, Mahn Je Kim et al., *The Economic and Social Modernization of the Republic of Korea*
93. Robert Repetto, Tai Hwan Kwon, Son-Ung Kim, Dae Young Kim, John E. Sloboda, and Peter J. Donaldson, *Economic Development, Population Policy, and Demographic Transition in the Republic of Korea*
94. Parks M. Coble, Jr., *The Shanghai Capitalists and the Nationalist Government, 1927–1937*
95. Noriko Kamachi, *Reform in China: Huang Tsun-hsien and the Japanese Model*
96. Richard Wich, *Sino-Soviet Crisis Politics: A Study of Political Change and Communication*
97. Lillian M. Li, *China's Silk Trade: Traditional Industry in the Modern World, 1842–1937*
98. R. David Arkush, *Fei Xiaotong and Sociology in Revolutionary China*
*99. Kenneth Alan Grossberg, *Japan's Renaissance: The Politics of the Muromachi Bakufu*
100. James Reeve Pusey, *China and Charles Darwin*

101. Hoyt Cleveland Tillman, *Utilitarian Confucianism: Chen Liang's Challenge to Chu Hsi*
102. Thomas A. Stanley, *Ōsugi Sakae, Anarchist in Taishō Japan: The Creativity of the Ego*
103. Jonathan K. Ocko, *Bureaucratic Reform in Provincial China: Ting Jih-ch'ang in Restoration Kiangsu, 1867–1870*
104. James Reed, *The Missionary Mind and American East Asia Policy, 1911–1915*
105. Neil L. Waters, *Japan's Local Pragmatists: The Transition from Bakumatsu to Meiji in the Kawasaki Region*
106. David C. Cole and Yung Chul Park, *Financial Development in Korea, 1945–1978*
107. Roy Bahl, Chuk Kyo Kim, and Chong Kee Park, *Public Finances During the Korean Modernization Process*
108. William D. Wray, *Mitsubishi and the N.Y.K, 1870–1914: Business Strategy in the Japanese Shipping Industry*
109. Ralph William Huenemann, *The Dragon and the Iron Horse: The Economics of Railroads in China, 1876–1937*

*110. Benjamin A. Elman, *From Philosophy to Philology: Intellectual and Social Aspects of Change in Late Imperial China*

111. Jane Kate Leonard, *Wei Yüan and China's Rediscovery of the Maritime World*
112. Luke S. K. Kwong, *A Mosaic of the Hundred Days:. Personalities, Politics, and Ideas of 1898*

*113. John E. Wills, Jr., *Embassies and Illusions: Dutch and Portuguese Envoys to K'ang-hsi, 1666–1687*

114. Joshua A. Fogel, *Politics and Sinology: The Case of Naitō Konan (1866–1934)*

*115. Jeffrey C. Kinkley, ed., *After Mao: Chinese Literature and Society, 1978–1981*

116. C. Andrew Gerstle, *Circles of Fantasy: Convention in the Plays of Chikamatsu*
117. Andrew Gordon, *The Evolution of Labor Relations in Japan: Heavy Industry, 1853–1955*

*118. Daniel K. Gardner, *Chu Hsi and the "Ta Hsueh": Neo-Confucian Reflection on the Confucian Canon*

119. Christine Guth Kanda, *Shinzō: Hachiman Imagery and Its Development*

*120. Robert Borgen, *Sugawara no Michizane and the Early Heian Court*

121. Chang-tai Hung, *Going to the People: Chinese Intellectual and Folk Literature, 1918–1937*

*122. Michael A. Cusumano, *The Japanese Automobile Industry: Technology and Management at Nissan and Toyota*

123. Richard von Glahn, *The Country of Streams and Grottoes: Expansion, Settlement, and the Civilizing of the Sichuan Frontier in Song Times*
124. Steven D. Carter, *The Road to Komatsubara: A Classical Reading of the Renga Hyakuin*
125. Katherine F. Bruner, John K. Fairbank, and Richard T. Smith, *Entering China's Service: Robert Hart's Journals, 1854–1863*

126. Bob Tadashi Wakabayashi, *Anti-Foreignism and Western Learning in Early-Modern Japan: The "New Theses" of 1825*
127. Atsuko Hirai, *Individualism and Socialism: The Life and Thought of Kawai Eijirō (1891–1944)*
128. Ellen Widmer, *The Margins of Utopia: "Shui-hu hou-chuan" and the Literature of Ming Loyalism*
129. R. Kent Guy, *The Emperor's Four Treasuries: Scholars and the State in the Late Chien-lung Era*
130. Peter C. Perdue, *Exhausting the Earth: State and Peasant in Hunan, 1500–1850*
131. Susan Chan Egan, *A Latterday Confucian: Reminiscences of William Hung (1893–1980)*
132. James T. C. Liu, *China Turning Inward: Intellectual-Political Changes in the Early Twelfth Century*
*133. Paul A. Cohen, *Between Tradition and Modernity: Wang T'ao and Reform in Late Ching China*
134. Kate Wildman Nakai, *Shogunal Politics: Arai Hakuseki and the Premises of Tokugawa Rule*
*135. Parks M. Coble, *Facing Japan: Chinese Politics and Japanese Imperialism, 1931–1937*
136. Jon L. Saari, *Legacies of Childhood: Growing Up Chinese in a Time of Crisis, 1890–1920*
137. Susan Downing Videen, *Tales of Heichū*
138. Heinz Morioka and Miyoko Sasaki, *Rakugo: The Popular Narrative Art of Japan*
139. Joshua A. Fogel, *Nakae Ushikichi in China: The Mourning of Spirit*
140. Alexander Barton Woodside, *Vietnam and the Chinese Model: A Comparative Study of Vietnamese and Chinese Government in the First Half of the Nineteenth Century*
*141. George Elison, *Deus Destroyed: The Image of Christianity in Early Modern Japan*
142. William D. Wray, ed., *Managing Industrial Enterprise: Cases from Japan's Prewar Experience*
*143. T'ung-tsu Ch'ü, *Local Government in China Under the Ching*
144. Marie Anchordoguy, *Computers, Inc.: Japan's Challenge to IBM*
145. Barbara Molony, *Technology and Investment: The Prewar Japanese Chemical Industry*
146. Mary Elizabeth Berry, *Hideyoshi*
147. Laura E. Hein, *Fueling Growth: The Energy Revolution and Economic Policy in Postwar Japan*
148. Wen-hsin Yeh, *The Alienated Academy: Culture and Politics in Republican China, 1919–1937*
149. Dru C. Gladney, *Muslim Chinese: Ethnic Nationalism in the People's Republic*
150. Merle Goldman and Paul A. Cohen, eds., *Ideas Across Cultures: Essays on Chinese Thought in Honor of Benjamin L Schwartz*
151. James M. Polachek, *The Inner Opium War*
152. Gail Lee Bernstein, *Japanese Marxist: A Portrait of Kawakami Hajime, 1879–1946*

- *153. Lloyd E. Eastman, *The Abortive Revolution: China Under Nationalist Rule, 1927–1937*
- 154. Mark Mason, *American Multinationals and Japan: The Political Economy of Japanese Capital Controls, 1899–1980*
- 155. Richard J. Smith, John K. Fairbank, and Katherine F. Bruner, *Robert Hart and China's Early Modernization: His Journals, 1863–1866*
- 156. George J. Tanabe, Jr., *Myōe the Dreamkeeper: Fantasy and Knowledge in Kamakura Buddhism*
- 157. William Wayne Farris, *Heavenly Warriors: The Evolution of Japan's Military, 500–1300*
- 158. Yu-ming Shaw, *An American Missionary in China: John Leighton Stuart and Chinese-American Relations*
- 159. James B. Palais, *Politics and Policy in Traditional Korea*
- *160. Douglas Reynolds, *China, 1898–1912: The Xinzheng Revolution and Japan*
- 161. Roger R. Thompson, *China's Local Councils in the Age of Constitutional Reform, 1898–1911*
- 162. William Johnston, *The Modern Epidemic: History of Tuberculosis in Japan*
- 163. Constantine Nomikos Vaporis, *Breaking Barriers: Travel and the State in Early Modern Japan*
- 164. Irmela Hijiya-Kirschnereit, *Rituals of Self-Revelation: Shishōsetsu as Literary Genre and Socio-Cultural Phenomenon*
- 165. James C. Baxter, *The Meiji Unification Through the Lens of Ishikawa Prefecture*
- 166. Thomas R. H. Havens, *Architects of Affluence: The Tsutsumi Family and the Seibu-Saison Enterprises in Twentieth-Century Japan*
- 167. Anthony Hood Chambers, *The Secret Window: Ideal Worlds in Tanizaki's Fiction*
- 168. Steven J. Ericson, *The Sound of the Whistle: Railroads and the State in Meiji Japan*
- 169. Andrew Edmund Goble, *Kenmu: Go-Daigo's Revolution*
- 170. Denise Potrzeba Lett, *In Pursuit of Status: The Making of South Korea's "New" Urban Middle Class*
- 171. Mimi Hall Yiengpruksawan, *Hiraizumi: Buddhist Art and Regional Politics in Twelfth-Century Japan*
- 172. Charles Shirō Inouye, *The Similitude of Blossoms: A Critical Biography of Izumi Kyōka (1873–1939), Japanese Novelist and Playwright*
- 173. Aviad E. Raz, *Riding the Black Ship: Japan and Tokyo Disneyland*
- 174. Deborah J. Milly, *Poverty, Equality, and Growth: The Politics of Economic Need in Postwar Japan*
- 175. See Heng Teow, *Japan's Cultural Policy Toward China, 1918–1931: A Comparative Perspective*
- 176. Michael A. Fuller, *An Introduction to Literary Chinese*
- 177. Frederick R. Dickinson, *War and National Reinvention: Japan in the Great War, 1914–1919*

178. John Solt, *Shredding the Tapestry of Meaning: The Poetry and Poetics of Kitasono Katue (1902–1978)*
179. Edward Pratt, *Japan's Protoindustrial Elite: The Economic Foundations of the Gōnō*
180. Atsuko Sakaki, *Recontextualizing Texts: Narrative Performance in Modern Japanese Fiction*
181. Soon-Won Park, *Colonial Industrialization and Labor in Korea: The Onoda Cement Factory*
182. JaHyun Kim Haboush and Martina Deuchler, *Culture and the State in Late Chosŏn Korea*
183. John W. Chaffee, *Branches of Heaven: A History of the Imperial Clan of Sung China*
184. Gi-Wook Shin and Michael Robinson, eds., *Colonial Modernity in Korea*
185. Nam-lin Hur, *Prayer and Play in Late Tokugawa Japan: Asakusa Sensōji and Edo Society*
186. Kristin Stapleton, *Civilizing Chengdu: Chinese Urban Reform, 1895–1937*
187. Hyung Il Pai, *Constructing "Korean" Origins: A Critical Review of Archaeology, Historiography, and Racial Myth in Korean State-Formation Theories*
188. Brian D. Ruppert, *Jewel in the Ashes: Buddha Relics and Power in Early Medieval Japan*
189. Susan Daruvala, *Zhou Zuoren and an Alternative Chinese Response to Modernity*
*190. James Z. Lee, *The Political Economy of a Frontier: Southwest China, 1250–1850*
191. Kerry Smith, *A Time of Crisis: Japan, the Great Depression, and Rural Revitalization*
192. Michael Lewis, *Becoming Apart: National Power and Local Politics in Toyama, 1868–1945*
193. William C. Kirby, Man-houng Lin, James Chin Shih, and David A. Pietz, eds., *State and Economy in Republican China: A Handbook for Scholars*
194. Timothy S. George, *Minamata: Pollution and the Struggle for Democracy in Postwar Japan*
195. Billy K. L. So, *Prosperity, Region, and Institutions in Maritime China: The South Fukien Pattern, 946–1368*
196. Yoshihisa Tak Matsusaka, *The Making of Japanese Manchuria, 1904–1932*
197. Maram Epstein, *Competing Discourses: Orthodoxy, Authenticity, and Engendered Meanings in Late Imperial Chinese Fiction*
198. Curtis J. Milhaupt, J. Mark Ramseyer, and Michael K. Young, eds. and comps., *Japanese Law in Context: Readings in Society, the Economy, and Politics*
199. Haruo Iguchi, *Unfinished Business: Ayukawa Yoshisuke and U.S.-Japan Relations, 1937–1952*
200. Scott Pearce, Audrey Spiro, and Patricia Ebrey, *Culture and Power in the Reconstitution of the Chinese Realm, 200–600*
201. Terry Kawashima, *Writing Margins: The Textual Construction of Gender in Heian and Kamakura Japan*
202. Martin W. Huang, *Desire and Fictional Narrative in Late Imperial China*

203. Robert S. Ross and Jiang Changbin, eds., *Re-examining the Cold War: U.S.-China Diplomacy, 1954–1973*
204. Guanhua Wang, *In Search of Justice: The 1905–1906 Chinese Anti-American Boycott*
205. David Schaberg, *A Patterned Past: Form and Thought in Early Chinese Historiography*
206. Christine Yano, *Tears of Longing: Nostalgia and the Nation in Japanese Popular Song*
207. Milena Doleželová-Velingerová and Oldřich Král, with Graham Sanders, eds., *The Appropriation of Cultural Capital: China's May Fourth Project*
208. Robert N. Huey, *The Making of 'Shinkokinshū'*
209. Lee Butler, *Emperor and Aristocracy in Japan, 1467–1680: Resilience and Renewal*
210. Suzanne Ogden, *Inklings of Democracy in China*
211. Kenneth J. Ruoff, *The People's Emperor: Democracy and the Japanese Monarchy, 1945–1995*
212. Haun Saussy, *Great Walls of Discourse and Other Adventures in Cultural China*
213. Aviad E. Raz, *Emotions at Work: Normative Control, Organizations, and Culture in Japan and America*
214. Rebecca E. Karl and Peter Zarrow, eds., *Rethinking the 1898 Reform Period: Political and Cultural Change in Late Qing China*
215. Kevin O'Rourke, *The Book of Korean Shijo*
216. Ezra F. Vogel, ed., *The Golden Age of the U.S.-China-Japan Triangle, 1972–1989*
217. Thomas A. Wilson, ed., *On Sacred Grounds: Culture, Society, Politics, and the Formation of the Cult of Confucius*
218. Donald S. Sutton, *Steps of Perfection: Exorcistic Performers and Chinese Religion in Twentieth-Century Taiwan*
219. Daqing Yang, *Technology of Empire: Telecommunications and Japanese Expansionism, 1895–1945*
220. Qianshen Bai, *Fu Shan's World: The Transformation of Chinese Calligraphy in the Seventeenth Century*
221. Paul Jakov Smith and Richard von Glahn, eds., *The Song-Yuan-Ming Transition in Chinese History*
222. Rania Huntington, *Alien Kind: Foxes and Late Imperial Chinese Narrative*
223. Jordan Sand, *House and Home in Modern Japan: Architecture, Domestic Space, and Bourgeois Culture, 1880–1930*
224. Karl Gerth, *China Made: Consumer Culture and the Creation of the Nation*
225. Xiaoshan Yang, *Metamorphosis of the Private Sphere: Gardens and Objects in Tang-Song Poetry*
226. Barbara Mittler, *A Newspaper for China? Power, Identity, and Change in Shanghai's News Media, 1872–1912*
227. Joyce A. Madancy, *The Troublesome Legacy of Commissioner Lin: The Opium Trade and Opium Suppression in Fujian Province, 1820s to 1920s*

228. John Makeham, *Transmitters and Creators: Chinese Commentators and Commentaries on the Analects*
229. Elisabeth Köll, *From Cotton Mill to Business Empire: The Emergence of Regional Enterprises in Modern China*
230. Emma Teng, *Taiwan's Imagined Geography: Chinese Colonial Travel Writing and Pictures, 1683–1895*
231. Wilt Idema and Beata Grant, *The Red Brush: Writing Women of Imperial China*
232. Eric C. Rath, *The Ethos of Noh: Actors and Their Art*
233. Elizabeth Remick, *Building Local States: China During the Republican and Post-Mao Eras*
234. Lynn Struve, ed., *The Qing Formation in World-Historical Time*
235. D. Max Moerman, *Localizing Paradise: Kumano Pilgrimage and the Religious Landscape of Premodern Japan*
236. Antonia Finnane, *Speaking of Yangzhou: A Chinese City, 1550–1850*
237. Brian Platt, *Burning and Building: Schooling and State Formation in Japan, 1750–1890*
238. Gail Bernstein, Andrew Gordon, and Kate Wildman Nakai, eds., *Public Spheres, Private Lives in Modern Japan, 1600–1950: Essays in Honor of Albert Craig*
239. Wu Hung and Katherine R. Tsiang, *Body and Face in Chinese Visual Culture*
240. Stephen Dodd, *Writing Home: Representations of the Native Place in Modern Japanese Literature*
241. David Anthony Bello, *Opium and the Limits of Empire: Drug Prohibition in the Chinese Interior, 1729–1850*
242. Hosea Hirata, *Discourses of Seduction: History, Evil, Desire, and Modern Japanese Literature*
243. Kyung Moon Hwang, *Beyond Birth: Social Status in the Emergence of Modern Korea*
244. Brian R. Dott, *Identity Reflections: Pilgrimages to Mount Tai in Late Imperial China*
245. Mark McNally, *Proving the Way: Conflict and Practice in the History of Japanese Nativism*
246. Yongping Wu, *A Political Explanation of Economic Growth: State Survival, Bureaucratic Politics, and Private Enterprises in the Making of Taiwan's Economy, 1950–1985*
247. Kyu Hyun Kim, *The Age of Visions and Arguments: Parliamentarianism and the National Public Sphere in Early Meiji Japan*
248. Zvi Ben-Dor Benite, *The Dao of Muhammad: A Cultural History of Muslims in Late Imperial China*
249. David Der-wei Wang and Shang Wei, eds., *Dynastic Crisis and Cultural Innovation: From the Late Ming to the Late Qing and Beyond*
250. Wilt L. Idema, Wai-yee Li, and Ellen Widmer, eds., *Trauma and Transcendence in Early Qing Literature*
251. Barbara Molony and Kathleen Uno, eds., *Gendering Modern Japanese History*

252. Hiroshi Aoyagi, *Islands of Eight Million Smiles: Idol Performance and Symbolic Production in Contemporary Japan*
253. Wai-yee Li, *The Readability of the Past in Early Chinese Historiography*
254. William C. Kirby, Robert S. Ross, and Gong Li, eds., *Normalization of U.S.-China Relations: An International History*
255. Ellen Gardner Nakamura, *Practical Pursuits: Takano Chōei, Takahashi Keisaku, and Western Medicine in Nineteenth-Century Japan*
256. Jonathan W. Best, *A History of the Early Korean Kingdom of Paekche, together with an annotated translation of* The Paekche Annals *of the* Samguk sagi
257. Liang Pan, *The United Nations in Japan's Foreign and Security Policymaking, 1945–1992: National Security, Party Politics, and International Status*
258. Richard Belsky, *Localities at the Center: Native Place, Space, and Power in Late Imperial Beijing*
259. Zwia Lipkin, *"Useless to the State": "Social Problems" and Social Engineering in Nationalist Nanjing, 1927–1937*
260. William O. Gardner, *Advertising Tower: Japanese Modernism and Modernity in the 1920s*
261. Stephen Owen, *The Making of Early Chinese Classical Poetry*
262. Martin J. Powers, *Pattern and Person: Ornament, Society, and Self in Classical China*
263. Anna M. Shields, *Crafting a Collection: The Cultural Contexts and Poetic Practice of the* Huajian ji 花間集 (*Collection from Among the Flowers*)
264. Stephen Owen, *The Late Tang: Chinese Poetry of the Mid-Ninth Century (827–860)*
265. Sara L. Friedman, *Intimate Politics: Marriage, the Market, and State Power in Southeastern China*
266. Patricia Buckley Ebrey and Maggie Bickford, *Emperor Huizong and Late Northern Song China: The Politics of Culture and the Culture of Politics*
267. Sophie Volpp, *Worldly Stage: Theatricality in Seventeenth-Century China*
268. Ellen Widmer, *The Beauty and the Book: Women and Fiction in Nineteenth-Century China*
269. Steven B. Miles, *The Sea of Learning: Mobility and Identity in Nineteenth-Century Guangzhou*
270. Lin Man-houng, *China Upside Down: Currency, Society, and Ideologies, 1808–1856*
271. Ronald Egan, *The Problem of Beauty: Aesthetic Thought and Pursuits in Northern Song Dynasty China*
272. Mark Halperin, *Out of the Cloister: Literati Perspectives on Buddhism in Sung China, 960–1279*
273. Helen Dunstan, *State or Merchant? Political Economy and Political Process in 1740s China*
274. Sabina Knight, *The Heart of Time: Moral Agency in Twentieth-Century Chinese Fiction*

275. Timothy J. Van Compernolle, *The Uses of Memory: The Critique of Modernity in the Fiction of Higuchi Ichiyō*
276. Paul Rouzer, *A New Practical Primer of Literary Chinese*
277. Jonathan Zwicker, *Practices of the Sentimental Imagination: Melodrama, the Novel, and the Social Imaginary in Nineteenth-Century Japan*
278. Franziska Seraphim, *War Memory and Social Politics in Japan, 1945–2005*
279. Adam L. Kern, *Manga from the Floating World: Comicbook Culture and the* Kibyōshi *of Edo Japan*
280. Cynthia J. Brokaw, *Commerce in Culture: The Sibao Book Trade in the Qing and Republican Periods*
281. Eugene Y. Park, *Between Dreams and Reality: The Military Examination in Late Chosŏn Korea, 1600–1894*
282. Nam-lin Hur, *Death and Social Order in Tokugawa Japan: Buddhism, Anti-Christianity, and the* Danka *System*
283. Patricia M. Thornton, *Disciplining the State: Virtue, Violence, and State-Making in Modern China*
284. Vincent Goossaert, *The Taoists of Peking, 1800–1949: A Social History of Urban Clerics*
285. Peter Nickerson, *Taoism, Bureaucracy, and Popular Religion in Early Medieval China*
286. Charo B. D'Etcheverry, *Love After* The Tale of Genji*: Rewriting the World of the Shining Prince*
287. Michael G. Chang, *A Court on Horseback: Imperial Touring & the Construction of Qing Rule, 1680–1785*
288. Carol Richmond Tsang, *War and Faith:* Ikkō Ikki *in Late Muromachi Japan*
289. Hilde De Weerdt, *Competition over Content: Negotiating Standards for the Civil Service Examinations in Imperial China (1127–1279)*
290. Eve Zimmerman, *Out of the Alleyway: Nakagami Kenji and the Poetics of Outcaste Fiction*
291. Robert Culp, *Articulating Citizenship: Civic Education and Student Politics in Southeastern China, 1912–1940*
292. Richard J. Smethurst, *From Foot Soldier to Finance Minister: Takahashi Korekiyo, Japan's Keynes*
293. John E. Herman, *Amid the Clouds and Mist: China's Colonization of Guizhou, 1200–1700*
294. Tomoko Shiroyama, *China During the Great Depression: Market, State, and the World Economy, 1929–1937*
295. Kirk W. Larsen, *Tradition, Treaties and Trade: Qing Imperialism and Chosŏn Korea, 1850–1910*
296. Gregory Golley, *When Our Eyes No Longer See: Realism, Science, and Ecology in Japanese Literary Modernism*

297. Barbara Ambros, *Emplacing a Pilgrimage: The Ōyama Cult and Regional Religion in Early Modern Japan*
298. Rebecca Suter, *The Japanization of Modernity: Murakami Haruki between Japan and the United States*
299. Yuma Totani, *The Tokyo War Crimes Trial: The Pursuit of Justice in the Wake of World War II*
300. Linda Isako Angst, *In a Dark Time: Memory, Community, and Gendered Nationalism in Postwar Okinawa*
301. David M. Robinson, ed., *Culture, Courtiers, and Competition: The Ming Court (1368–1644)*
302. Calvin Chen, *Some Assembly Required: Work, Community, and Politics in China's Rural Enterprises*
303. Sem Vermeersch, *The Power of the Buddhas: The Politics of Buddhism During the Koryŏ Dynasty* (918–1392)
304. Tina Lu, *Accidental Incest, Filial Cannibalism, and Other Peculiar Encounters in Late Imperial Chinese Literature*
305. Chang Woei Ong, *Men of Letters Within the Passes: Guanzhong Literati in Chinese History, 907–1911*
306. Wendy Swartz, *Reading Tao Yuanming: Shifting Paradigms of Historical Reception (427–1900)*
307. Peter K. Bol, *Neo-Confucianism in History*
308. Carlos Rojas, *The Naked Gaze: Reflections on Chinese Modernity*
309. Kelly H. Chong, *Deliverance and Submission: Evangelical Women and the Negotiation of Patriarchy in South Korea*
310. Rachel DiNitto, *Uchida Hyakken: A Critique of Modernity and Militarism in Prewar Japan*